A HISTORY OF SECRET SOCIETIES

A HISTORY OF
SECRET
SOCIETIES

by

ARKON DARAUL

A CITADEL PRESS BOOK
Published by Carol Publishing Group

Carol Publishing Group Edition, 1997

A Citadel Press Book
Published by Carol Publishing Group
Citadel Press is a registered trademark of Carol Communications, Inc.

Editorial, sales and distribution, rights and permissions inquiries
should be addressed to Carol Publishing Group, 120 Enterprise Avenue,
Secaucus, N.J. 07094

In Canada: Canadian Manda Group, One Atlantic Avenue, Suite 105,
Toronto, Ontario M6K 3E7

Carol Publishing Group books may be purchased in bulk at special
discounts for sales promotions, fund-raising, or educational purposes.
Special editions can be created to specifications. For details, contact
Special Sales Department, Carol Publishing Group, 120 Enterprise Avenue,
Secaucus, N.J. 07094

Manufactured in the United States of America
ISBN 0-8065-0857-4

15   14   13   12   11   10   9   8   7

Contents

LINE ILLUSTRATIONS

KEY TO SYMBOLS IN THE TEXT

Foreword

ALMOST everyone who has written about secret societies has attempted a definition of what such a society is: yet no satisfactory description of the phenomenon has yet been attained. This is because there are so many variants surrounding the central fact of the existence of the society that what will identify one society will not fit another.

Not all secret societies are entirely secret: many of their members may be known (as in the case of the Freemasons); their objectives (as with the Rosicrucians) may be stated publicly; their teachings (as those of the Assassins) may be available to all. The secrecy of the society is not always confined to the few. In most primitive tribal initiations (which exactly resemble many civilized secret societies) all the adults are members. This latter fact means that the society is working not against established authority, but for it, removing the validity of the argument that all secret associations are dedicated to the "destruction of properly constituted authority".

It is interesting to note how students of this strange branch of human activity have tended to miss the fact that the secret society is an amalgam of many elements which are found in ordinary life. There is the exclusivity of membership, the importance attaching to being a member. This is found in clubs and associations which are not in any way secret: found among thousands of coteries of individuals everywhere and in all eras. Then there is the use of signs, passwords and similar materials. These, too, perform a function in human organization everywhere. Thirdly, there is the objective of the society. This may be almost anything, and is found in all manner of pressure-groups wherever humanity congregates.

There is the shared experience of the rituals and the belief (the 'myth') of the society. Every clan, nation, even family has such

9

myths and rituals, which come to have a special meaning for the participants.

These are some of the materials for the secret society. The uniqueness of the true secret society is that certain aspects of human thought which are particularly compelling are combined to train and maintain the efforts of a group of people to operate in a certain direction.

It is the undesirable activities of some secret societies and their very air of mystery which has given them the reputation of being strange, abnormal associations. When, however, their beliefs become those of the majority, they cease to be considered anti-social. It is as simple as that.

The secret organizations dealt with in this book have been chosen in such a way as to illustrate the widest variety of their forms, rituals and beliefs. Much of the material has been obtained at first-hand and is published for the first time.

Secret societies are generally considered to be anti-social: to contain elements which are distasteful or harmful to the community at large. Such is undoubtedly the case—sometimes. Communism and Fascism function as secret societies in countries where they are prohibited by law. Christianity was a secret society in Rome, and was considered by the authorities from the start to be a dangerous innovation. The same was true of Islam. It can be said that at least some of the believers in these creeds, working in secret, were genuinely devout believers that what they practised was for the eventual good of society. The Arabs today consider that the Jews constitute a dangerous secret society which is dedicated to the overwhelming of the world. The Druses and Yezidis in Syria and Iraq think the same of the Arabs. Freemasons and Catholics hold almost precisely similar ideas about each other. It is impossible, incidentally, to divorce the study of secret societies from religion, because even avowedly criminal societies so often have religious origins or pretensions. If one takes the position that social right and wrong should be the mentor in estimating the value of the secret society, a stumbling-block of similar magnitude appears. In Borneo, initiates of the hunting societies considered it meritorious and necessary to hunt heads. In Polynesia, infanticide and debauch were considered essential for initiation into societies where the tribal code needed members who indulged in these things, as pillars of society. In Africa, North America, Melanesia and elsewhere, initiation into the highest degrees of clan life (and consequent status as a man and a just man at that) involved undergoing trials which not infrequently resulted in the death or madness of the candidate.

Since the earliest recorded times, the official administration of any given country has been concerned with maintaining the *status quo* and defending society as constituted against minority groups which sought to function as 'states within states', or to overthrow the authority of the time. Few of such efforts have been permanently successful, and it seems unlikely from the sociological point of view that they ever will be. The human desire to be one of the elect is something which no power has yet been able to reduce, let alone overcome. Whether this is a good or a bad thing depends entirely upon one's point of view and one's commitments at the time of judging the question. This book does not pretend to be an exhaustive account of secret societies: none such has ever been nor ever will be written. But in these pages will be found some of the characteristic forms which secret societies and cults have taken—successfully and otherwise. None of them can be regarded as good from every point of view. But all of them can be considered evil, from one standpoint or another: democracy by autocrats, banditry by the law-abiding, mysticism by the materialist.

I

The Old Man of the Mountains

TWO men in the year 1092 stood on the ramparts of a medieval castle—the Eagle's Nest—perched high upon the crags of the Persian mountains: the personal representative of the Emperor and the veiled figure who claimed to be the incarnation of God on earth. Hasan, son of Sabah, Sheikh of the Mountains and leader of the Assassins, spoke. "You see that devotee standing guard on yonder turret-top? Watch!"

He made a signal. Instantly the white-robed figure threw up his hands in salutation, and cast himself two thousand feet into the foaming torrent which surrounded the fortress.

"I have seventy thousand men—and women—throughout Asia, each one of them ready to do my bidding. Can your master, Malik Shah, say the same? And he asks me to surrender to his sovereignty! This is your answer. Go!"

Such a scene may be worthy of the most exaggerated of horror films. And yet it took place in historical fact. The only quibble made by the chronicler of the time was that Hasan's devotees numbered "only about forty thousand." How this man Sabah came by his uncanny power, and how his devotees struck terror into the hearts of men from the Caspian to Egypt, is one of the most extraordinary of all tales of secret societies. Today, the sect of the Hashishin (druggers) still exists in the form of the Ismailis (Ishmaelites), whose undisputed chief, endowed by them with divine attributes, is the Aga Khan.

Like many another secret cult, the Assassin organization was based upon an earlier association. In order to understand how they worked and what their objectives were, we must begin with these roots.

It must be remembered that the followers of Islam in the seventh century A.D. split into two divisions: the orthodox, who regard Mohammed as the bringer of divine inspiration; and the Shiahs, who consider that Ali, his successor, the Fourth Imam (leader), was more important. It is with the Shiahs that we are concerned here.

From the beginning of the split in the early days of Islam, the Shiahs relied for survival upon secrecy, organization and initiation. Although the minority party in Islam, they believed that they could overcome the majority (and eventually the whole world) by superior organization and power. To this end they started a number of societies which practised secret rites in which the personality of Ali was worshipped, and whose rank and file were trained to struggle above all for the accomplishment of world dominion.

One of the most successful secret societies which the Shiahs founded was centred around the Abode of Learning in Cairo, which was the training-ground for fanatics who were conditioned by the most cunning methods to believe in a special divine mission. In order to do this, the original democratic Islamic ideas had to be overcome by skilled teachers, acting under the orders of the Caliph of the Fatimites, who ruled Egypt at that time.

Members were enrolled, on the understanding that they were to receive hidden power and timeless wisdom which would enable them to become as important in life as some of the teachers. And the Caliph saw to it that the instructors were no ordinary men. The supreme judge was one of them; another was the commander-in-chief of the army; a third the minister of the Court. There was no lack of applicants. In any country where the highest officials of the realm formed a body of teachers, one would find the same thing.

Classes were divided into study groups, some composed of men, others of women, collectively termed Assemblies of Wisdom. All lessons were carefully prepared, written down and submitted to the Caliph for his seal. At the end of the lecture all present kissed the seal: for did the Caliph not claim direct descent from Mohammed, through his son-in-law Ali and thence from Ismail, the Seventh Imam? He was the embodiment of divinity, far more than any Tibetan lama ever was.

The university, lavishly endowed and possessing the best manuscripts and scientific instruments available, received a grant of a quarter of a million gold pieces annually from the Caliph. Its external form was similar to the pattern of the ancient Arab universities, not much different from Oxford. But its real purpose was the complete transformation of the mind of the student.

Students had to pass through nine degrees of initiation. In the first, the teachers threw their pupils into a state of doubt about all conventional ideas, religious and political. They used false analogy and every other device of argument to make the aspirant believe that what he had been taught by his previous mentors was prejudiced and capable of being challenged. The effect of this, according to the Arab historian, Makrizi, was to cause him to lean upon the personality of the teachers, as the only possible source of the proper interpretation of facts. At the same time, the teachers hinted continually that formal knowledge was merely the cloak for hidden, inner and powerful truth, whose secret would be imparted when the youth was ready to receive it. This 'confusion technique' was carried out until the student reached the stage where he was prepared to swear a vow of blind allegiance to one or other of his teachers.

This oath, together with certain secret signs, was administered in due course, and the candidate awarded the first degree of initiation.

The second degree took the form of initiation into the fact that the Imams (successors of Mohammed) were the true and only sources of secret knowledge and power. Imams inspired the teachers. Therefore the student was to acknowledge every saying and act of his appointed guides as blessed and divinely inspired. In the third degree, the esoteric names of the Seven Imams were revealed, and the secret words by which they could be conjured and by which the powers inherent in the very repetition of their names could be liberated and used for the individual especially in the service of the sect.

In the fourth degree, the succession of the Seven Mystical Law-givers and magical personalities was given to the learner. These were characterized as Adam, Noah, Abraham, Moses, Jesus, Mohammed and Ismail. There were seven mystical 'helpers': Seth, Shem, Ishmael, Aaron, Simon, Ali, and Mohammed, the son of Ismail. This last was dead, but he had a mysterious deputy, who was the Lord of the Time: authorized to give his instructions to the People of Truth, as the Ismailis called them-selves. This hidden figure gave the Caliph the power to pretend that he was acting under even higher instructions.

The fifth degree named twelve apostles under the seven pro-phets, whose names and functions and magical powers were de-scribed. In this degree the power to influence others by means of personal concentration was supposed to be taught. One writer claims that this was done merely by the repetition, for a period of three years to train the mind, of the magical word AK-ZABT-I.

To obtain the sixth degree involved instruction in the methods of analytical and destructive argument, in which the postulant had to pass a stiff examination. The seventh degree brought reve-lation of the Great Secret: that all humanity and all creation were one and every single thing was a part of the whole, which in-cluded the creative and destructive power. But, as an Ismaili, the individual could make use of the power which was ready to be awakened within him, and overcome those who knew nothing of the immense potential of the rest of humanity. This power came through the aid of the mysterious power called the Lord of the Time.

To qualify for the eighth degree, the aspirant had to believe that all religion, philosophy and the like were fraudulent. All that mattered was the individual, who could attain fulfilment only through servitude to the greatest developed power—the Imam. The ninth and last degree brought the revelation of the secret that there was no such thing as belief: all that mattered was action.

And the only possessor of the reasons for carrying out any action was the chief of the sect.

As a secret society, the organization of the Ismailis as outlined above was undoubtedly powerful and seemed likely to produce a large number of devotees who would blindly obey the orders of whomever was in control of the edifice. But, as with other bodies of this kind, there were severe limitations from the point of view of effectiveness.

Perhaps the phase of revolt or subversion planned by the society did not in the end get under way; perhaps it was not intended to work by any other means than training the individual. Be that as it may, its real success extended abroad only (in 1058) to Baghdad, where a member gained temporary control of Baghdad and coined money in the Egyptian Caliph's name. This sultan was slain by the Turks, who now entered the picture, and the Cairo headquarters was also threatened. By 1123, the society was closed down by the Vizier Afdal. The rise of Turkish power seemed to have discouraged the expansionist Cairo sect so strongly that they almost faded out, and little is heard of them after that date.

It was left to Hasan, son of Sabah, the Old Man of the Mountains, to perfect the system of the ailing secret society, and found an organization which has endured for nearly another thousand years.

Who was Hasan? He was the son of a Shiah (Ali-worshipper) in Khorasan, a most bigoted man, who claimed that his ancestors were Arabs, from Kufa. This assumption was probably due to the fact that such a lineage bolstered up claims to religious importance, then as now, among Moslems. The people of the neighbourhood, many of them also Shiahs, stated very decisively that this Ali was a Persian, and so were his forebears. It is generally thought that this is the truer version. As the Governor of the Province was an orthodox Moslem, Ali spared no efforts to assume the same guise. This is considered to be completely permissible—the Doctrine of Intelligent Dissimulation. As there was some doubt as to his reliability in the religious sense, he retired into a monastic retreat,

'Tree of Life' design embroidered on the altar–cloth and robes of a modern secret society. This design is Assyrian, and seen in mystery–cult use in places as far apart as India, Syria and Germany.

and sent his son Hasan to an orthodox school. This school was no ordinary one. It was the circle of disciples presided over by the redoubtable Imam Muwafiq, about whom it was said that every individual who enrolled under him eventually rose to great power.

It was here that Hasan met Omar Khayyám, the tentmaker-poet and astronomer, later to be the poet laureate of Persia. Another of his schoolmates was Nizam-ul-Mulk, who rose from peasanthood to become prime minister. These three made a pact, according to Nizam's autobiography, whereby whichever rose to high office first would help the others.

Nizam, the courtier, became Vizier to Alp-Arslan the Turkish sultan of Persia, in a relatively short time. He helped Omar, in accordance with his vow, and secured him a pension, which gave him a life of ease and indulgence in his beloved Nishapur, where many of his *Rubá'iyát* poems were written. Meanwhile Hasan remained in obscurity, wandering through the Middle East, waiting for his chance to attain the power of which he had dreamed. Arslan the Lion died, and was succeeded by Malik Shah. Suddenly, Hasan presented himself to Nizam, demanding to be given a place at court. Delighted to fulfil his childhood vow, the vizier obtained for him a favoured place, and relates what transpired thus in his autobiography:

"I had him made a minister by my strong and extravagant recommendations. Like his father, however, he proved to be a fraud, hypocrite and a self-seeking villain. He was so clever at dissimulation that he appeared to be pious when he was not, and before long he had somehow completely captured the mind of the Shah."

Malik Shah was young, and Hasan was trained in the Shiah art of winning people over by apparent honesty. But Nizam was still the most important man in the realm, with an impressive record of honest dealing and achievements. Hasan decided to eliminate him.

The king had asked in that year, 1078, for a complete accounting of the revenue and expenditure of the empire, and Nizam told him that this would take over a year. Hasan, on the other hand, claimed that the whole work could be done in forty days, and offered to prove it. The task was assigned to him. And the accounts were prepared in the specified time. Something went wrong at this point. The balance of historical opinion holds that Nizam struck back at the last moment, saying "By Allah, this man will destroy us all unless he is rendered harmless, though I cannot kill my playmate." Whatever the truth may be, it seems that Nizam managed to have such disparities introduced into the final calligraphic version of the accounts that when Hasan started to read them they appeared so absurd that the Shah, in fury, ordered him to be exiled. As he had claimed to have written the accounts in his own hand, Hasan could not justify their incredible deficiencies.

Hasan had friends in Isfahan, where he immediately fled. There survives a record of what he said there, which sheds interesting light upon what was in his mind. One of these friends, Abu-al-Fazal, notes that Hasan, after reciting the bitter tale of his downfall, shouted these words, in a state of uncontrollable rage: "If I had two, just two, devotees who would stand by me, then I would cause the downfall of that Turk and that peasant."

Fazal concluded that Hasan had taken leave of his senses, and tried to get him out of this ugly mood. Hasan took umbrage, and insisted that he was working on a plan, and that he would have his revenge. He set off for Egypt, there to mature his plans.

Fazal was himself later to become a devotee of the Assassin chief, and Hasan, two decades later, reminded him of that day in Isfahan: "Here I am at Alamut, Master of all I survey: and more. The Sultan and the peasant Vizier are dead. Have I not kept my vow? Was I the madman you thought me to be? I found my two devotees, who were necessary to my plans."

Hasan himself takes up the story of how his fortunes fared after the flight from Persia. He had been brought up in the secret doctrines of Ismailism, and recognized the possibilities of power inherent in such a system. He knew that in Cairo there was a powerful nucleus of the society. And, if we are to believe the words of Fazal, he already had a plan whereby he could turn their followers into disciplined, devoted fanatics, willing to die for a leader. What was this plan? He had decided that it was not enough to promise paradise, fulfilment, eternal joy to people. He would actually *show* it to them; show it in the form of an artificial paradise, where houris played and fountains gushed sweet-scented waters, where every sensual wish was granted amid beautiful flowers and gilded pavilions. And this is what he eventually did.

Hasan chose a hidden valley for the site of his paradise, described by Marco Polo, who passed this way in 1271:

"In a beautiful valley, enclosed between two lofty mountains, he had formed a luxurious garden stored with every delicious fruit and every fragrant shrub that could be procured. Palaces of various sizes and forms were erected in different parts of the grounds, ornamented with works of gold, with paintings and with furniture of rich silks. By means of small conduits contained in these buildings, streams of wine, milk, honey and some of pure water were seen to flow in every direction. The inhabitants of these places were elegant and beautiful damsels, accomplished in the arts of singing, playing upon all sorts of musical instruments, dancing, and especially those of dalliance and amorous allurement. Clothed in rich dresses, they were seen continually sporting and amusing themselves in the garden and pavilions, their female guardians being confined within doors and never allowed to appear. The object which the chief had in view in forming a garden of this fascinating kind was this: that Mahomet having promised to those who should obey his will the enjoyments of Paradise, where every species of sensual gratification should be found, in the society of beautiful nymphs, he was desirous of it being understood by his followers that he also was a prophet and a compeer of Mahomet, and had the power of admitting to Paradise such as he should choose to favour. In order that none without his licence should find their way into this delicious valley, he caused a strong and inexpungable castle to be erected at the opening to it, through which the entry was by a secret passage."

Hasan began to attract young men from the surrounding countryside, between the ages of twelve and twenty: particularly those whom he marked out as possible material for the production of killers. Every day he held court, a reception at which he spoke of the delights of Paradise . . . "and at certain times he caused draughts of a soporific nature to be administered to ten or a dozen youths, and when half dead with sleep he had them conveyed to the several palaces and apartments of the garden. Upon awakening from this state of lethargy their senses were struck by all the delightful objects, and each perceiving himself surrounded by lovely damsels, singing, playing, and attracting his regards by the most fascinating caresses, serving him also with delicious viands and exquisite wines, until, intoxicated with excess and enjoyment, amidst actual rivers of milk and wine, he believed himself assuredly in Paradise, and felt an unwillingness to relinquish its delights. When four or five days had thus been passed, they were thrown once more into a state of somnolency, and carried out of the garden. Upon being carried to his presence, and questioned by him as to where they had been, their answer was 'in Paradise, through the favour of your highness'; and then, before the whole court who listened to them with eager astonishment and curiosity, they gave a circumstantial account of the scenes to which they had been witnesses. The chief thereupon addressing them said: 'We have the assurance of our Prophet that he who defends his Lord shall inherit Paradise, and if you show yourselves to be devoted to the obedience of my orders, that happy lot awaits you'. "

Suicide was at first attempted by some; but the survivors were early told that only death in the obedience of Hasan's orders could give the key to Paradise. In the eleventh century it was not only credulous Persian peasants who would have believed such things were true. Even among more sophisticated people the reality of the gardens and houris of paradise were completely accepted. True, a good many Sufis preached that the garden was allegorical —but that still left more than a few people who believed that they could trust the evidence of their senses.

The ancient *Art of Imposture*, by Abdel-Rahman of Damascus, gives away another trick of Hasan's. He had a deep, narrow pit sunk into the floor of his audience-chamber. One of his disciples stood in this, in such a way that his head and neck alone were visible above the floor. Around the neck was placed a circular dish in two pieces which fitted together, with a hole in the middle. This gave the impression that there was a severed head on a metal plate standing on the floor. In order to make the scene more plausible (if that is the word) Hasan had some fresh blood poured around the head, on the plate.

Now certain recruits were brought in. "Tell them," commanded the chief, "what thou hast seen." The disciple then described the delights of Paradise. "You have seen the head of a man who died, whom you all knew. I have reanimated him to speak with his own tongue."

Later, the head was treacherously severed in real earnest, and stuck for some time somewhere that the faithful would see it. The effect of this conjuring trick plus murder increased the enthusiasm for martyrdom to the required degree.

There are many documented instances of the recklessness of the fidayeen (devotees) of the Ismailis, one witness being a Westerner who was treated a century later to a similar spectacle to that which had appalled the envoy of Malik Shah. Henry, Count of Champagne, reports that he was travelling in 1194 through Ismaili territory. "The chief sent some persons to salute him and beg that, on his return he would stop at and partake of the hospitality of the castle. The Count accepted the invitation. As he returned, the Dai-el-Kebir (Great Missionary) advanced to meet him, showed him every mark of honour, and let him view his castle and fortresses. Having passed through several, they came at length to one of the towers which rose to an exceeding height. On each tower stood two sentinels clad in white. 'These,' said the Chief, pointing to them, 'obey me far better than the subjects of your Christians obey their lords;' and at a given signal two of them flung themselves down, and were dashed to pieces. 'If you wish,' said he to the astonished Count, 'all my white ones shall do the came.' The benevolent Count shrank from the proposal, and candidly avowed that no Christian prince could presume to look for such obedience from his subjects. When he was departing, with many valuable presents, the Chief said to him meaningly, 'By means of these trusty servants I get rid of the enemies of our society.'

Further details of the mentality of Hasan are given in what is supposed to be an autobiographical account of his early days: and it probably is in fact such, because the method of his conversion does seem to follow the pattern which has been observed in fanatics, of whatever religious or political persuasion.

He was, he says, reared in the belief of the divine right of the Imams, by his father. He early met an Ismaili missionary (Emir Dhareb) with whom he argued strenuously against the Emir's particular form of the creed. Then, some time later, he went through a bout of severe illness, in which he feared to die, and began to think that the Ismaili doctrine might really be the road to redemption and Paradise. If he died unconverted, he might be damned. Thus it was that as soon as he recovered he sought out another Ismaili propagandist, Abu Najam, and then others. Eventually he went to Egypt, to study the creed at its headquarters.

He was received with honour by the Caliph, due to his former position at the Court of Malik Shah. In order to increase their own importance, the high officials of the Court made a good deal of public play of the significance of the new convert; but this fact seemed in the end to help Hasan more than it did them. He entered into political intrigue and was arrested, then confined in a fortress. No sooner had he entered the prison than a minaret collapsed, and in some unexplained way this was interpreted as an omen that Hasan was in reality a divinely protected person. The Caliph, hurriedly making Hasan a number of valuable gifts, had him put aboard a ship sailing for north-west Africa. This gave him the funds which he was to use for setting up his 'paradise'—and also, through some quirk of fate, the disciples whom he sought.

A tremendous storm blew up, terrifying the captain, crew and passengers alike. Prayers were held, and Hasan was asked to join. He refused. "The storm is my doing; how can I pray that it abate?" he asked. "I have indicated the displeasure of the

24

Almighty. If we sink, I shall not die, for I am immortal. If you want to be saved, believe in me, and I shall subdue the winds.'

At first the offer was not accepted. Presently, however, when the ship seemed on the point of capsizing, the desperate passengers came to him and swore eternal allegiance. Hasan was still calm; and continued so until the storm abated. The ship was then driven on to the sea-coast of Syria, where Hasan disembarked, together with two of the merchant passengers, who became his first real disciples.

Hasan was not yet ready for the fulfilment of his destiny as he saw it. For the time being, he was travelling under the guise of a missionary of the Caliph in Cairo. From Aleppo he went to Baghdad, seeking a headquarters where he should be safe from interference and where he yet could become powerful enough to expand. Into Persia the road led him, travelling through the country, making converts to his ideas, which were still apparently strongly based upon the secret doctrines of the Egyptian Ismailis. Everywhere he created a really devoted disciple (fidayi) he bade him stay and try to enlarge the circle of his followers. These circles became hatching-grounds for the production of 'self-sacrificers', the initiates who were drawn from the ranks of the most promising ordinary converts. Thus it was that miniature training centres, modelled upon the Abode of Learning, were in being within a very few months of his return to his homeland.

During his travels, a trusted lieutenant—one Hussein Kahini—reported that the Iraki district where the fortress of Alamut was situated seemed to be an ideal place for proselytism. Most of the ordinary people of that place, in fact, had been persuaded into the Ismaili way of thinking. The only obstacle was the Governor —Ali Mahdi—who looked upon the Caliph of Baghdad as his spiritual and temporal lord. The first converts were expelled from the country. Before many months, however, there were so many Ismailis among the populace that the Governor was compelled to allow them to return. Hasan, though, he would not brook. The prospective owner of Alamut decided to try a trick. He offered the Governor three thousand pieces of gold for "the amount of land which could be encompassed by the hide of an ox". When Mahdi agreed to such a sale, Hasan produced a skin, cut it into the thinnest possible thongs, and joined them together to form a string which encompassed the castle of Alamut. Although the Governor refused to honour any such bargain, Hasan produced an order from a very highly placed official of the Seljuk rulers, ordering that the fortress be handed over to Hasan for three thousand gold pieces. It turned out that this official was himself a secret follower of the Sheikh of the Mountain.

The year was A.D. 1090. Hasan was now ready for the next part of his plan. He attacked and routed the troops of the Emir who had been placed in the governorship of the Province, and welded the people of the surrounding districts into a firm band of diligent and trustworthy workers and soldiers, answerable to him alone. Within two years the Vizier Nizam-ul-Mulk had been stabbed to the heart by an assassin sent by Hasan, and the Emperor Malik Shah, who dared to send troops against him, died in grave suspicion of poison. Hasan's revenge upon his class-fellow was to make him the very first target of his reign of terror. With the king's death, the whole realm was split up into warring factions. For long the Assassins alone retained their cohesion. In under a decade they had made themselves masters of all Persian Irak, and of many forts throughout the empire. This they did by forays, direct attack, the poisoned dagger, and in any other manner which seemed expedient. The orthodox religious leaders pronounced one interdict after another against their doctrines; all to no effect.

By now the entire loyalty of the Ismailis under him had been transferred from the Caliph to the personality of the Sheikh of the Mountain, who became the terror of every prince in that part of Asia, the Crusader chiefs included. "Despite and despising fatigues, dangers and tortures the Assassins joyfully gave their lives whenever it pleased the great master, who required them either to protect himself or to carry out his mandates of death. The victim having been pointed out, the faithful, clothed in a white tunic with a red sash, the colours of innocence and blood, went on their mission without being deterred by distance or danger. Having found the person they sought, they awaited the favourable moment for slaying him, and their daggers seldom missed their aim."

Richard the Lionheart was at one time accused of having asked the 'Lord of the Mountain' to have Conrad of Montferrat killed; a plot which was carried out thus: "Two assassins allowed themselves to be baptized and placing themselves beside him, seemed intent only on praying. But the favourable opportunity presented itself; they stabbed him and one took refuge in the church. But hearing that the prince had been carried off still alive, he again forced himself into Montferrat's presence, and stabbed him a second time; and then expired, without a complaint, amidst refined tortures." The Order of the Assassins (i) had perfected their method of securing the loyalty of human beings to an extent and on a scale which has (ii) seldom been paralleled.

The Assassins carried on the battle on two fronts. (iii) They fought whichever side in the Crusades served their purposes. At the same time they continued the struggle against the Persians. The son and successor of (iv) Nizam-ul-Mulk was laid low by an Assassin dagger. The Sultan, who had succeeded his father Malik Shah   Fig. A and gained power over most of his territories was marching against them. One morning, however, he awoke with an Assassin weapon stuck neatly into the ground near his head. Within it was a note, warning him to call off the proposed siege of Alamut. He came to terms with the Assassins, powerful ruler though he undoubtedly was. They had what amounted to a free hand, in exchange for a pact by which they promised to reduce their military power.

Hasan lived for thirty-four years after his acquisition of Alamut. On only two occasions since then had he even left his room: yet he ruled an invisible empire as great and as fearsome as any man before—or since. He seemed to realize that death was almost upon him, and calmly began to make plans for the perpetual continuance of the Order of the Assassins.

2

The Latter Days of the Assassins

THE ruler of one of the most terrifying organizations the world has ever known was without a lineal successor. He had had both of his sons killed: one for carrying out an unauthorized murder, the other for drinking wine; certainly a case of "do as I say, not as I do". He called his two most trusted lieutenants from the strongholds which they maintained on his behalf: Kia Buzurg-Umid (Kia of Great Promise) and Abu-Ali of Qaswin. Kia was to inherit the spiritual and mystical aspect, while Abu-Ali attended to the military and administrative affairs of the Order. It is said that Hasan bin Sabah died almost immediately afterwards, in 1124, at ninety years of age; having given the world a new word; assassin. 'Assasseen' in Arabic signifies 'guardians', and some commentators have considered this to be the true origin of the word: 'guardians of the secrets".

The Organization of the Order, under Hasan, called for Missionaries (Dayes), Friends (Rafiq) who were disciples, and Fidavis, devotees. The last group had been added by Hasan to the Ismaili original, and these were the trained killers. Fidavis wore white, with a girdle, cap or boots of red. In addition to careful coaching in where and when to place the dagger in the victim's bosom, they were trained in such things as languages, the dress and manners of monks, merchants and soldiers, any of whom they were ready to impersonate in carrying out their missions. The chief was known as Sayedna (Our Prince, Leader), and, popularly (because of the mountain stronghold of Alamut), as the Sheikh of the Mountain. This is the figure referred to in Crusaders' writings as 'Sydney', or 'Senex de Monte', the first word being a literal translation of the word 'Pir': Persian for Ancient, or Sage. There were three Great Missionaries, who ruled three territories. After the Friends and Fidavis came the Laziks, aspirants who were being trained for membership of the society, but were as yet uninitiated.

Hasan reduced the original number of degrees of initiation from nine to the mystical number of seven. A similar number of regulations formed the Rules of the Order. This, in fact, comprised the working plan of the spreading of the Faith. The First Rule was that the Missionary must know human psychology in such a way as to be able to select suitable people for admission to the cult; and was summed up in the mnemonic: *Cast no seeds upon rocks*. The second rule of procedure was the application of flattery and gaining the confidence of the prospective member. Third came the casting of doubt into the mind, by superior knowledge. Fourthly, the teacher must apply an oath to the student never to betray any of the 'truths' which were to be revealed to him. Now he was told, as the fifth stage, that Ismailism was a powerful secret organization, supported by some of the most important figures of the time. After this, the aspirant was questioned and studied, to discover whether he had absorbed the opinions of the teacher and attached himself sufficiently into a position of dependence upon his ideas. At this stage he was asked to meditate upon the meaning of the reported saying of the prophet that "Paradise lies in the shadow of swords". In the final degree, many difficult passages of the Koran were explained in terms of allegory.

How is it that the rules of this extraordinarily successful Order are known in such detail? It so happened that when the Mongols eventually overthrew Alamut by force of arms, their chief, Halaku ('Destruction') Khan, asked his chief minister to examine their library. This most learned man, 'Father of Kings' Jawani, later wrote a careful book in which he detailed the organization of the Assassins, whose name he attributed to the use of the drug Hashish, which they were said to use in stupefying candidates for the ephemeral visit to 'paradise'.

It is possible that recruits were made in another way than by selecting gullible, fully grown youths. Legend has it that Hasan, once master of Alamut, used to buy unwanted children from their parents, and train them in implicit obedience and with the sole desire to die in his service.

Buzurg-Umid ('Great Promise'), the second Grand Master, maintained the power of the Assassins on much the same pattern: building new forts, gaining fresh converts, terrorizing those whom he did not want to have killed and using them to further his designs of world conquest. Sultan Sanjar of Persia, in spite of several expeditions against the Viper's Nest, as Alamut was now being called, could do little about him. Ambassadors on each side were slain; a notable religious leader was captured by the Assassins, given a mock trial and flung into a furnace. The Grand Master at this time seldom put on the field more than two thousand men at a time: but it must be remembered that they were killers acting under an iron discipline, and more than a match for any organized army that they might ever have to face. Now the Order began to spread in Syria, where the continued contact with the Crusaders was established.

The warriors of the Cross were in fairly effective control of an area extending from the Egyptian border to Armenia in the north. Bahram, a Persian leader of the Assassin cult from Astrabad, gained control of a mighty fortress in Syria, in the region known as the Valley of Demons (Wadi-el-Jan), and from there spread out from one fort to another. The Grand Prior Bahram now moved to an even more substantial fortified place, Massyat. Bahram's successor, Ismail the Lash-Bearer, planted a trained devotee on the saintly Vizier of Baghdad, into whose confidence he worked his way to such an extent that this Assassin, now called the 'Father of Trust', was actually made Grand Judge of Baghdad.

The Crusaders had by now been about thirty years in the Holy Land, and the Assassins decided that they could usefully form an alliance with them aimed against Baghdad. A secret treaty was therefore made between the Grand Master and Baldwin II, King of Jerusalem, whereby the Ismaili Grand Judge would have opened the gates of Baghdad treacherously to the Crusaders, if the fortified city of Tyre were handed over to the Assassins for their part in the transaction.

Something went wrong. The judge had ordered an underling to open the city's gates. This servant had told the military commander of Damascus, who lost no time in killing the man, the Vizier and six thousand people believed to be secret Assassins within the city. The Damascus garrison fell upon the Crusaders and beat them back in a thunderstorm which the Christian warriors attributed to divine anger at their unworthy pact, and the Assassins as an attempt by the powers of Nature to allow the Crusaders into the city under its cover.

Meanwhile the Grand Master was indulging in an orgy of destruction of individual rulers who opposed his creed; the list is interminable, but this is a fair example: "The celebrated Aksunkur, Prince of Mosul, was a warrior equally dreaded by the Christians and the Assassins. As this Prince, on his return from Ma'ara Masrin, where the Moslem and Christian hosts had parted without venturing to engage, entered the Mosque at Mosul to perform his devotions, he was attacked at the moment when he was about to take his usual seat by eight Assassins, disguised as dervishes. Three of them fell below the blows of the valiant Emir; but ere his people could come to his aid, he had received his death-wound and expired."

The fanaticism which inspired the killers was shared, it seems, by other members of their families, who had been thoroughly trained in the bloody creed: for the historian Kamal-ed-Din relates, "On this occasion when the mother of one of the youths who attempted Aksunkur's life heard that he had been slain, she painted her face and donned the gayest raiment and ornaments, rejoicing that her son had been found worthy to die the glorious death of a martyr in the cause of the Imam. But when she saw him return alive and unscathed, she cut off her hair and blackened her countenance, and would not be comforted."

Things thus continued for the fourteen years and a quarter of the Second Grand Master's rule. When he died he nominated his son Kia Mohammed as his successor. Under Mohammed the killings continued, a part of the sea-coast of Palestine came into Assassin hands, and the cult leaders reaffirmed their overt belief in orthodox Islam. In public, Ismailis were ordinary Moslems; the secret doctrine of the divinely guided leader was not to be discussed with the uninitiated.

But this most successful of secret societies soon showed that its strength ultimately depended upon a powerful leader: and Kia Mohammed was no such. Little by little it became obvious that his own son, Hasan the Hated, was the stronger personality. Now Hasan, through some magnetic power, was able to capture the imagination of the Assassins, soon having it believed that he himself was none other than the Power of All Powers, the Hidden Imam, who had been mentioned by the first Grand Master; an incarnation of all greatness. So important was he that he was the fountain of power, and others only held a measure of authority because he allowed them to have it.

This final absurdity was lapped up by members who had been conditioned to believe in things which were not, shall we say, exactly self-evident to the ordinary man. The doctrine of the all-powerful Invisible Imam was a part of Ismailism; and Hasan was ready even during his early manhood to assume the role. But, since his father was able to assert himself by having some two hundred and fifty of Hasan's followers murdered, he thought it wiser to hold his hand. In 1163 his chance came. Mohammed died, and Hasan II issued an order to all Ismailis to collect below the castle of Alamut.

Never before had such an assembly of killers, fanatics and dedicated perverters of the truth been seen. Hasan, probably in a state of megalomania, assured them that he had received a message from the Almighty that as from now, all the bonds of religion were loosed: everyone might do as he liked. It was not necessary to keep up pretences. And, furthermore, he, Hasan, was none other than the Hidden Imam. His word was law; and he was a form of the divinity, not merely relaying instructions from above.

There was one further obstacle. According to Ismaili doctrine, the Hidden Imam was to be of the Family of Hashim, the blood of Mohammed the Prophet. Such descendants were known and revered: and it was common knowledge that Hasan II was not one of them. He overcame this difficulty by stating that he was not in fact the true son of Kia Mohammed the Persian, but an adopted child of the Caliphial family of Egypt. This pretence was carried on for four years, during which the crazed Hasan showed that he was not as mad as he might have been, by consolidating quite efficiently the power of the cult. Eventually, he was assassinated by his brother-in-law, Namwar ('The Famous'). Now the father-to-son succession seemed to be established. Mohammed II, son of Hasan II, began the cultivation of letters and sciences which was to distinguish successive Grand Masters of the Order. It was a conceit of his, in the time of the greatest flowering of Persian literature, that he was supreme among poets and philosophers. He used his assassins, too, to drive this point well home. The Imam Razi, one of the greatest thinkers of the time, refused to acknowledge the Assassins as the most advanced theologians: so Mohammed II sent an envoy to him, promising either a swift death by dagger or a pension of several thousand gold pieces a year. Suddenly the learned Imam's discourses seemed to lose their bite. One day, soon afterwards, he was asked why he did not attack the Assassins as of old. "Because," said the old man, with a nervous glance around the assembly where a murderer might lurk, "their arguments are so sharp, and pointed."

For thirty-five years Mohammed II ruled the Ismailis with a rod of iron; the only law was that of obedience to the Assassin will. The observances of ritual Islam were abolished. A new star had arisen: a power to stiffen resistance to Crusader penetration; Saladin, who was to become an implacable foe of the Assassins.

The Syrian branch of the cult grew in power, while the activities of the Eastern Assassins were carried out much more quietly, with missionaries being sent to India, Afghanistan, even the remote Pamir Mountains which straddle China and Russia, where even today adherents of the sect are to be found. Saladin had overcome

the other Ismaili branch and original home of Assassinism—
Egypt—and restored the true faith to the people of the Nile. He
now had enough booty for ten years' war against the Crusaders
in Palestine, and troops to spare. His first task was to unify the
forces of Islam; and this he determined to do by force if necessary.
Sinan, Ancient of the Assassin cult in Syria, decided to oppose
this terrible enemy of the Fatimites. Three assassins fell upon
Saladin and nearly killed him. This made the sect a priority target
for the Saracen chief. The Old Man of the Mountain, for his
part, now unleashed a succession of fanatics, in every kind of
disguise, upon Saladin. By 1176, Saladin decided that an end
must be put to the cult. He invaded their territory and started to
lay it waste, when the Assassin chief offered him freedom of action
to fight the Crusaders, and no further attempt upon his life, if the
cult were spared. These terms were agreed to, and henceforth no
Assassin ever again attempted to molest Sultan Saladin.

This period introduces Sinan as yet another strange and terrible
Assassin leader. He had decided that he was the incarnation of all
power and deity, and that he would live the part. Sinan was never
seen to eat or drink, sleep, or even to spit. Between sunrise and
sunset he stood on a pinnacle of rock, dressed in a hair-shirt, and
preached his own power and glory to delighted Assassins. Thus,
at one and the same time, there were two chiefs of the Order, each
busily telling his own followers that he, and he alone, was God.
Hasan in Persia, Sinan in Syria, each commanded legions of
devoted killers, all committed by oath to follow his path.

When Mohammed II died, he was succeeded by his son
Jalaludin, who completely reversed the orders that the Assassins
were to have no outward religious observances. He felt that he
could do a great deal by adopting the cloak of orthodox piety,
and sent ambassadors far and wide to announce his maintenance
of the true faith. He went so far as to curse his predecessors
publicly, in order to convince the incredulous that such a people
as the Assassins could turn over a new leaf. As a result of what
would today be called a long-term and comprehensive propaganda plan, he was acknowledged as a religious leader by half

the orthodox monarchs of Islam, and (the first Assassin to be so styled) came to be termed Prince Jalaludin.

Jalaludin died in 1203, after twelve years of leadership of the cult, handing over to Alaeddin (Aladdin), a child of nine years of age. Weak, inefficient, stupid, Alaeddin made little mark upon history. It is said that his main activity was tending sheep, to which he was passionately attached, and he even had a small hut built in a sheepfold, where he spent most of his time. He was extraordinarily cruel, in spite of the contact with the sheep, and continued to terrorize in time-honoured fashion any person, great or small, who did not pay tribute or otherwise co-operate with the organization.

The Assassins' hands, ears and eyes were everywhere. Once fully initiated, a man might be sent to a place a thousand miles away, there to take up residence and live: waiting for the moment when orders came to him from Alamut to fulfil his fatal destiny. A story is told of the court of the Shah of Khwarism, thus: "The Ismaili ambassador spent some time with the Vizier. One day, after a splendid banquet when the wine which they had been drinking in violation of the law had mounted into their heads, the ambassador told the Vizier by way of confidence that there were several Ismailis among the pages, grooms, guards and other persons who were immediately about the Sultan. The Vizier, dismayed and at the same time curious to know who these dangerous attendants were, besought the ambassador to point them out to him, giving him his napkin as a pledge that nothing evil should happen to them. Instantly, at a sign from the envoy, five of the persons who were attendants in the chamber stepped forth, avowing themselves to be concealed Assassins. 'On such a day and at such an hour,' said one of them, an Indian, to the Vizier, 'I might have slain thee without being seen or punished; and if I did not do so it was only because I had no orders from my superiors.' "

The Vizier begged for his life. But word got to the Sultan, who ordered the Assassins to be apprehended and burned alive, and "the five chamberlains were cast on the flaming pyre, where they

35

died exulting at being found worthy to suffer in the service of the great Sheikh of the Mountain." The Assassins had the last laugh, for an order arrived immediately afterwards from Alamut, that the Shah must pay ten thousand pieces of gold as compensation for each man killed—which he did.

Another subsidiary activity which the Assassins delighted in was the holding captive in Alamut of useful, rare and distinguished personages who could be of value to them in educational, military or other spheres. One was a physician, another a famous astronomer, a third the greatest painter in Persia, who worked to the order of the chief alone.

The end of a chapter was near, for the Mongol hordes under Halaku, lieutenant of Chinghiz, were steadily destroying all the civilization of Islam which lay in their inexorable path westwards. Rukneddin, son of Alaeddin, succeeded him and tried at first to turn the Mongol tide. After a series of encounters, pitched battles, intrigues and counter-intrigues, Rukneddin was taken. He played for time as long as he could, but was eventually murdered in his own turn by the victorious Mongol chief's men. Assassin power in Persia was broken, and what remained of the members were ordered—none knows by whom—to conceal their faith and await a signal that the cult was in full operation again. Alamut was silenced, and the Syrian headquarters alone remained.

It was a long time until the Mamluk Sultan of Egypt was able to overcome the Mongol thrust. In 1260, however, he carried the banners of Islam victoriously against them, and restored the fortress of Alamut and other properties to the Assassins, who were strongly surviving underground. They soon found that they had exchanged one master for another, for the Egyptians were now employing them for their own purposes. Ibn Batuta, the great traveller of the fourteenth century, found them well entrenched in their former strong places, being used as the "arrows of the Sultan of Egypt with which he reaches his enemies."

The supposed suppression of the creed which followed the Mongol destruction did not in fact take place. Copying each other, historians have asserted that Assassinism died six hundred years ago. Now and again, however, fresh facts of their continued existence still come to light. In the eighteenth century an Englishman, the British Consul at Aleppo in Syria, was at pains to make this better known: "Some authors assert," he writes, "that these people were entirely extirpated in the thirteenth century by the Tartars . . . but I, who have lived so long in this infernal place, will venture to affirm that some of their spawn still exists in the mountains that surround us; for nothing is so cruel, barbarous and execrable that is not acted, and even gloried in, by these cursed Gourdins."

The Assassins were widely dispersed throughout Asia. The rise of the Thugs, the secret society of assassination of India, followed the Mongol invasion of Persia. Indeed, at least one of the Thug recognition-signals (Ali bhai Salam!) indicates salutations to Ali, the descendant of the Prophet most greatly revered by the Assassins. Ismailis, not all of them recognizing the one chief, reside in places as far apart as Malaya, East Africa and Ceylon. They would not necessarily feel that they are Assassins in the same sense as the extremists who followed the old Sheikhs of the Mountains; but at least some of them revere the descendants of the Lords of Alamut to the extent of deification.

The modern phase of Ismailism dates from 1810, when the French Consul at Aleppo found that the Assassins in Persia recognized as their divinely-inspired chief a reputed descendant of the Fourth Grand Master of Alamut, who then lived at Kehk, a small village between Isfahan and Tehran. This Shah Khalilullah "was revered almost like a god and credited with the power of working miracles . . . the followers of Khalilullah would, when he pared his nails, fight for the clippings; the water in which he washed became holy water."

The sect next appear to the public gaze through an odd happening. In 1866, a law case was decided in Bombay. There is in that city a large community of commercial men known as Khojas: "A Persian," the record tells us, "Aga Khan Mehalati (i.e., a native of Mehelat, a place situate near Khek) had sent an agent to Bombay to claim from the Khojas the annual tribute due from them to him, and amounting to about £10,000. The claim was resisted, and the British court was appealed to by Aga Khan. Sir Joseph Arnold investigated his claim. The Aga proved his pedigree, showing that he descended in a direct line from the fourth Grand Master of Alamut, and Sir Joseph declared it proved; and it was further demonstrated by the trial that the Khojas were members of the ancient sect of the Assassins, to which sect they had been converted four hundred years before by an Ishmaelite missionary, who composed a work which has remained the sacred book of the Khojas."

In the First Afghan War, the then Aga Khan contributed a force of light cavalry to the British forces. For this he was awarded a pension. Hitti, in his *History of the Arabs*, notes (p. 448, 1951 edition) that the Assassin sect, known as Khojas and Malwas, gave over a tenth of their revenues to the Aga Khan, who "spends most of his time as a sportsman between Paris and London." The influence of the new form of organization and training, as well as initiatory techniques, of the Assassins upon later societies has been remarked by a number of students. That the Crusaders knew a good deal about the Ismailis is shown from the detailed descriptions of them which survive. S. Ameer Ali, an Orientalist of considerable repute, goes further in his assessment: "From the Ismailis the Crusaders borrowed the conception which led to the formation of all the secret societies, religious and secular, of Europe. The institutions of Templars and Hospitallers; the Society of Jesus, founded by Ignatius Loyola, composed by a body of men whose devotion to their cause can hardly be surpassed in our time; the ferocious Dominicans, the milder Franciscans—may all be traced either to Cairo or to Alamut. The Knights Templar especially, with their system of grand masters, grand priors and religious devotees, and their degrees of initiation, bear the strongest analogy to the Eastern Ismailis."

Fig. B

3

The Rise of the Knights Templar

IN A.D. 1118 nine knights, concerned for the welfare of pilgrims to the Holy Land, bound themselves together in the creation of a knightly Order. In under two hundred years this organization had become one of the most powerful single entities—if not the greatest—in Europe. A few years later it was utterly destroyed. The zeal of religion, the conditioning which made men support a dedicated cause with all their might, was likewise the instrument of their destruction. Nothing less than religious fervour could have smashed the Order: as nothing less could have created it.

Were the Knights Templar devil-worshippers, secret Saracens, indulging in obscene orgies? Did they adore a head, spit on the Cross, use the word 'Yallah' (O Allah!) in their rituals? Did they learn their ways from the terrible sect of the Assassins? Nobody really knows the answers; but the story of the rise and fall of the Templars is something well worth studying.

The original objective of the Order, which immediately became the subject of applause throughout Christendom, was to combine the two functions of monk and knight, to live chastely and fight the Saracens with the sword and spirit. The Sweet Mother of God was chosen as their patroness; and they bound themselves to live in accordance with the rules of St. Augustine, electing as their first leader Hugh de Payens. King Baldwin II granted them a part of his palace to live in, and gave them a grant towards their upkeep.

They vowed to consecrate their swords, arms, strength and lives to the defence of the mysteries of the Christian faith; to pay complete and utter obedience to the orders of the Grand Master; to fight whenever commanded, regardless of perils, for the faith of Christ as they understood it. Among the vows taken were those which forbade their yielding even a foot of land to the enemy, and not to retreat, even if attacked in the proportion of three to one. They chose the name *militia templi*—soldiers of the Temple —after the temple supposedly built by Solomon in Jerusalem, near which they had been assigned quarters by the King.

Philip the Fair.

Some say that the Templars derived the idea of their Order from that of the Hospitallers, who looked after Catholic pilgrims to Palestine; for there was little hospitality to be had from the native Orthodox Christians of those parts. Others hold that there was an even older Order from which they received their inspiration. No reliable evidence on this point is, however, available. Although the Templars were so poor that two men had to share a horse (and their Seal commemorated this decades after they became one of the richest communities of their time), they soon attracted favourable notice and support. Only one year after their establishment, Fulk, Count of Anjou, who had come to Jerusalem on a pilgrimage, joined as a married member and gave them an annual grant of thirty pounds of silver. This example was soon followed by other devout Western princes.

For the first nine years of their existence, the knights continued to live a life of chastity and poverty, in accordance with their vows. They adopted a striped white and black banner, called the *Beauséant*, after their original piebald horse; and this word also became their battle-cry. Special raiment they had none, and they wore whatever clothes were given to them by the pious. But little by little, as one writer puts it, they were to become "haughty and insolent".

Baldwin of Jerusalem, who had been a prisoner in the hands of the Saracens and knew of their disunity, realized at about this time that Islam must eventually unite against the Christian invasion, and he decided that the Templars would prove ideal allies in the battles which were to come. In 1127, therefore, he sent two Templars with his strong recommendation to the Pope, applying for official recognition of the Order by the Holy See. They had an introduction to St. Bernard himself, the Abbot of Clairvaux, who was known to be an admirer of theirs, and who was a nephew of one of their envoys. Then the Grand Master himself arrived in Europe, and received the eulogistic opinion of the Abbot: "They go not headlong into battle, but with care and foresight, peacefully, as true children of Israel. But as soon as the fight has begun, they rush without delay upon the foe . . . and know no fear . . . one has often put to flight a thousand; two, ten thousand . . . gentler than lambs and grimmer than lions; theirs is the mildness of monks and the valour of the knight." This testimonial was a part of the campaign to help the Templars in their efforts at recognition. On the 31st January, 1128, the Master appeared before the Council of Troyes. This formidable body consisted of the Archbishops of Rheims and Sens, ten bishops and a number of abbots—including St. Bernard himself—presided over by the Cardinal of Albano, the Papal legate. They were approved; and Pope Honorius chose for them a white mantle, completely plain. The red cross was added by order of Pope Eugenius III in 1146.

Hugh de Payens now took his delegation through France and England, and collected a number of recruits. Gifts and grants were showered upon the Order; lands, rents and arms were forthcoming from all quarters. Richard I of England was enthusiastic about them. By 1133, King Alfonso of Aragon and Navarre, who had fought the Spanish Moors in twenty-nine battles, had willed his country to them; although when the Moors finally laid him low his nobles prevented the Templars from claiming their rights.

In 1129 the Master, accompanied by three hundred knights, recruited from the noblest houses of Europe, led a huge train of pilgrims to the Holy Land. It was at this time that the Templars formed part of the Christian contingent which, allied with the Assassins, tried to take Damascus. Were they (as the Orientalist von Hammer alleges) connected in some secret way with the Assassins? It is an historical fact that the Assassins were prepared to adopt Christianity if they could gain greater power thereby: Christianity, that is, on the surface. Hammer points to the similarity of the two organizations. The followers of Hasan Ibn Sabah were in contact with the Templars, and had a similar method of organization. They were in existence before the Templars were formed: "The Ismailians (Assassins) was the original, and the Order of the Templars, the copy."

The balance of Western opinion is against this contention; more particularly because, one feels from wide reading of historians, great sympathy is felt for the cruelly treated and arbitrarily dispossessed Templars. Thus Keightley, who made a close study of the Order, attacks those who would claim that the Templars were an Assassin branch: "When, nearly thirty years after their institution, the Pope gave them permission to wear a cross on their mantle, like the rival Hospitaller Order, no colour could present itself so well suited to those who daily and hourly exposed themselves to martyrdom as that of blood, in which there was so much of what was symbolical. With respect to internal organization it will, we apprehend, be always found that this is for the most part of the growth of time and the product of circumstances; and is always nearly the same where these last are similar."

The famous question of the three thousand gold pieces paid by the Syrian branch of the Assassins to the Templars is another matter which has never been settled. One opinion holds that this money was given as a tribute to the Christians; the other, that it was a secret allowance from the larger to the smaller organization. Those who think that the Assassins were fanatical Moslems, and therefore would not form any alliance with those who to them were infidels, should be reminded that to the followers of the Old Man of the Mountains only he was right, and the Saracens who were fighting the Holy War for Allah against the Crusaders were as bad as anyone else who did not accept the Assassin doctrine.

Grave charges against the Templars during the Crusades included the allegation that they were fighting for themselves alone. More than one historical incident bears this out. The Christians had besieged the town of Ascalon in 1153, and were engaged upon burning down the walls with large piles of inflammable materials. Part of the wall fell after a whole night of this burning. The Christian army was about to enter, when the Master of the Temple (Bernard de Tremelai) claimed the right to take the town himself. This was

The original Seal of the Templars.

because the first contingent into a conquered town had the whole spoils. As it happened, the garrison rallied and killed the Templars, closing the breach. There seem good grounds for believing that the power which they had gained caused the Templars to devote their efforts as much to their own Order's welfare as to the cause of the Cross, in spite of their tremendous sacrifices for that cause. Having no loyalty to any territorial chief, they obeyed their Master alone, and hence no softening political pressure could be put upon them. This might well have led to an idea that they were an invisible super-state; and this does show some similarity with the invisible empire of the Assassins. If none can deny their bravery, their high-handedness

43

and exclusivity in less than a hundred and fifty years after their founding gave them the reputation of considering themselves almost a law unto themselves.

"One of the most disgraceful acts which stain the annals of the Templars," says even one of their ardent admirers, "occurred in the year 1155, when Bertrand de Blancford (whom William of Tyre calls a 'pious and Godfearing man') was Master of the Order. In a contest for the supreme power in Egypt, which the viziers, bearing the proud title of Sultan, exercised under the phantom-caliphs, Sultan Abbas who had put to death the Caliph his master found himself obliged to fly from before the vengeance of the incensed people. With his harem and his own and a great part of the royal treasures, he took his way through the desert. A body of Christians, chiefly Templars, lay in wait for the fugitives near Ascalon. The resistance offered by the Moslems was slight and ineffectual; Abbas himself was either slain or fled, and his son Nasiredin professed his desire to become a Christian. The far larger part of the booty of course fell to the Templars; but this did not satisfy their avarice. They sold Nasiredin to his father's enemies for 60,000 pieces of gold, and stood by to see him bound hand and foot and placed in a sort of cage or iron-latticed sedan, on a camel to be conducted to Egypt, where a death by protracted torture awaited him."

It was not the Templars alone who were guilty of arrogance and worse. The Hospitallers had deteriorated from their first fine beginnings; and the annals of both Orders are not innocent of unpleasantness, though they are indeed well filled with tales of glory. The Hospitallers, for instance, refused to pay tithes to the Patriarch of Jerusalem, even going so far as to erect immense buildings in front of the Church of the Holy Sepulchre, as a practical demonstration of their own importance. When the Patriarch entered this church, they rang their bells so loudly that he could not make himself heard. There is an occasion recorded when "the congregation was assembled in church, the Hospitallers rushed into it in arms, and shot arrows among them as if they were robbers or infidels. These arrows were collected and hung up on Mount Calvary, where Christ had been crucified, to the scandal of these recreant knights. On applying to Pope Adrian IV for redress, the Syrian clergy found him and his cardinals so prepossessed in favour of his enemies—bribed by them, as was said—that they had no chance of relief."

This, then, was the background of the rise of the Templars, and the flavour of their environment. If one adds to these elements the fact that various very heterodox sects—gnostic, Manichae and the rest—still lurked in the Holy Land, together with a great deal of magic and superstition of every kind, there is a possibility, to say the least, that the Templars were infected by it. The contention which has been made, that such heresies and archaic religions and practices did not survive until the Templar period, is demonstrably false, although much play has been made of it by those who would defend the Order; for do such sects not endure there until this day? This is not to say that the Templars were guilty of the practices which formed the substance of the confessions later to be wrung from them by barbaric torture, which we will examine in due course. But a secret tradition and magical rites may well have played a part in their hidden lore and practices. It should also be remembered that towards the end there were Templars who were of actual Palestinian birth, who would have every opportunity of absorbing the unorthodox beliefs of the many schools of a magico-religious nature which existed in the area. The Grand Master Philip of Nablus (1167), for instance, was a Syrian, and many Crusaders were Levantine lords, whatever their original blood, speaking Arabic with perfection.

It was in 1162 that the Magna Carta of the Order was obtained by the Templars: the Bull *Omne Datum Optimum*, often described as the keystone of their power. Through this instrument they were able to consolidate their authority and preserve their secrets against intrusion. They were to find, too, that it did much to excite the envy of their opponents.

Pope Adrian IV had died, and two rival popes were elected: Alexander III by the Sicilian group, and Victor III by the imperial party. At first the Templars acknowledged Victor; but in 1161 they switched their allegiance to Alexander. There was probably some sort of secret arrangement behind this, for by January 7th of the following year the famous Bull was issued. By the terms of this document, the Templars were released from all spiritual ties except to the Holy See; they were permitted to have special burial-grounds in their own houses; they could have chaplains of their own; they had no tithes to pay; and were allowed to receive tithes. Nobody who had once entered the Order could leave it, except to join one with a stricter discipline. The stage was set for clerical hatred of the Templars and Hospitallers (who had similar privileges), although the advantages to the Pope from the combined support of these two Orders could hardly be overestimated.

In 1184 an incident occurred which inspired a great deal of distrust of the Order, although the rarity of its occurrence should have underlined the fact that it was nothing of much consequence. The English knight Robert of St. Albans left the Templars, became a Moslem and led an army for Saladin against Jerusalem, then in the hands of the Franks. The charge against the Templars that they were secret Mussulmans or allies of the Saracens does not seem borne out by the fact that Saladin accused them of treacherous truce-breaking and other crimes and—unlike his usual chivalrous self—took a solemn oath that he would execute such Templar captives as he could obtain, as "beyond the limits of Islam and infidelity alike." Nor did they make any attempt to invoke any religious bond with Saladin when they were captured, as we know from the Arabic *Life of Saldin* written contemporaneously by his secretary, Qadi Yusuf. Strong evidence of this is given in the events which followed the terrible Battle of Hittin. Two years before, Saladin had made a pact with the Assassins that they would give him a free hand to continue his Holy War against the Franks. On July 1st, 1187, he captured Tiberias. He attacked nearby Hittin at dawn on Friday, July 3rd. Thirty thousand Crusaders were captured, including the King of Jerusalem. No Templar is mentioned in the detailed Arab account as asking for mercy on religious or other grounds, although all knew that Saladin had issued a war-cry: "Come to death, Templars!" The Grand Master, Gerard of Ridefort, and several other knights were among those taken. Saladin offered them their lives if they would see the light of the True Faith. None accepted, and all these knights were beheaded except, admittedly, the Templar Grand Master. A non-Templar, Reginald of Chatillon, tried to invoke the sacred code of Arab hospitality, and other Crusaders claimed that they were Moslems, and were spared: none of them Templars or Hospitallers. Reginald and the Templars collectively were sentenced to death for breaking the truce and the "war crime" of killing unarmed pilgrims to Mecca. Arab accounts include only a few references which could be construed as indicating any collusion with the Christian army. One says that on the Friday at midday (the battle lasted for two days), Sultan Saladin issued the attack cry to be passed along the Saracen host, "On for Islam!", at which the striped banner of the Templars was raised, "and the Emir Lion-of-the Faith said, 'Are those Sultan (Saladin) Yusef's allies, of whom I have heard from the Reconnaisance men?' " This cannot be regarded as anything at all conclusive. The only other reference is to a body of Templars who went over to the Saracen side, and whose supposed descendants survive to this day as the Salibiyya (Crusader) tribe in north Arabia.

This engagement spelt the end of real Western power in Palestine for over seven hundred years, although it did stimulate the unsuccessful Third Crusade. Although the Templars—and some other Crusaders—were still in the Holy Land, they had lost almost all of their possessions there. But in the West lay the real seat of their power. At this time their European possessions numbered over seven thousand estates and foundations. Although principally concentrated in France and England, they had extensive properties in Portugal, Castile, Leon, Scotland and Ireland, Germany, Italy and Sicily. When Jerusalem was lost, their headquarters were transferred to Paris. This building, like all their branch churches, was known as the Temple. It was here that the French King Philip the Fair took refuge in 1306, to escape a civil commotion. It is said that this visit gave him his first insight into the real wealth of the order: the fabulous treasures which his hosts showed him giving the bankrupt monarch the idea to plunder the knights on the pretext that they were dominated by heresies.

Philip the Fair was not entirely without some grounds for attacking the Templars. In 1208 we find Pope Innocent III, a great friend of the Order, censuring them publicly for "Causing their churches to be thrown open for Mass to be said every day with loud ringing of bells, bearing the cross of Christ on their breasts but not caring to follow his doctrines which forbid giving offence to the little ones who believe in him. Following the doctrines of demons, they affix their cross of the Order upon the breast of every kind of scoundrel, asserting that

The last Grand Master of the Templars, in captivity.

whoever by paying two or three pence a year became one of their fraternity could not, even if interdicted, be deprived of Christian burial . . . and thus they themselves, being captive to the devil, cease not to make captive the souls of the faithful, seeking to make alive those whom they knew to be dead. . . ."

The first sign of an attempt to bring some sort of physical restraint upon the Templars came from Henry III of England. In 1252 he hinted that he might try to seize some of the property of the Order: "You prelates and religious," he said, "especially you Templars and Hospitallers, have so many liberties and charters that your enormous possessions make you rave with pride and haughtiness. What was imprudently given must therefore be prudently revoked; and what was inconsiderately bestowed must be considerately recalled."

The Master of the Templars immediately replied: "What sayest thou, O King? Far be it that thy mouth should utter so disagreeable and silly a word. So long as thou dost exercise justice thou wilt reign; but if thou infringe it, thou wilt cease to be King!"

4

The Fall of the Knights Templar

THE haughty Templars of the fourteenth century owned land and revenues, gained steadily in honour and importance. They might have had thrones had they wanted them; for such was their power towards the end that, banded together (as one historian points out), they could have overcome more than one of the smaller countries of Europe. Perhaps, though, they aimed even higher than that. If their eventual aim was world hegemony, they could not have organized themselves better, or planned their aristocratic hierarchy more thoroughly. The pride, arrogance and complete confidence and self-sufficiency of the Order is something which shows through even the least inspired pages of the chroniclers. Their power was legendary:

"Everywhere they had churches, chapels, tithes, farms, villages, mills, rights of pasturage, of fishing, of venery, of wood. They had also in many places the right of holding annual fairs which were managed and the tolls received by some of the brethren of the nearest houses or by their donates or servants. The number of their preceptories is, by the most moderate computation, rated at nine thousand; the annual income of the Order put at about six millions sterling: an enormous sum for those times! Masters of such a revenue, descended from the noblest houses in Christendom, uniting in their persons the most esteemed secular and religious characters, regarded as the chosen champions of Christ and the flower of Christian knights, it was not possible for the Templars, in such lax times as the twelfth and thirteenth centuries, to escape falling into the vices of extravagant luxury and overweening pride."

The Order, when fully developed, was composed of several classes: chiefly knights, chaplains and serving-brothers. Affiliated were those who were attached to the Order and worked for it and received its protection, without taking its vows. This affiliation was said to be derived from the Arab 'clientship' association, analogous to blood-brotherhood in tribal associations.

A candidate for knighthood should prove that he was of a knightly family and entitled to the distinction. His father must have been a knight, or eligible to become one. He had to prove that he was born in wedlock. The reason for this last requirement was said to be not only religious: there was the possibility that a political head such as a king or prince might influence the Order by managing to have one of his bastard sons enter it, later perhaps to rise to high rank therein, and finally attaching it to the service of his dominion.

The candidate had to be unmarried and free from all obligations. He should have made no vow, nor entered any other Order; and he was not to be in debt. Eventually the competition for admission was so great from eligible people that a very high fee was exacted from those who were to be monk-warriors of the Temple.

All candidates were to be knighted before entry into the Order. But the period of probation which was originally demanded was before very long entirely abolished. No young man could be admitted until he was twenty-one years of age, because he was to be a soldier as well as a monk, and this was the minimum age at which he could bear arms.

When a new knight was admitted to the Order, the ceremony was held in secret. This fact, and persistent rumours, caused the belief that certain ceremonies and tenets were put into practice which deviated more than a little from the rituals of the Church. The ceremony was held in one of the Order's chapels, in the presence of the assembled chapter alone.

The Master (or the Prior, who took his place in chapels other than those at which he was present) opened the proceedings: "Beloved brethren, ye see that the majority are agreed to receive

this man as a brother. If there be any among you who knows anything of him, on account of which he cannot lawfully become a
brother, let him say it; for it is better that this should be signified
beforehand than after he is brought before us."

If no objection was lodged, the aspirant was sent to a small
room with two or three experienced knights, to coach him in
what he had to know: "Brother, are you desirous of being associated with the Order?" If he agreed, they would dwell upon the
trials and rigours of being a Templar. He had to reply that for
the sake of God he was willing to undergo anything and remain
in the Order for life; they asked him if he had a wife or was
betrothed; had he made vows to any other Order; did he owe
money more than he could pay; was he of sound mind and body;
was he the servant of any person?

After satisfactory answers, the result was passed to the Master.
The assembled company was then asked again if they knew
anything that might disqualify him. If none objected, they
were asked: "Are you willing that he should be brought in, in
God's name?" The knights answered, "Let him be brought in, in
God's name."

He was now again asked by his sponsors if he still desired to
enter the Order. Receiving an affirmative reply, they led him to
the chapter, where he folded his hands and flung himself upon
his knees: "Sir, I am come before God and before you for the
sake of God and our Dear Lady, to admit me into your Society,
and the good deeds of the Order as one who will be all his life
long the servant and the slave of the Order."

"Beloved brother," answered the receptor, "you are desirous
of a great matter, for you see nothing but the outward shell of
our Order. It is only the outward shell when you see that we have
fine horses and rich caparisons, that we eat and drink well and
are splendidly clothed. From this you conclude that you will be
well off with us. But you know not the rigorous maxims which
are in our interior. For it is a hard matter for you, who are your
own master, to become the servant of another. You will hardly
be able to perform, in future, what you wish yourself. For when

you may wish to be on this side of the sea, you will be sent to the other side; when you will wish to be in Acre, you will be sent to the district of Antioch, to Tripolis, or to Armenia; or you will be sent to Apulia, to Sicily, or to Lombardy, or to Burgundy, France, England, or any other country where we have houses and possessions.

"When you will wish to sleep, you will be ordered to watch; when you will wish to watch, then you will be ordered to go to bed; when you will wish to eat, then you will be ordered to do something else. And as both we and you might suffer great inconvenience from what you have mayhap concealed from us, look here on the holy evangelists and the word of God and answer the truth to the questions which we shall put to you; for if you lie you will be perjured, and may be expelled the Order, from which God keep you!"

Now all the former questions were asked on Holy Writ.

If the answers proved acceptable, the receptor continued:

"Beloved brother, take good care that you have spoken the truth to us: for should you have spoken false on any one point, you might be put out of the Order—from which God keep you! Now, beloved brother, attend strictly to what we shall say unto you. Do you promise to God, and to our dear Lady Mary to be, all your life long, obedient to the Master of the Temple, and to the Prior who shall be set over you?"

"Yea, sir, with the help of God!"

"Do you promise to God, and to our dear Lady Mary, to live chaste of your body all your life long?"

"Yea, sir, with the help of God!"

"Do you promise to God, and to our dear Lady Mary, to observe all your life long, the laudable manners and customs of our Order, both those which are already in use and those which the Master and Knights may add?"

"Yea, Sir, with the help of God!"

"Do you promise to God, and to our dear Lady Mary, that you will, with the strength and powers which God has bestowed on you, help as long as you live to conquer the Holy Land of

53

Jerusalem; and that you will, with all your strength, aid to keep and guard that which the Christians possess?"

"Yea, Sir, with the help of God!"

"Do you promise to God, and to our dear Lady Mary, never to hold (leave) this Order for stronger or weaker, for better or worse, than with the permission of the Master, or the chapter which has the authority?"

"Yea, Sir, with the help of God!"

"Do you finally promise to God, and to our dear Lady Mary, never to be present when a Christian is unjustly and unlawfully despoiled of his heritage, and that you will never, by counsel or by act, take part therein?"

"Yea, Sir, with the help of God!"

"In the name, then, of God, and our dear Lady Mary, and in the name of St. Peter of Rome, and of our father the Pope, and in the name of all the brethren of the Temple, we receive to all the good works of the Order which have been performed from the beginning, and shall be performed to the end, you, your father, your mother, and all of your family whom you will let have share therein. In like manner do you receive us to all the good work which you have performed and shall perform. We assure you of bread and water and the poor clothing of the Order, and labour and toil enow."

The candidate was admitted. The white mantle with its red cross was placed by the Master over the neck of the candidate, and clasped firmly by him. The Chaplain recited the 132nd psalm and the prayer of the Holy Ghost, and each brother repeated a paternoster.

Then the Master and the Chaplain kissed the new entrant on the mouth. As he sat down before the Master, the latter delivered him a sermon on his duties.

Knights were equipped more lightly than other Crusaders, and were issued with shield, sword, lance and mace. They were allocated three horses each, plus an esquire, who was either a serving-brother or a layman, perhaps a youth from a noble family anxious to become a knight in his own turn.

Retired knights were looked after by the Order, became counsellors at meetings, and were eventually buried in coffins in their Templar habit, with the legs crossed. Many Templar gravestones show the Knight with his feet upon a dog.

It was Philip the Fair of France, bankrupt and fearful of the growing power of the warriors of the Temple, who laid the conspiracy for the suppression of the Order for all time. It has been hinted that Philip had some forewarning that a plot against the throne was afoot; that the Templars, frustrated in their attempts to win back the Holy Land, were about to turn upon Pope and King alike and try to overcome all Christendom. In 1305, Pope Clement had been crowned through the assistance of the French King; and Philip was ready to bring all the power of Church and State against the Knights of the Temple.

There had been continual rivalry between the Templars and the Hospitallers; and Clement, six months after his enthronement, wrote asking them to visit him for a conference, ostensibly for the purpose of making plans for aiding the kings of Armenia and Cyprus. The Pope was, however, hoping that he could effect a reconciliation between the two Orders, which would in turn strengthen his own position as their only ultimate head. William de Villaret, Master of the Hospital, was fully engaged in an attack upon the Saracens of Rhodes when the invitation arrived, and could not obey it; but Jacques de Molay, Grand Master of the Temple, decided to accept. He handed over the defence of Limassol in Cyprus to the Order's Marshal, collected sixty knights, packed 150,000 gold florins plus much other treasure, and set sail for France.

At Paris, de Molay was received with honours by the King who was plotting his downfall. In Poitiers, he met Clement, and discussed the possibilities of a fresh Crusade. De Molay opined that only a complete alliance of all Christendom could be of any avail against the Moslems, and that the amalgamation of the two Orders was not a good idea. The Grand Master returned to Paris; and almost at once rumours began to circulate about certain serious charges to be preferred against the Order. Troubled by this campaign, the Master (together with Rimbaud de Caron, Preceptor of Outremer; Jeffrey de Goneville, Preceptor of Aquitane, and Hugh de Peraudo, Preceptor of France) returned to Poitiers to justify the Order before the Pope.

An audience took place, about April of 1307, in which the Pope mentioned the charges which had been made. The commission understood that their answers satisfied Clement, and returned to the capital in good heart. But this was just the beginning.

The method by which the charges were originally said to have been made was through a former Templar who had been expelled from the Order for heresy and other offences. This Squin de Flexian found himself in prison, together with another man (a Florentine named Noffo Dei), and they thought (or were told) that they could obtain their release and a pardon for the crime of which they were currently accused if they would testify against the Order. One account has it that de Flexian called for the governor of the prison, saying that he had a disclosure to make which he could tell the King personally; and which would be more to him than the conquest of a whole kingdom. Another chronicle has it that both men were degraded Templars, and had been actively engaged in the revolt against the King during which Philip had been forced to take refuge with the Templars. It is further stated that Cardinal Cantilupo, the Chamberlain to the Pope, who had been in association with the Templars since he was eleven years old, had confessed some of their doings to his master.

Ten main charges were made by de Flexian against the Order:

Latter-day Templar seal.

1. Each Templar on his admission swore never to quit the Order, and to further its interests by right or wrong.

2. The heads of the Order are in secret alliance with the Saracens, and they have more of Mohammedan infidelity than Christian faith. Proof of the latter includes that they make every novice spit upon the cross and trample upon it, and blaspheme the faith of Christ in various ways.

3. The heads of the Order are heretical, cruel and sacrilegious men. Whenever any novice, on discovering the iniquity of the Order, tries to leave it, they kill him and bury the body secretly by night. They teach women who are pregnant by them how to procure abortion, and secretly murder such newborn children.

4. They are infected with the errors of the Fratecelli; they despise the Pope and the authority of the Church; they scorn the sacraments, especially those of penance and confession. They pretend to comply with the rites of the Church simply to avoid detection.

5. The superiors are addicted to the most infamous excesses of debauchery. If anyone expresses his repugnance to this, he is punished by perpetual captivity.

6. The Temple-houses are the receptacle of every crime and abomination that can be committed.

7. The Order works to put the Holy Land into the hands of the Saracens, and favours them more than the Christians.

8. The Master is installed in secret and few of the younger brethren are present at this ceremony. It is strongly suspected that on this occasion he repudiates the Christian faith, or does something contrary to right.

9. Many statutes of the Order are unlawful, profane and contrary to Christianity. The members are therefore forbidden under pain of perpetual confinement to reveal them to anyone.

10. No vice or crime committed for the honour or benefit of the Order is held to be a sin.

These charges were later augmented by others which were collected through testimony from other enemies of the Order, and included such assertions as the use of the phrase *Ya Allah*

(O Allah!) and the adoration of an idol called the Head of Baphomet.

Philip and his advisers prepared in great secrecy for the descent upon this powerful organization. On the 12th of September, 1307, sealed letters were sent to all governors and Royal officers throughout France, instructing them to arm themselves on the twelfth of the next month and open the seal orders—and to act upon them forthwith. By the morning of Friday, October 13th,

Grand Inspecteur Franc-Maçonnique.

Cyphers used by secret societies.

almost every Templar in France was in the hands of the King's men. Hardly one seems to have had any warning. On the day before his arrest, the Grand Master had actually been chosen by the King to be a pall-bearer at a State funeral.

The secret orders had it that all Templars were to be seized, tortured and interrogated. Confessions were to be obtained from them; pardon might be promised if they confessed. All their goods were to be expropriated.

The King himself took possession of the Temple at Paris as soon as the Grand Master and his knights were arrested. The next day the University of Paris assembled, together with canons and other functionaries and ministers; and the Chancellor declared that the knights had been proceeded against for heresy. Two days later the University met in the Temple and some heads of the Order, including the Grand Master, were interrogated. They are said to have confessed to 'forty years' guilt'.

Whether de Molay and others confessed on that occasion or not, the King was emboldened to publish an accusation, in which he called the knights "polluters of the air and devouring wolves". A public meeting was called in the Royal Gardens and addressed by monks and representatives on this subject.

Edward II was the son-in-law of the French Philip, and to him was sent a priest who invited the English monarch to act at once against the Order in Britain. Edward almost at once wrote to say that the charges seemed to him to be incredible. But Pope Clement wrote on November 22nd to London, assuring Edward that the Master of the Temple had confessed of his own free will that knights on their admission to the Order denied Christ. Others had admitted idolatry and other crimes. He therefore called upon the King of England to arrest all Templars within his domains, and to place their lands and goods in custody until their guilt or innocence should be ascertained.

Before he received this missive, Edward seems to have been sorely troubled by the allegations. He wrote, on November 26th, to the Seneschal of Agen, asking about the charges. On the 4th of December he wrote to the kings of Portugal, Castile, Aragon and Sicily, asking "what they had heard, and adding that he had given no credit to it". He wrote to the Pope himself on December 10th, expressing disbelief of what the French King said, and begging His Holiness to instittute an enquiry. By December 15th, when the Papal Bull arrived, Edward felt that he must act upon it without question. On December 26th he wrote to the Pope that his orders would be obeyed. In the interim, Edward had sent word to Wales, Scotland and Ireland that the Templars were all to be seized, as in England; but they were to be treated with kindness.

On October 19th, less than a week after they had been arrested, 140 prisoners were being tortured by the Dominican Imbert, in the Paris Temple. Promises and the rack produced many confessions. Thirty-six of the examinees died during these proceedings. Throughout France the racks worked overtime, and the confessions poured forth. Many of these were contradictory and confused; perhaps there is little wonder of that.

The Pope now seemed a little uneasy at the arbitrary methods which were being employed. Philip wrote sharply to him saying that he, the King, was doing God's work, and rendered accounts to God alone. He offered to turn over all the goods of the Templars to the service of the Holy Land, Clement, still a weakling, merely stipulated that the inquisitions of each Bishop should be confirmed by a Provincial Council, and that the examination of the heads of the Order should be reserved to himself. Now we hear a constant succession of confessions and retractions, allegations that the heads of the Order confessed completely and spontaneously to the Pope himself. The Pope himself, for some unexplained reason, tried to escape to Bordeaux, but was stopped by the King. Now he was the monarch's captive as well as his creation.

Detailed confessions of individual Templars have been kept on record, many of them undoubtedly obtained by extreme racking and other tortures. The Templars who were prepared to defend the Order in court were brought to Paris, to the number of five hundred and forty-six. Deprived of their knightly habits and the sacraments of the Church, they had no means to acquire defence counsel. Their numbers rose to nine hundred, and now they clamoured for the presence of the Grand Master, who was held elsewhere. An Act of Accusation in the name of the Pope was drawn up, and seventy-five Templars drew up the Defence.

The accusation had it now that "At the time of their reception they were made to deny God, Christ, the Virgin, etc., and in particular to declare that Christ was not the true God, but a false prophet, who had been crucified for his own crimes and not for the redemption of the world. They spat and trampled upon the cross, especially on Good Friday. They worshipped a cat, which sometimes appeared in their chapters. Their priests, when celebrating Mass, did not pronounce the words of consecration. They believed that their Master could absolve them from their sins. They were told at their reception that they might abandon themselves to all kinds of licentiousness. They had idols in all their provinces, some with three faces, some with one. They worshipped these idols in their chapters, believed that they could save them, regarded them as the givers of wealth to the order and of fertility to the earth; they touched them with cords which they afterwards tied around their own bodies. Those who at the time of their reception would not comply with these practices were put to death or imprisoned."

The reply of the Templars denied every charge and stated that they had been subjected to every kind of illegality since their arrest. Fifty-four of the knights who had volunteered to defend the Order were committed to the flames, having been declared relapsed heretics, before the trials had even started.

Four years to the day after the first arrests, the Pope led a convocation of one hundred and fourteen bishops to come to a final decision about the Templar Order. The prelates of Spain, England, Germany, Denmark, Ireland and Scotland called for the Templars to be allowed to defend themselves. The Pope retorted by closing the Session almost at once. Out of fifteen hundred to two thousand Templars who were in hiding in the vicinity, nine knights actually came forward to testify for the Order. The Pope doubled his guard and sent a message to the King to do the same, as there was still danger from the hidden knights. They were not heard. Only one Italian prelate and three French ones voted to prevent the Order from putting in its defence.

Now Philip, deciding that something should be done to hasten affairs, set off for Venice and the conference. His arrival had an electric effect. On his sole authority the Pope almost immediately abolished the Order in a secret consistory. This was on March 22nd, 1313. On May 2nd, when the Bull was published, the Order ceased officially to exist. The Grand Master, assumed but not proved to be guilty, was sentenced to perpetual imprisonment. Most of the other knights were released, and many of these passed their remaining days in poverty. De Molay and one of his chiefs, Guy of Auvergne, proclaimed their innocence on the public stage to which they had been taken to have sentence announced. The King, upon hearing this, immediately had them committed to the flames.

5

The Path of the Sufi

TWELVE men sit on sheepskin rugs, arranged in a circle on the floor of a large room in a country house in Sussex, England. They are of various ages; each wears an orange robe over his Western clothes. They look towards the leader of the circle as the man opposite him remarks: "We are all here, Master." It is Thursday night, and the meeting of Sufis is paralleled in a thousand lodges throughout Asia and Africa—and some in Europe and America as well.

Softly, somewhere a drum starts to beat. The leader, an olive-skinned man in his late thirties, holds up his right hand, the fingers extended: "Love! Blessings! The principles are five. Meditation of the mind upon contact with the Infinite; abstinence and restraint in order to produce the greater power; generosity in all things; travel and movement, internal and external; belief in the unity of all power."

All present incline their heads, intoning the cabbalistical word, *Yaahuuuu*, with something of the reasonance of the "Amen" which follows a prayer.

We are at a Sufi meeting. Who are our companions? Three of them are Orientals, settled in Britain, and carrying on various avocations. The fourth is a young architect, who joined Sufism when he was a soldier in the Middle East. He knows some Arabic, and has studied the mystical literature of the saints of the Order. Another, rather older, is a lawyer who was recruited several years ago, after reading an article on Sufism and putting an advertisement in a newspaper in an effort to trace any member of the cult who might be in Britain. Two further members are commercial men, who have their own businesses. The rest are a mixture of employed people who have come straight from their London offices to this country place to spend the greater part of the night in their observances, and people of more or less independent means, attracted to the message which the Order offers.

Why has the Oriental cult of Sufism an appeal for materialistic Westerners? What is it all about, anyway?

The People of the Path believe, as the early anchorites of Arabia did, that a certain nobility of mind and purpose resides within every human being. This is the basis of what distinguishes them from their fellow-men. This it is the task of the Sufi teacher to discover and develop in the individual. By the mental and physical methods of 'development' which are practised, it is believed that the human being finds his true place in life.

Is Sufism a religion; a way of life; something like Yoga—just a ramp? It is none of these things, and yet it is a secret cult whose members believe that it gives them something which they have unconsciously sought for years. In this respect, at least, it resembles a religion. It is rooted in the Persian and Arab literature of the mystics who sought communion with an eternal principle through the cultivation of ecstatic states. But at the same time it is immensely practical. A Sufi is what a Westerner might call a hundred-percenter. This attribute alone might enable a person to get ahead in his own sphere, without much of the mind-training and discipline which Sufism inculcates. "If you are writing a letter," says the Sufi dictum, "write it as if all the world will judge you by this letter alone."

Yet the Sufis believe that if a person were to take their principles alone or piecemeal and applied them, this would result in an unbalanced personality. Sufism, they maintain, must be followed as a training system in its entirety.

How does one become a Sufi? This is extraordinarily difficult. Sufis are not allowed to seek converts. This is because the disciple must obey every order of his superior, even unto death. If, the Sufis say, they were to recruit people by promising them worldly or even spiritual advancement, they would be accused of merely trying to get people into their power. In the countries where Sufism is deeply rooted, there is no lack of applicants. And, of course, many young men and women are brought up on the path by their parents, for there is no celibacy in Sufism.

Sufism enjoys a somewhat equivocal position in the countries of Islam, where it has its widest currency. This is because the orthodox religionists tend to frown upon a system which they believe is designed to set the individual free (after an appropriate period of training) from the restrictions of religion. At the same time, countless thousands of Sufi teachers' shrines are revered by the masses; innumerable classical books have been composed by Sufis; some of the greatest national heroes of Eastern lands belonged to one or other of the four main Orders of the Sufi Way.

That there is a supernatural element in Sufism cannot be denied. Members believe (and literature abounds with supposed examples of it) that the members of the higher degrees of initiation are capable of influencing the minds of men and even events in a totally inexplicable manner. And this belief is one which is as adamantly held by the Western members of the Orders.

"My little daughter of six was dying of an incurable disease," one British Sufi told me, "and I asked the Master to bless her. He raised his hands, palms forwards, towards me, and said, '*Baraka bashad*' (may the blessing be), and she was cured in three days." This exactly coincides with innumerable tales which are current in countries of the East where hopeless cases are taken from Western-style hospitals to Sufi mystics for the application of their *baraka*. This is the power which is passed from the Sheikh (Master) to his disciple, and from one generation of Sufis to another.

If we return to our English Sufi meeting, we can see how another aspect of Sufism works. One member places his right hand to his neck, as a signal to the Master that he wants to speak. The Sheikh inclines his head. "I seek advice. I am dealing in motor-cars and other machinery. I have the choice of putting all my capital into a number of used cars or of building new garages.

I have not enough capital to do both. Which is the better alternative?"

The Sheikh momentarily places the tips of his fingers over his eyes. "I shall send the decision to you after this session, as soon as as we have finished."

The assistant Sheikh makes a signal that he wishes to speak. "We seek guidance upon the question of the headquarters of the Order. Would you indicate whether we should try to buy the building in which we hold our contemplation retreats?" The Sheikh looks upwards. "Let a fund be started. No money is to be borrowed; it is against the Rule of the Order. When there is sufficient money, buy."

Now the Sheikh starts to repeat certain syllables in rapid succession, and the sounds are taken up by the rest of the company: "Ishk! Ya Hu! Ya Haadi! Ya Haadi!"

These, roughly translated, mean, Love, O He! O Guide, Director! In common with the Arab cabbalists, the Sufis believe that every sound contains power; the repetition of certain sounds with certain intentions causes a focus to be attained. The result of that focus is to cause the human mind to project power, in accordance with the meaning of the sound.

For operations of treatment of disease, for example, the company or individual will repeat "O Protector" (Ya Hafiz) as many as three hundred thousand times. Material goods are increased by concentrating upon the invocation *Ya Mughni* ("O Enricher"). This is not thought of as a form of magic, because the relationship between the thing desired and the word is believed to be a cause-and-effect one. If you believe in anything strongly enough, in other words, it will happen.

A part of the evening is set aside for concentration upon various objectives of the Order in this manner. Then, in ones and twos, the members carry out their own silent repetitions, designed to liberate the innate faculties which their 'Director' believes should be developed. Added to the repetitions are physical exertions. The body may sway from side to side with the beat of the drum or the words intoned by the Sheikh. Or the head may be nodded backwards and forwards, while the Sufi carries out his exercises designed to cause him 'illumination', in which he gains a glimpse of perfect fulfilment.

Meanwhile, awaiting his turn, a candidate for initiation sits in an adjoining room, wondering what is in store for him. He is a young man, scarcely twenty years of age. He has been introduced to the Path through what is considered to be the best of all ways of entry: through the desire to emulate. It is thought that a potential Sufi is destined for great things if he has noticed something unusual and impressive about a Sufi, and asks him how he developed this gift, ability or characteristic.

We are in a Sufi lodge, whose collective noun is the Halka, or circle. The initiation varies slightly according to the Order which is represented. In this (Nakshbandi) Lodge, of the Order which is known as the Painters, the intending members must be prepared to comply with the instructions and the means of spiritual development given him by the Master (Murshid). This is contained in the Rules for Initiates, laid down by Ahmad Yasawi, one of the thirteenth-century Adepts; and these rules are memorized by every intending member:

1. I surrender myself to the direction of the Murshid, helpless in his hands as a corpse in the hands of those who lay it out; glad to do so because I know that this is the right way.

2. I will polish my mind, in such a way as to follow the instructions which will develop my capacities to the utmost limit.

3. Regarding the powers which are liberated in me, I will never make use of them except for the good of humanity; knowing that such attempted adverse use would harm only me.

4. I will serve the Murshid, seeing in his personality that which will be my personality, and in his greatness, and in my greatness, the benefit of all and the divine all-power.

5. Doubts and uncertainties are to be expected. These I will ignore, after I have allowed myself to know why they exist.

6. I will practise loyalty and steadfastness unto death; and hereby endow, both symbolically and if asked, practically, the

Order in the person of my Guide and Murshid, with all my property and all my expectations in this life.

7. Utter silence of secrets is my oath; and I will show respect for those who are set up over me, without quibble. I am the friend of the friends of the Order and the Murshid who exemplifies it; the enemy of the enemies of the same.

The youth has completed his military service, is now studying accountancy. His first contact with a Sufi was when he was working as a part-time assistant in a restaurant. Here he noticed a man among the customers who always seemed "on top of every situation. His methods of discussion with the people who came into the place were so controlled, and his perception, especially of atmosphere, so profound, that I plucked up enough courage to ask him how one did it. It may have been because I had not yet acquired enough self-confidence. But I am glad that I did it."

The way to initiation, however, was devious. At more than one point the youth thought that his mentor was more than half mad. He took him for long walks, telling him that one day he might tell him something of value, but that he would have to have patience. How much patience did he have? Sometimes, after the first meeting, he deliberately misconstrued something that the young man said, and accused him of being stupid. Listening to the way in which he tested him—for patience, tact, moral probity and sheer endurance—one felt that there could be few who would stand the pace: in Britain today, at any rate.

I asked the sponsor whether this was the standard procedure. He laughed. "Not exactly in that form. One goes by intuition, you know, old boy."

Eventually, the youth was given a book containing references to Sufism to read, then questioned upon them. Finally, he was asked to write a complete account of his life to date, taking as long as he liked over it, and writing it in the form and detail which seemed appropriate.

Now he was brought to a meeting for his initiation. He had already been asked whether he was prepared to surrender his personal sovereignty to another person, and had agreed to do so.

The members of the Circle are styled by various names, which describe household or other offices. This is probably a survival of the time when most Sufis were organized into communities. There may be, for instance, the Cupbearer, the Cook, the Groom and the Carpet-layer. Other Orders have the Soldier, Cavalier, Emir; or the brother, nephew, uncle, and so on. In this particular case, the Swordbearer (taken from the motif of a ruler's court) is the sponsor for our neophyte.

He leaves the assembly, goes into the antechamber, and asks the candidate if he is ready. Upon being told that he is, he teaches him the secret sign of salutation of the Order. This is the first identification signal learnt. He leads the youth back to the Halka. At the entrance to the chamber, the newcomer removes his shoes and waits while the Swordbearer walks to where the master sits. "I bring a newcomer, seeking the protection of the Order."

"Protection and blessings be upon him!"

"He is one who seeks admission to our Path. He has washed his hands of life; he is reconciled to the submission to the Chief of Chiefs; he bows in salutation to the Emir of Emirs; he begs to say that he has completed his novitiate with (naming himself). And now he seeks the admission to the Company."

"Why does he not speak for himself?"

"He is here to speak."

"Come forward, then, and take my hand."

The candidate comes forward, bows before the Murshid, and kisses his hand, afterwards raising his own to his head, tips of the fingers of the right hand in the centre of the forehead.

"Describe what you know of the Rules for Initiates."

The candidate now recites the Rules as already given. He pauses after each rule, to be asked: "Do you swear?"; and replies, "I swear"; upon which the master of the Halka raises his hand and the other members intone *Ya Hai* (O Living One!).

The disciple may now take his place in the Circle, and is handed his terracotta-coloured robe, a staff and a bowl. This is the regalia of the wandering dervish, and serves to remind him of the dedication of the Order to: uniformity in outward appearance (the robe); work and authority (the staff); and inner and bodily nutriment (the bowl).

There are many paths within the Order which the initiate may take; all will depend upon what his natural bent is: what are his inner capabilities, which will be 'developed' by the training which he is to receive. Early in his training, which takes place primarily with a designated teacher from the circle, he is given the poem of the Sufi mystic Nadim to commit to memory. It purports to describe the False Sufi:

"Who fears man, accuses, slanders, claims exclusive right; Who preaches travelling, not to disciples properly enrolled; Who purports to explain the Path through assemblies other than those of initiates;

Who denounces a father, son, uncle or other relative; Who panders to the desires of the raw (immature) in giving them promise of things that they may want: not the things which they must have."

Many Sufis go through training courses, as they would be termed in the West, designed to bring out various characteristics which they are thought to need in order to have a balanced personality. If the newcomer is impetuous, he must learn calm; if irritable, he must be made forbearing; if ambitious, his ambition must be directed.

It is more than likely that Sufism has influenced the modern schools of mysticism which are known in the West, as well as the monastic Orders of the Middle Ages. Many writers have tried to show that Sufism arose from Gnosticism, from Egyptian religion, was influenced by Buddhism, Yoga, Christianity, Mithraism. But no such effort has been wholly successful. The problem is that it is not enough to say that such-and-such a phenomenon or belief occurs in, say, Shintoism, and also in Sufism: hence that a cause-and-effect relationship is to be deduced.

What do the Sufis themselves say about their history? To them, Sufism is the blending of mind-training with successful living which comes in association with what until recently has generally been considered to be religious ecstasy. They do not, however, differentiate between one thing and the other. Mankind, they say, has certain capabilities, certain ideas, certain capacities for experience. These things are all related. The goal is the Ideal Man, who shall use every aspect of his experience to be "In the World and yet not Of the World." These teachings have been passed down to the elect since the beginning of time.

The modern phase, and the fully documented one, begins with Islam. Forty-five people, calling themselves Seekers, banded together during the first year of the Prophet's mission in Mecca, and called themselves Companions of the Shrine, or Temple. They devoted themselves to reflection and the improvement of their inner and outer selves. Their objective was to do good to others, and to rise to the greatest heights of achievement of which man was capable.

These people may have been drawn from a tribe in Arabia— called the Bani Muzar—who for centuries attended the Temple of Mecca, and called themselves the Servants of the Temple. This Temple, today called the Holy Temple, is the point towards which Moslems turn in prayer, and to which they carry out their annual pilgrimage. Tradition has it that it was built by the first men, and that it was rebuilt by Abraham.

Those who believe in a secret doctrine within Islam state that the Family of Abraham, who were traditional guardians of the Temple in Mecca for time uncounted before Mohammed, had been taught the Sufi Path, and passed it on.

Mohammed himself was of the lineage of Abraham, through the Quraish tribe, guardians of the Temple at Mecca. His progeny are highly respected by the Sufis, who say that they alone are the true inheritors of the secret doctrine.

Some historians say that the word 'Sufi' is derived from the Arabic word *Suf* (wool); because Sufis dressed in woollen cloth; others that it is derived from the Greek *Sophia* (wisdom) and that the Sufis are the Wise Ones. Many Sufis deny this. If they had chosen the name because of the wool, they say, it would by their symbolism mean that they regarded themselves as sheep. As for wisdom, the title "Wise One" is a low degree of initiation, and could not be used as descriptive of the Sufi Path as a whole. Members of the esoteric branches work out the meaning of the word by cabbalistic numerology:

S=The Earth; (letter *suad*);
U=The Perfect Man, Elevator of Rank; (letter *wau*);
F=Power, angels (letter *fa*);
I=Supporter, Lord (letter *ya*).

This association of numbers, runs the secret doctrine, totals 186, which number can be split up by the *abjad*-notation to mean Recompense for Effort—Power—Rising to Success. Thus it will be seen that the Sufi cabbalist believes that words and numbers have interchangeable meanings; and that the name for the cult is based upon a mnemonic of its strivings.

There are varying degrees of initiation in Sufism. Promotion from the one to another is through the decision of the Teacher to whom one is attached. In the Bektashi Order (which provided the Turkish Empire with the Janissaries) the organizational degrees are thus:

1. *Ashiq* (devotee), who is a postulant but not fully initiated;
2. *Muhib* (dedicated), who has been assigned a Master;
3. *Baba* (father), Master of a Halka;
4. *Khalifa* (deputy), Prior.

In this Order, the initiate must pass through a doorway, composed of two pillars which curve and meet at the top. The entrance symbolizes entry into real knowledge and illumination. He must not touch the pillars or step on the threshold. The Bektashis consider that Ali—son-in-law of the Prophet and his fourth successor—passed down the inner wisdom of their initiation. The pillars commemorate those at the Temple of Mecca (Safa and Marwa) between which all pilgrims must pass.

The attachment of the initiate to a teacher is considered to be a part of the training to enable him to overcome the restrictions of selfishness, as a first stage. Part of his struggle as a Sufi is against the self, which he cannot remould at one blow. The fundamental principle of the cult is unity. Unity means that, eventually, some-where, all things are one; all thought, all matter, all power. It is not possible for a person to understand this (even though he may accept it as an intellectual postulate) until he has experienced it in mystical or ecstatic reverie.

Sainthood, or illumination, is the stage of perfection of the

Sufi, when he becomes identi-fied with all power and all being. Ordinary Islam does not officially take cognizance of saints, yet the myriad popular tombs and places of pilgrimage throughout the world of Islam are almost without exception those of Sufis.

How secret is Sufism? This is something which is very difficult to answer. In the first place, the Orders require initiation, pass-words and signs. Secondly, some of their esoteric literature is hard to understand, and has its own

Detail from a Moslem coat-of-arms shows heraldic eagle bearing Sufi oct-agonal calligraphic motto on its breast. (Arms of the Princes of Paghman, hereditary Sufi Chiefs.)

technical terminology. Yet on the other hand, it is a canon of belief that a Sufi does not progress merely by passing through degrees and intitiations; the 'blessing' (*baraka*, sometimes called Power) must come upon him. If this is so, and the baraka is passed on from another Sufi, the conclusion is that there should be no need for secrecy; because no outsider could experience what the Sufis are undergoing in their raptures.

The answer to this, given by Sufis themselves, is that atmo-sphere plays a part in the cultivation of enlightenment. Strangers are a barrier and also a superfluity. Sufism is not for an audience. Again, the word 'Secret' is used in a special sense. It refers to one or more of the inner experiences of the mind, and not to the mere possession of formal knowledge. In this way Sufism differs from those schools of initiation which used to hold actual secrets, such as those of philosophy or how to work metals, or even how one could supposedly control spirits.

The disciplines of the Orders are six in number; and it depends upon his teacher as to which one is to be used by which Sufi. First comes traditional ritual worship; then recitation of the Koran; after that the repetition of certain formulas; now "Striving" or effort for a goal; then physical exercises, breath-control and the like; and finally contemplation on individual themes, then on complicated ones.

Sufis are to be found in every department of life, because few of them practise retirement from the world, except for short periods of reflection. Architecture and the arts are traditionally represented by a greater number of them than otherwise; but there are military Sufis, commercial Sufis, teachers, travellers, contemplatives, healers and the rest. Some of them combine more than one attribute.

Some of them are women; and Rabiyya, one of the greatest ecstatics of the East, was a Sufi mystic. She, like others before and after her, stresses the fact that the stage of mystical illumination, release and understanding of the meaning of life, is only the first of two halves. The Sufis say that, after reaching that stage (unlike any other mystical school on record), the Sufi must "return to the world" and must put his experiences into practice. This is the point at which his infallibility is first encountered. It is believed that he is now endowed with a perception far greater than that of ordinary men and women; and that he is "Rightly Guided": will now always take the course, hold the opinion, or follow the path which is for the best. This is because he is in harmony with the pattern of life which is almost all hidden to those who have not been through his training.

There are many traditional centres of Sufism, and all the major Orders trace their spiritual pedigree through dozens of teachers. Heredity is also acknowledged in the transmission of the lore. The Musa-Kazim family, who have ruled Paghman (in Afghanistan) for seven centuries, are directly descended from Mohammed and are the traditional heads of the Nakshbandi Order. They are also said by some to preserve a special training system which is granted only to a very few initiates. It is by means of this system that they have been able to produce an apparently endless succession of princes, military leaders, savants and successful men in many walks of life. It is from this family, by tradition, that the office of Caliph of All Islam is to be filled.

On the whole, the effect of Sufism upon society has been creative and wholesome. Sufis do not suffer from fanaticism, are not connected with magic (though they are thought to have special, extra-normal powers) and hold to the principle of honour and effort to an astonishing extent. Alone among what may be termed secret cults, they have not been successfully challenged with heterodox activities; and the phrase 'the word of a Sufi' is proverbial. Attempts have been made to popularize Sufism in the West in a similar manner to that which is used with odd cults of personality. But, with the exception of the schools which have been set up on an experimental basis, the 'society Sufism' has never caught on. It is probable that the message is not susceptible to popularization on a theoretical basis alone; just as the English translations of Sufi literature by erudite non-initiates are held by Sufis to be faulty to a degree. And the people who are real Sufis must, by definition, work and teach as Sufis; which is a slow and arduous path. In the West, if not in the East, there are very few shining examples of Sufi personalities to attract large followings.

Fig. C

But the Path of the Sufi is likely to exercise a fascination over men's minds for many a year yet; and its influence in the West is undoubtedly increasing.

6

The Secret Rites of Mithra

THE cult of Mithra, intercessor between man and the Persian divine power Ormuzd, was once an extremely widespread one. From its origins in Persia, the faith spread to Babylonia, Greece and finally the Roman Empire, where it struggled against Christianity at the latter's inception. Christianity won, with the decline of the material virtues of the Romans, but there are people who worship the solar deity yet, and even London has its Mithra temple.

Mithra was said to give his worshippers success in this world as well as security and happiness in the next. He was originally a genie, the worldly representative of the invisible power which ruled the affairs of men. Later (and the cult probably has a history of over six thousand years) he became thought of by his devotees as being not just one of the twenty-eight genii, but the only one which mattered, and the only one who could cater for the wishes and needs of the people. Thus it was that the ancient Aryan worship of Ahura-Mazda, the supreme being, was displaced by that of one of his representatives. Although archaeological research has produced little to give a clear picture of the rituals and beliefs of the Mithraists, a considerable amount of secret lore still survives in the East—from India to Syria—which gives one a good idea of exactly how the members of the cult thought, and what their magical ceremonies were.

Three ritualistic objects are used by Mithraists: the crown (equivalent to the sun, and power of the supernatural kind), the hammer or club (symbolizing creative activity of mankind) and the bull, which stands for nature, virility, increase. By the proper understanding of these objects and what they represent, Mithraists have it that the ordinary man can transcend his environment, can become great, or successful, or can achieve what he wants to do; and enters a delightful after-life. What must he give in exchange? Nothing but worship to the principle which presides over all destiny.

One reason for the loss of importance of the cult undoubtedly is that admission was restricted to those who were thought worthy to receive the blessings which would come through the proper beliefs and use of the magical powers presided over by the Mithra priests. Christianity, for instance, was open to a far greater section of the population, even although the Christian mysteries were not accessible everywhere to all until relatively late. At the same time, some of the Mithraist ceremonials were of such obvious emotional appeal that scholars are agreed that the purely ritualistic side of Christianity owes much to those of the sun-god of the Persians.

The lowest degree of intiation was known as the Sacrament, and could be administered to anyone, theoretically, who could be relied upon to keep a secret, and who would eventually develop into a regular and devout worshipper. This degree was called that of The Crow, and it symbolized, according to present-day Mithraists, the death of the new member, from which he would arise reborn as a new man. This death spelt the end of his life as an unbeliever and cancelled his allegiance to former and unaccepted beliefs. The use of the word 'crow' probably derives from the ancient Persian practice of exposing their dead to be eaten by carrion birds—which is still carried on by the Parsi community in India, who follow parts of ancient Iranian religion as supposedly taught by Zoroaster. But if the crow symbolized death, it was also the delegate privileged to take over the human body after death. This meant that, in a sense, it was superior to humanity. Thus it was that the member of the cult was superior to the ordinary run of mortals.

The candidate descended seven steps into the temple, which was an underground one, fashioned in the shape of a cavern, and made to look as much as possible like a natural cave. Initiation tests now took place. The newcomer was pursued by 'wild beasts' (priests

76

in animal skins), 'demons' and all sorts of terrors. He had to fast for three days. In this debilitated, altered and plastic state, he was given a lecture by a priest on the responsibilities which were now his. Among these were the necessity to call brother only those who had been initiated. All family ties were severed; nothing mattered except doing one's job well, and carrying out the worship of Mithra. The final ceremony took place amid the clash of cymbals, the beating of drums and the unveiling of a statue of Mithra himself. This latter showed Mithra as a man, carrying a bull by the hind legs. Now the symbolism of this piece of sculpture was explained to him. The bull, in addition to symbolizing fecundity, was representative of animal passion. It was through invocations to Mithra that mankind first discovered how to overcome this force, and how to discipline himself. Therefore the secret of religion was partly that the worshipper must restrain himself physically in order to attain power over himself and over others. This graphic teaching of the diversion of sexual power into psychic channels shows that the Mithraists followed in essence the pattern of all mystical schools which believed in the production of power through discipline. In this they are clearly distinguished from the more primitive and less important orgiastic schools, which merely practised indiscriminate indulgence, mass immorality, and so on.

The neophyte then drank a little wine from the cymbal, to show that he realized that the cymbal is the means whereby ritual ecstasy comes, which puts him in touch with the 'higher powers'.

Two long lines of initiates knelt on either side of the low stone benches which traversed the crypt, as the new member, accompanied by the priests who were initiating him, walked along the central aisle for the Eating of the Bread. A number of pieces of dry bread were placed on a drum, similar to those which were being softly beaten by one of the priests. The candidate ate one morsel, signifying that he accepted Mithra as the source of his food. This bread, according to their beliefs, had been exposed to the rays of the sun to absorb some of its quality; and thus the worshipper was partaking of the nature of the sun itself in this ritual observance. Now he was taught the password of the cult, which was to identify him to other members, and which he was to repeat to himself frequently, in order to maintain the thought always in his mind: "I have eaten from the drum and drunk from the cymbal; and I have learned the secret of religion."

This is the cryptic phrase which an early Christian writer, Maternus, reports as being taught to the Mithraists "by a demon".

The second degree of initiation was called The Secret, and during this the candidate was brought to a state of ecstasy in which he was somehow made to believe that he had seen the statue of the god actually endowed with life. It is not likely that there was any mechanical method by which this was done, because no such apparatus has been found in Mithraic temples unearthed. The candidate was brought up to the idol, to which he offered a loaf of bread and a cup of water. This was to signify that he was a servant of the god, and that "By what sustains my life I offer my entire life to your service." The grade of Soldier may show that the military arts were responsible for a good deal of the power of Mithra worship in ancient Persia. Certain it is, in any case, that this degree greatly appealed to the Roman warriors who formed a very large part of the rank and file of the cult during its Western expansion. A sign similar to a cross, signifying the sun, was made on the forehead of the initiate, who was thus marked as owned by the deity. A crown was placed before him, hanging from the point of a sword. This he took and placed it aside with the words: "Mithra alone is my crown." The Persian crown, it will be remembered, from which pattern all present-day crowns are eventually derived, is a golden sun-disc, with a hole in the centre for the head. It is jagged at the edges (representing the sun's rays), and these projections are turned up, to make what is still known in Western heraldry as the Oriental crown.

Now the candidate has to prove himself in a mock combat with soldiers and animals in a number of caves. When the Emperor Commodus went through this degree of initiation, he actually killed one of the participants, although he was supposed only to make a symbolic slaying.

Passed through the Soldier degree, the Mithraist was eligible, after a lapse of time, to be promoted to the rank of Lion. He was taken again to the cavern, and honey was smeared upon his brow, as opposed to the water which had been used in his acceptance into the earlier degree—his 'baptism'. The degree of Lion was taken only by those who had decided to dedicate themselves completely to the cult, and who would henceforth have no truck with the ordinary world. The Lion was, then, a sort of priest, but rather more of a monk. He was trained in the rites of the cult and told certain secrets.

The degree of Lion of Mithras could be conferred only when the sun was occupying the Zodiacal Sign of Leo (about July 21st to August 20th) during the Persian month of Asad, The Lion. There is a good deal of astrological lore in Mithraism, and also an admixture with cabbalistic numerology. The Greek branch of the Mithraists, for example, worked out that the numerical equivalent of the name (spelt by them Meitras) was 365, and thus corresponded to the number of days in the solar year. In the purely magical sense, Mithraism has it that both the name of the god and the rank which the individual holds in the cult have magical power. Thus, if a person wants to achieve anything, he has to concentrate upon the word 'Mithra', while preparing for himself the ceremonial repast and beating alternately a drum and cymbals.

That the effect of initiation was to produce someone of upright character is amply evidenced by literature of the Roman times, in which the Mithraists were generally considered to be thoroughly trustworthy and improved people. Even their enemies could reproach their own followers with the vitality of the Mithraist creed. Tertullian, in his *De Corona*, which he composed in the third Christian century, upbraids the Christians, inviting their attention to the Mithraists as examples:

"You, his fellow-warriors, should blush when exposed by any soldier of Mithra. When he is enrolled in the cave, he is offered the crown, which he spurns. And he takes his oath upon this moment, and is to be believed. Through the fidelity of his servants the devil puts us to shame."

There were seven degrees of initiation in all, although there are some branches of the ecstatic side of the lore which include certain others, making the total twelve. After Lion came the Persian, then the Runner of the Sun, then Father, and finally, Father of Fathers. The twelfth degree, it is said, is King of Kings, and, properly, this can be held only by the supreme king: and preferably the Shahinshah (King of Kings) of Persia.

This very ancient cult, from which more than one present-day secret society may well be derived, is thus seen to contain many of the elements which underlie organizations of this sort. It is a training system; it attempts to produce in its members a real or imagined experience of contact with some supreme power. The magical element is there, too, shown in the belief in the power of certain names to achieve things which cannot be done by men. Mithraism was not an anti-social society, in the sense that it did not conflict in its aims with the objectives of the countries in which it flourished. And hence it did not threaten the established order. It was tolerant of other creeds, which meant that it did not attempt to supplant them. Its greatest festival, the Birth of the Sun, on the 25th of December, became Christianized; and it is claimed by those who still believe in its mysteries and celebrate them, that Christianity did not so much supplant Mithraism as absorb it, accepting some of its externals and diverting them to its own use. Perhaps incongruously, a present-day follower of Mithra in England recently likened this phenomenon to the eclipse of the Liberal Party, "because the two other Parties have taken over its objectives, and widened the basis. Only the actual initiates of Mithra know what has been lost in the process." So the young man in the Phrygian bonnet, sometimes seen as the conqueror of the bull, or even as a man with a lion's head, still has his devotees. And the sun still shines.

(i)

(ii)

(iii)

(iv)

(v)

(vi)

Fig. D

7

The Gnostics

AN extraordinary number of exceedingly bizarre talismans and inscribed stones bear witness to the power of the secret Gnostic organizations which flourished in various forms during the few centuries immediately before and after the rise of Christianity in the Middle East. One of the oddest emblems of these schools was the figure of Abraxas. A human body clothed in a Roman soldier's garb wielded a battle-axe, as if threatening an enemy. In its left hand it carried an elliptical shield, upon which the words of power IAO and SABOATH were sometimes written. The head of this fearsome being was that of a cock, with open beak. For legs it had twin serpents, coiling to either side. Underneath the figure sometimes lay a conventionalized thunderbolt.

Who was Abraxas? His name, in accordance with cabbalistic computation, is decoded to mean "three hundred and sixty-five" —the number of days in the year. There was no god or idol belonging to the society: the Abraxas figure merely represented the aspects of power which went to make up the supreme intelligence, the all-power. The body was man himself; the bird stood for intelligence, and the hailing of light which is the cock's habit at dawn. The tunic represented the need for struggle, the arms the protection and power given by the dedication to the Gnosis— knowledge. The shield was wisdom, the club or whip, power. The two snakes meant *nous*, insight, and *logos*, understanding.

By means of this diagram Gnostic teachers inculcated the theory that man comes to his full power by developing certain facets of his mind. He must struggle to arrive at *gnosis*; but this knowledge is of the mystical kind, and is not the mere collection of facts. Great stress was laid upon personal mystical experience, to and through which the initiate was guided under conditions of great secrecy.

The Gnostics did not confine their studies, or their teachings, to any one religion, but borrowed illustrations from all that were accessible to them. This caused them to be considered Christian heretics, Jews, who were trying to undermine Christianity, remnants of the Persian sun-worshippers. They have been widely studied by early Christian sages, and it is upon the opinions of these latter that many conclusions have been formed. Little or no investigation of these 'People of Wisdom' has been done by research workers on the spot—in Asia and North Africa—where strong and interesting traces of their beliefs and practices still remain.

The main teaching states that there is a supreme being or power which is invisible and has no perceptible form. This power is the one which can be contacted by mankind, and it is through it that man can control himself and work out his destiny. The various religious teachers through the ages, putting their creeds in many different ways, were in contact with this power, and their religions all contain a more or less hidden kernel of initiation. This is the secret which the Knowers can communicate to their disciples. But the secret can be acquired only through exercising the mind and body, until the terrestrial man is so refined as to be able to become a vehicle for the use of this power. Eventually the initiate becomes identified with the power, and in the end he attains his true destiny as a purified personality, infinitely superior to the rest of unenlightened mankind.

The symbolism in which this teaching is concealed, the methods by which the mystical power is attained, vary from one Gnostic society to another. But the constant factor is there: the attainment of that which humankind unconsciously needs. The Gnostic claims that within every man and woman there is an unfulfilled urge which cannot be given proper expression in the normal way because there is no social means by which it can be fulfilled. This

feeling has been put into man in order that he may seek the fulfilment which the Gnostics can give him. His search for complete-
ness in love, trade, professions, theology is vain and unsuccessful.

The theories of the various schools of Gnosticism with which
the Christian clerics came into contact are very much secondary
to the rituals and practices which are used to produce the Gnosis,
the enlightenment. This has not been fully understood by too
many writers, who devote much space to trying to work out the
beliefs of the Knowers by a perusal of their writings, or by reports
which have been given them by others.

Symbol of Power of Gnostic Society.

What were—and are—the Gnostic practices? First, discipleship
and the inculcated belief that the initiate must struggle, must
devote himself as much as possible to the identification with the
power which inspires all. Secondly, there are two kinds of men,
those who are bound to the earth and to matter, and those who
can refine themselves. It is from the latter class that aspirants are
chosen. Thirdly, the methods by which the divine illumination
may come are many and varied; and it is the province of the
teacher to choose which path he will give to his disciple to follow.
Some Gnostics believed that frenzy and excitement would
produce the necessary liberation of the mind from the fetters of
the body; others considered that this could be done best by
fasting and meditation. Present-day Gnostic practice in the East has

it that different methods suit different temperaments: and this may be one cause for the historical confusion as to which branch of 'heretics' practised what.

The Gnostics believed themselves to be intellectual aristocrats: their knowledge was only for the few who were ready to receive it. And this is what made them a secret cult, not the fear of persecution. They had their own passwords, in shaking hands they tickled the palm as an identification signal, and they helped one another in every conceivable way.

They could not be called pantheists, because they considered that the doctrine was secondary to the experience of religion; and the theologians and ordinary priesthood of any religion did not approve of that. They were not, in fact, a religion like most others, because they stressed the importance of the individual before that of the community. Those who were more enlightened were more important in every possible way, because they were valuable, refined, aristocrats. At the same time they taught that providing the wellbeing of the Gnostics was assured, so was that of the community at large. This meant that they could subscribe to the outward doctrines of any religion, and could continue to operate under many different politico-religious systems. Gnosticism profoundly influenced men's minds even in Europe up to and after the Middle Ages, and its basic way of thinking is probably an underlying factor in other secret societies whose members would be surprised to know it.

Terrible obscenities and other crimes have been laid at the door of the Gnostics by the early ecclesiastical writers. Although there is little doubt that some of them did believe in mass ecstasy, it seems unlikely that their secrets were well enough known to enable the commentators to assess them. The belief that certain special men could control their destiny and obtain extra powers through dedication to Gnostic practices meant that, inevitably, there was a belief in magic. The myriad Gnostic 'gems' (inscribed stones) decorated with serpents, cabbalistic names and the rest, are more likely to be proofs of initiation and talismans than mere identification tokens presented to ensure admission to meetings, as some authors have thought. The reason for supposing this is that (1) the 'gems' are very similar in many respects to talismans in use by other communities; and (2) they can often be interpreted as containing magical messages or 'diagrammatical invocations'.

Altar of a Western secret society with Sufi and Gnostic affinities. The knot-motif symbolises the 'Great Secret' of the Society.

Ethically speaking, Gnostic belief is that there are two principles: that of good and that of evil. A balance must be struck between these forces; and the balance is in the hands of the Gnostic—the Knower—partly because nobody else can tell whether an action is for the eventual good of the individual or the community. This secret knowledge comes through the mystical insight which the supermen-Gnostics attained.

The rise of individuals who wrongly believed that they had

attained to Gnosis—all-knowledge—some of whom were leaders of Gnostic societies, produced notorious characters. Those who followed the way of the Ophite branch glorified the serpent who tempted Eve. They did this because this snake by his actions brought knowledge into the world. Basilides was a leader who taught that Jesus did not die on the cross. Since matter and material things were considered to be a part of the inferior, non-spiritual world, the sect known as the Cainites called upon everyone to destroy those things which belonged to the world.

These deviations and aberrants have attracted the greatest attention—as is natural—and the quieter teachers of the creed have received less attention. The pious horror with which the less respectable Gnostics were viewed by the early Christian fathers has stamped itself for ever on Western literature and belief about the Enlightened Ones. But, in more than one place in the Middle East, as well as in small groups in Western Europe, there are still followers of various schools of Gnosticism. They mainly follow the ideas held by Valentinus, with some variations. This school teaches its initiates that matter is more evil than good; that man must be purified by mental concentration; that after death man will rejoin that from which he has been severed, and will be unified with those whom he loves. They also believe that all matter will eventually be destroyed by fire.

The Mandaeans, a small but tenacious community which dwells in Iraq, follow an ancient form of Gnosticism, which practises initiation, ecstasy and some rituals which have been said to resemble those of the Freemasons.

8

The Castrators of Russia

QUITE one of the most extreme secret cults of recent time is the Skoptsi ('Castrated') of Russia and the Balkans. The fact that they carried out castration as a part of their religious rites caused them to be considered to be insane. But, as one recent psychologist has pointed out, the movement spread in so many directions, numbered so many thousands of people, and continued for so long, that it cannot be regarded but as a psychological state which fulfilled some sort of deep inner need. This need, it is true, might have been implanted by suggestion.

Mad fanatics there were within their ranks, from the Caucasus to Hungary. But "the Skoptsi reckon among their members men of comparative culture and position", as a bewildered contemporary writer puts it.

Although given a Christian framework, the cult of the castrated and castrators was descended from ideas found in the old mystery religions. Ascetics, monks and saints felt that they could attain affinity with the divine through self-mortification. Worshippers of classical mother-goddesses, and particularly their priests, celebrated their devotion by the sacrifice of their genitalia.

Although it is widely assumed that debauches accompanied the celebration of mystic rites among the ancients, in which indiscriminate sexual relations played a large part, there is considerable evidence to show that at least in many forms of the fertility cult it was the suppression of the mating urge, or its diversion into ecstatic channels, which was sought.

This seems to be what the Castrators did.

Skoptsism in its modern form started about 1757, among members of the Sect of the Flagellants: the people who lashed and mutilated themselves as a means to attain a state of excitement and coma which is to be found in religious and secret sects throughout the world. Although debauches of self-inflicted wounding were going on in almost epidemic fashion, the Russian Government heard officially of the secret sect only in 1771.

Rasputin, the mad mystic of Russia, was a Flagellant. Their ceremonies are touched upon by Prince Yousopov thus: "They claimed to be inspired with the Word and to incarnate Christ . . . a monstrous combination of the Christian religion with pagan rites and primitive superstitions. . . . The purpose of these radenyi, or ceremonies, was to create a religious ecstasy, an erotic frenzy. After invocations and hymns, the faithful formed a ring and began to sway in rhythm, and then to whirl round and round, spinning faster and faster . . . the master of ceremonies flogged any dancer whose vigour abated. The radenyi ended in a horrible orgy, everyone rolling on the ground in ecstasy or in convulsions."

A peasant called Andrei Ivanov was arrested, tried and convicted of having induced thirteen other peasants to mutilate themselves. In this act, accompanied by orgies of singing and dancing, he was helped by one Kondratji Selivanov, a peasant of Stolbovo, in the Province of Orel.

The legal investigation took place in St. Petersburg, during which there was considerable popular incredulity that people could act thus without apparent reason. The baffled court sentenced Ivanov to the knout. He was then exiled to Siberia, and is thought to have died there.

But Selivanov was still at liberty. Fleeing to the district of Tambov, he started to preach the doctrine that salvation and fulfilment came only through the supreme sacrifice, the 'Baptism of Fire'. He soon attracted a disciple, Alexander Ivanov Shilov, and made many converts. The members met regularly, worked themselves up into a wild and uncontrollable frenzy—and encouraged each other to self-mutilation. In 1775 the revered leader, by now plump and facially hairless (the consequences of his eunuchry), was in Moscow itself, preaching his doctrine, and enrolling disciples. Seized in Moscow he was given a taste of the knout and sent to Siberia, from which he was soon to escape. Several of his followers were beaten judicially, then sent to penal servitude in the fortress of Dortmund. Others, who had not yet committed the sacrifice, were warned, and forbidden to preach the cult.

But the movement spread, to the utter bewilderment of the State. In 1797 Selivanov appeared again in Moscow, where the Emperor, intrigued by such an aberration, gave him an audience —and sent him to a madhouse.

The accession of Alexander I, a mystical-minded Czar, gave Selivanov his chance. Alexander was dominated by a strange woman who believed in magic and thought that Selivanov was a saint. This Baroness Krüdner arranged for him to be released from the asylum, and gave him the entrée to aristocratic circles. House after noble house was opened to him, and filled with his enthusiastic disciples of all ranks. He numbered among his followers one extremely powerful figure, who early helped him and the other Skoptsi in every way: State Councillor Alexei Michaelov Jelanski, a secret member of the cult, himself castrated and also a castrator of new recruits.

Selivanov was before long set up in a splendid house by his disciples. They contributed towards his upkeep, worked ceaselessly to increase the membership among influential people, and indulged in ceremonies which, they believed, gave them joy in this life and entry to the next on their own terms.

The master's home was called the House of God, or, sometimes, Heavenly Zion. Sometimes, again, it was referred to as the New Jerusalem. Selivanov was a reincarnation of Christ, who was himself the embodiment of an earlier, undefined deity. His transmigration was not direct, having been through the body of Peter III, who had been born, they claimed, of the immaculate virgin Elizabeth Petrovna.

This Empress ruled in actuality, it is said, for two years only. After this, she transferred her power to a woman of the court who resembled her. Changing her name to Akulina Ivanovna, she dedicated herself to the cult. She lived at first at the house of the Skoptsi prophet Filimon (prophets were those who had induced twelve people to castrate themselves) in the Province of Orel. Then she moved to a sanctuary behind a wall, where she was worshipped by the faithful until 1865. Secret reports state that she was believed to be able to transfer her divine powers to a selected person, when on the point of death; thus keeping up the ability to give the Skoptsi their hallucinatory experiences of divine kinship.

The supposed history of Selivanov is no less unusual. He was born, says the legend, in Holstein, and as soon as he reached manhood he castrated himself utterly, and convinced many others that this was the way to salvation. He was helped in this, if we are to believe the story, because he was able to perform miracles, which he said was only because he had made the sacrifice.

Inheriting the throne as Peter III, he was compelled to marry. His bride, Catherine II, soon felt that his deficiencies were such that she must have him removed, by assassination. The Emperor, however, was warned in time. He changed clothes with a sentry, who was killed in his place. He later took the form of the peasant Selivanov. Meanwhile the Empress learned of the facts, but it suited her plans to have it thought that she was a widow. The soldier was buried with full Imperial honours. Disciples pointed to Selivanov's undoubted popularity with people of quality as one indication of his former life.

Shilov, the believers asserted, was the forerunner and merely the announcer of the Redeemer Selivanov. The 'Book of the Passion of (Selivanov) The Redeemer' tells how Emperor Paul I had Selivanov brought back to metropolitan Russia, to hand him his crown, as he recognized him as his father.

But this was not possible, because Selivanov, of course, demanded that Paul be castrated, in order to become a proper member of the true faith. As a result, Selivanov was imprisoned by the perverse Paul, who valued his genitals more than his redeemer.

It is further claimed that when Alexander came to the throne and had the mystic released, he also joined the sect and induced his wife to do likewise. Certain it is that Selivanov was protected at court, and it was only the Government which considered him a threat to public safety.

Selivanov, when the Government decided to confine him to the monastery of Suzdal, gave out that he would live for ever; and this belief continued long after his death. It is said that the legend is still believed. In due course, he will reappear and take control of all Russia; and everyone will be castrated. Present-day followers of the cult (at least until recently in the Balkans, and currently quite secretly in the Lebanon and Turkey) have modified the teachings. Each member is allowed to have two children, after which he must be castrated and can fulfil himself in the way which, the sect insists, was his destiny.

The reason for the Castrators revering Peter III is that it was this Czar who removed the ordinances against the Flagellants and treated them kindly. He actually was the son of the Duke of Holstein. There is no reason to believe that Akulina Ivanovna was in fact the Empress Elizabeth. It was stated by the police authorities that she was born into the peasantry in the Province of Tamboff, and her real name was Karassanova.

Selivanov died in 1832, at a very advanced age, in the monastery of Spasso-Euphemius. One of his most fanatical lieutenants—'Captain' Sosonovitch—was placed in another monastery, where he was re-converted to Orthodox Christianity, and revealed the innermost secrets of the cult to the Abbot.

The cult showed a remarkable propensity for spreading. A Russian doctor who prepared maps of its diffusion, taken from the accounts of people who had been caught and tried during a succession of cases in the early nineteenth century, showed that up to 1839 the cult had centres in most Russian provinces. These, of course, embraced people of several different races and temperaments. Great concentrations of the 'People of God' existed as far apart as St. Petersburg, the Black Sea area and the borders of the White Sea. Even by 1822 the spread had been extraordinary.

Most of the gold- and silver-smiths of the capital belonged to it, and the Crimea was thoroughly infiltrated with the doctrine.

In the middle of the nineteenth century, the Emperor Nicholas took severe measures against Skoptsism. Hundreds were caught and sent to Siberia, but this seemed only to increase the epidemic. The Balkans became a seat of propaganda, and more and more orgies of self-mutilation were reported. Whole guilds of traders (hackney-carriage drivers, carpenters and builders) were reputed to be infected.

Following a decline in activity, which was wrongly thought to spell the beginning of the end, the cult burst out with renewed fury in the 1870s. The Skoptsi had something to communicate; they had to have recruits. But they were also a secret society; and this combination has led to an interesting reflection about them. More than one theorist claims that there was a secret which was confided to the members, only after they had been castrated. By making a sacrifice of this magnitude, the member would not only be proved to be worthy; he would not have very much to go back to if he were to revert. The secret, according to a confession of one who is referred to as "a Skopez who had gone mad," was the means whereby one man or woman can gain absolute power over another, and appear to cause miracles. The inner teaching, said a young man who heard such things discussed by his parents when he was almost in his cradle, and who escaped before puberty to avoid the enthusiastic attentions of his nearest and dearest, was that a man can have the power of a god. This power is immensely greater and more fulfilling than obeying the dictates of fate in a procreative activity which has been imposed upon one. Only by sacrificing the organ of such indulgence could a person cultivate the taste for greater, 'real' power.

They would at first only admit Russians to the sect, a barrier which was removed in 1902. Writing of this restriction in 1874, one disgusted commentator asks "is it that they can in no other nationality find people mad enough to submit to their rites?"

Nothing seemed to stop the enthusiasm, the visions, the immense vigour of the Castrators. In 1865 the inhabitants of an area bordering the Sea of Azov complained to the Russian Government that the sect was spreading daily. Mutilated men and women in their hundreds were found by police investigators. The cult here seemed to centre around a 'prophetess', a peasant woman by the name of Babanin, who was believed to have the power to cure all ills by the touch, to speak with the voices of the dead (who resided within her) and to be able to procure favours for anyone, in any part of Russia, through telepathic hypnotism. All these beliefs, of course, were attributed to the new power which she had obtained by embracing the creed and suffering an operation in accordance with its rules. She and a number of her followers were banished to Siberia. Soon, however, it was found that her community was but a branch of a greater centre.

The town of Morchansk, in the Province of Tambov, was witnessing remarkable scenes of mass and instant conversion, hallucinations and the ever-growing power of the sinister Skoptsi. On the last night of the year 1869, the chief of police of the town was at a party. About midnight, he was called out of the room, and handed a letter by a servant of an important merchant, asking for the release of three women of the sect who were in custody. They would be returned to their prison in the morning. Ten thousand roubles in cash were enclosed with the letter. The matter was immediately turned over to the Criminal Investigation Department. The merchant—one Ploticyn—was arrested on an attempted bribery charge, and his house searched.

His home was found to consist of a cluster of houses, built over four immense underground cellars. From these vaults a huge amount of treasure in gold and bank notes was unearthed. But the damning evidence was an extensive correspondence with numerous wealthy merchants in various parts of Russia—including a well-known St. Petersburg millionaire. The letters showed that all were members of the cult and were engaged in activities ranging from increasing their influence through bribery and recruitment to preparing for the overthrow of the State. People interviewed stated that the reason for asking for the temporary release of the three women cultists was that they were needed to help to produce the ritual ecstasy which the sect was indulging in. It was believed that by using some of the prisoners in their rites, they would all be enabled to go free in some magical manner. This, of course, is nothing less than the principle of sympathetic magic: "like affects like". Going on this assumption, they would have made use of policemen and jailers, too, if they could get hold of them, to bring this element into the magical activities.

Ploticyn was deprived of his dignities and his civil rights, and banished to Siberia, along with twelve other men and nineteen women members of the movement. The correspondence and plots discovered led now to the attempted uprooting of the Skoptsi in other parts of the Russian Empire. Nearly two years were occupied with the trials of the accused, high and low, who were daily being discovered. Such horrors were revealed, and such important people implicated, that it was forbidden to publish further details of the cases.

The purpose of the uprooting of the sect was officially looked upon as a matter of internal security rather than religious discipline. Thus it is that we hear little of torture being applied to obtain confessions or reversal to the original faith. But documents and confessions elicited by whatever means give a fair picture of the 'official' beliefs and method of worship of the Skoptsi.

The 'Baptism of Fire' was stated to be the way to eternal salvation, and it was also referred to as the Seal of God. The Great Seal was the euphemism for the removal of the entire organ, and this was considered to be the highest form of dedication. The Lesser Seal was ordinary castration. Normal marital relations between man and woman were considered sinful. Parents, in giving life to their children, committed a very mortal sin. This was the reason given for making the neophyte, before initiation, write the names of his progenitors on paper and trample them underfoot. It should be mentioned, however, that this practice was claimed by the members of some communities to be a symbolic one in which the candidate formally indicated his severance from worldly ties. Variations, as already noted, allowed two children to be born before initiation; and it is reported that only one child was allowed in some groups of the order.

In a typical Saturday night Skoptsi religious ceremony, men and women were led in the singing of hymns by one or more 'prophets'. These songs were often composed of apparently barbarous words, and the compelling rhythm of the tunes seems to have been the main instrument of producing frenzy. During the singing one or other of the leaders present would apparently pass into some form of trance, and give out orders and prophecies to all and sundry. These ejaculations were carefully written down and abided by if at all possible.

The final part of the proceedings was the frenzied dancing which was carried out in such a violent manner as to give the impression that the dancer was possessed by spirits. The dance most often used resembled shamanistic displays among the Mongols. The arms were held outwards from the sides, and moved up and down to the beat of a small drum. Then, with the body twitching as if it wanted involuntarily to step forward, the dancer would put his left foot forward by two jerky steps, followed by the right. The music varied from a really thundering rhythm on percussion instruments, to a form of dance which seemed to resemble the waltz-step of later days.

Sometimes the dancers, in imitation of one of their leaders, would mimic frenziedly his or her hand-gestures, something like a team of athletes doing callisthenics.

The initiation of a new entrant does not follow this pattern at all, oddly enough. It might be expected that recruitment would take place after participation in an orgy such as has been described. But in the case of the Skoptsi, it was the individual who was first worked up to a stage of piety, excitement, a consciousness of sin and a desire to participate in the activities of the group which seemed to him to have so much power and mystery.

It might almost be said that the instructor, once he had found a victim, conditioned him by remaining, as it were, one step behind him in his mounting excitement and desire to join a privileged class. In the final vow before the ritual of castration, the victim promised "of his own free will to come to the Redeemer, and to keep secret from the Emperor, princes, parents, relatives and friends, everything that is connected with these holy affairs; to submit to persecution, torture, fire and even death, before revealing any part of the mysteries to enemies."

The Skoptsi built their meeting-places with some care, in order to preserve themselves from intrusion. They claimed, of course, that the plan of the buildings and the method of their arrangement were essential to the production of the power which they were using. The general pattern was a room, built as far as possible from any other dwelling-house, though surrounded by barns and other buildings. Either in the middle of this enclosure, where there was a courtyard, or within the room itself, the orgies were held. There were always a number of secret doors which led into fields, and each member knew which was his own emergency exit. This provided against congestion in the case of attack, and the probability that some, at least, of the worshippers might escape. In escaping, the senior members would pass through a bee-house, placed there to discourage the attentions of any party investing the premises.

There was a special garb worn for the devotions. The men wore long white, wide shirts closed at the neck and with long sleeves—of quite an Oriental pattern. A girdle was tied around the waist, and large baggy trousers completed the outfit. The women "wear blue gowns of nankeen; in the towns, of chintz. They, moreover, cover their heads with white cloths."

All wore white stockings at times; and at other times were said to be barefooted. In their hands were white handkerchiefs, which they called flags. Members not yet castrated are termed 'donkeys' or 'goats'; while the others are white 'lambs' or 'doves'.

In order to absorb a part of the divinity of the renowned Shilov, small pieces of bread were eaten, which had been placed in holes of a monument which had been erected to him. It was claimed by a priest, a spy who cultivated certain Skoptsi leaders on Church orders, that there was a "communion of flesh and blood". This (possibly fictitious) practice was said to take the particularly obnoxious form of cannibalism which could be expected among a community with castration tenets.

Castration is called the Baptism of Fire by the sect because, according to their beliefs, it was originally carried out with a red-hot iron. Because of human weakness this was amended to allow a sharp knife to be employed. Christ, they hold, and the early Christians, all practised it. It seems, however, that it is the act rather than the instrument with is all-important. This is borne out by statistics published by the authorities, as follows:

Knife	Razor	Hatchet	Scythe	Iron, Glass, Tin, etc.
164	108	30	23	17

The exact location of the operation varied a good deal. In 620 cases investigated by the police, ninety-six were carried out in houses, nineteen castrations in prisons, forty-one in baths, thirty-two in barns, six in cellars, one hundred and thirty-six in woods, 223 on roads and in fields—and so on. If the authorities were unable to account for the strange beliefs and practices of the Skoptsi, they were at least going to comply with filling in the appropriate form under 'Where the Offence was Committed'.

Women members were almost as fanatical as men: forty per cent as fanatical, that is to say. "Within them," we are informed, "the operation is as fearful as it is revolting: and yet we find women among the operators. Among forty-three peasant women who acted in this capacity, five had actually operated upon men." Four members in ten were females, on average.

The Skoptsi cast their net wide in search of converts; and in 1815 it was remarked that if the numbers of their aristocratic adherents were small compared to the peasants within their ranks, this was merely because in Russia most people were peasants. One report states that "their numbers, in the matter of proportions of peasants to people of quality, approximate to the usual relationship of numbers in terms of rank."

A sampling by class is still extant: "Four ladies and four gentlemen of the nobility, ten military and five naval officers, fourteen civil servants, nineteen priests, 148 merchants, 220 citizens, 2,736 peasants (of whom 827 were women), 119 landowners, 443 soldiers and soldiers' wives and daughters."

The attempts at suppression of the sect served in many cases only to increase its power; a fact which had been foreseen and was actively canvassed by the members. Skoptsi, who had been placed

Secret cyphers.

in the care of monks, converted whole monasteries to their teachings, in spite of the horror with which they had been viewed on entry. The unpopularity of the clergy and the police actually provided a large number of cases of emulation on the part of individuals who wanted to share their fate. Observers were convinced that the only way to stop the spread of the cult was to deport its members to unpopulated places, and leave them there to die out. Another obstacle to the crushing of the movement, much noted during the beginning of the twentieth century, was the fact that the Skoptsi endowed churches, paid large sums of money to priests and officials, and generally became looked upon as benefactors by large numbers of people who were thus prevented from doing their duty to protect society against them.

The riddle of the power of the Skoptsi has had some light thrown upon it by more recent psychological research. Noting that the active emasculation and self-mutilation is a very old form of religious activity, Dr. K. A. Menninger (*Man Against Himself*, London, 1938, pp. 248ff.) believes that this cult and others like it originated with a self-destructive urge which can be found, or developed, in many people. It is related, he thinks, in common with many other psychological thinkers, to all forms of self-mortification, whether done in the name of religion or otherwise. There are to this day people in many parts of the world who will claim that self-mutilation is but a step to the attainment of mystical insight. That it is associated with the idea of sacrifice seems in no doubt at all. What is still in dispute is whether all forms of self-mortification are merely mental states, or whether there is, in fact, some inner resource which can be tapped by these means. Few people would go to the irremediable lengths of the Skoptsi in order to find out. The methods employed with such success in mass conversions by the Skoptsi may depend upon the existence of 'teachers' fanatical enough to drive home a dominant idea into the minds of suggestible people. If this is so, and there is no secret knowledge such as has been hinted at in Skoptsi confessions, it is unlikely that the cult will have as startling a future as its past. In Soviet periodicals references to the survival of the sect continue, as in material coming from Roumania where descendants of early refugees are to be found.

(i)

(ii)

(iii)

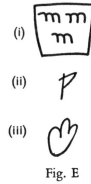

Fig. E

9

The Charcoal-Burners

AMONG the secret societies of Italy none was more comprehensive in its political objectives than that of the Carbonari. In the early 1820s they were more than just a power in the land, and boasted branches and sub-societies as far afield as Poland, France and Germany. The history of these 'Charcoal-burners', according to themselves, started in Scotland.

A certain Queen Isabel of Scotland, they relate, was on the throne when King Francis of France first made contact with the happy, democratic mystics who formed the original Carbonari. He had strayed across the frontiers of his kingdom, and (since everyone is assumed to know that Scotland shares a frontier with France) it was a matter of only a short time before he ran into our heroes. Should it be claimed that there was no Queen Isabel of Scotland at the time of Francis I, it may be remembered that the first wife of Robert the Bruce was a lady of this name, and she was indeed to be found during the early part of the fourteenth century in rural exile in her homeland. The question of the land-frontier between the two countries cannot be so easily explained, however.

Now, continues our charcoal historian, there was a band of noble-minded people dwelling in this rugged land. They had escaped from the yoke of tyranny, and took refuge in the woods. For the purpose of avoiding suspicion of ulterior motives, they took to charcoal-burning, which is described as the industry *par excellence* of Scotland.

"Under the pretence of carrying their charcoal for sale, they introduced themselves into the villages, and bearing the name of real Carbonari (charcoal-makers) they easily met their supporters, and communicated their mutual plans. They made themselves known to each other by signs, touches and words. As there were no houses in the forests, they devised rectangular huts, made from branches. They set up a government, which was a law-making body. This was a triumvirate: the members of it ruled for three years, and they presided over three *vendite* (lodges). The first was legislative, the second administrative, and the third judicial. The last-named was called the High Lodge, and Carbonari obeyed only their own laws.

"These lodges were sub-divided into a number of smaller units —known as *barracas*—each one started by a Good Cousin of some distinction among his fellows, who was in contact with the High Lodge, and was known as the Grand Master (*Gran Maestro*)."

In this forest also lived a mystic, a hermit known as Theobald. He became a member, supported them, and was given the rank of Protector of the Carbonari. Thus they continued, carrying out their plans and meetings.

"It happened that Francis I, King of France, hunting on the frontiers of his kingdom, next to Scotland, in following a wild beast parted from his courtiers. Night came on and he lost himself in the forest. He came upon one of the small lodges (barracas) and asked for shelter. It was granted, and the Good Cousins unanimously ministered to him all that he was in need of. Francis admired the happiness of these Carbonari, and their mystic discipline. He thought that he saw something mysterious and singular in it, and revealed himself to them as the King of France. He earnestly asked to be told their secret and their objects. They told him, and he was full of admiration; he desired to be admitted to the Order, and promised to be their protector. He joined, and the following morning he returned to his courtiers. When he went back to France, he scrupulously fulfilled his undertaking, declaring himself Protector of the Carbonari, and he increased their numbers. The Order now spread through Germany, France and England."

Known as 'forest Masonry', Carbonarism practised, in contravention of local custom and Papal attitudes, complete freedom of religion; and from time to time formed powerful alliances with other secret societies, some of which may have in their turn influenced it. It became extremely popular in France, numbering in the first quarter of the nineteenth century numerous important French savants among its members. Under Louis XVIII and Charles X, over twelve thousand Parisian Freemasons were also Carbonari.

The principles of the organization are partly dealt with in the "General Doctrine of the Order", extracted from the first chapter of the official (though secret) Statutes of Carbonarism:

Article I. Good Cousinship is principally founded upon faith and virtue.

Article II. The place of meeting is called the *Baracca:* the space surrounding it, the Forest or Wood; the interior of the lodge is the *Vendita*.

Article III. The Members are called Good Cousins. They are divided into two classes: Apprentices and Masters.

Article IV. Tested virtue and purity of morals, and not Pagan (uninitiated) qualities, render men worthy to belong.

Article V. Six months must elapse before an Apprentice can become a Master. He must, principally, practise good works, help the unfortunate, show humility, have no hostility towards Carbonari, and enrich his heart with virtue.

Article VI. It is forbidden to talk directly or indirectly against religion.

Article VII. All conversation on religion in general, or against good morals, is forbidden.

Article VIII. Every Good Cousin Carbonaro is under an obligation to preserve inviolate the secrecy of the Mysteries of the Order.

Article IX. No Good Cousin may communicate any decision of his Vendita to those who belong to another one, much less to an uninitiated person.

Article X. Members are reminded that they must be

most careful in talking with people whom they do not know well. They must be especially watchful in their own family circle.

The objective of this society was to constitute a body of men who would be subject to the orders of a central body. When the organization was in powerful being, it could take what action seemed necessary: probably of a political nature, against even established governments or military formations. From the earliest recorded period of its existence, it formed a state within a state.

The regulations, the frequent meetings, the discussion of mystical matters and the common practising of certain rites, produced a bond sufficient to weld the Carbonari into an association which came near to dominating Italy. A fair idea of the symbolism and the artificial 'shared experience' which members underwent is available in the secret documents of the society. As in the case of most secret societies, the place where the meetings were held was specially arranged.

The Vendita, say the instructions, was represented by a room of planks covered with wood. The floor was brick, the interior furnished with backless seats. At the end there was a block supported by three legs; on the two sides were two other blocks of similar size, for the assistants. On the first block—that of the Grand Master—were the following symbolic objects: a linen cloth; water; salt; a cross; leaves; sticks; fire; earth; a crown of white thorns; a ladder; a ball of thread and three ribbons, one blue, one red and one black.

There was also to be a radiant triangle, with the initial letters of the password of the Master Degree in its middle. On the left was a triangle, with the arms of the Lodge painted upon it. On the right-hand side were three triangles, each with the initial letters of the sacred words of the first rank. These triangles were to be translucent. When apprentices were admitted, "the symbolical picture of the Vendita and the emblems on the patents (which are a repetition of it) were explained after a discourse on the natural liberty of man, its forfeiture by the perseverance of the wicked, and the necessity for recovering it by the efforts of the Society. The Initiated were addressed more openly as soon as they had shown an aptitude for seizing allegories, or when they belonged to a more enlightened class of society."

Two written lectures have been found: one aiming at the less educated, the other at the intellectuals. The first is a short one, in which the Grand Master explains that certain sages discovered that the way to gain the necessary ends of justice and welfare for the people was to found secret societies. The other explains the need for ceaseless effort for the Society, by allegories based upon forest examples:

"The trunk of the *tree* which you see expresses the surface of the earth on which the Good Cousins are dispersed. It denotes also the sky spread equally over all; and it shows us that our wants are equal, and our interests the same. The roots of the tree mark its stability. Its green foliage and the strength by which it resists the storm, show that it never grows old. As our first parents after losing their innocence covered their shame with leaves, the Good Cousins should conceal the faults of their fellow men, and particularly those of the Society.

"The *white linen* in which you have been received is the product of a plant which has been transformed by labour. So we too should purify and cleanse ourselves by continual effort. As we were wrapped in linen when we were born, so we will be regenerated to virtue.

"*Water* cleansed us when we came from the womb. It teaches us here to purify ourselves from vice, in order to enjoy the pleasures of virtue.

"*Salt*, which preserves things which deteriorate, warns us to keep our hearts from corruption.

"The *crown of white thorns* placed upon our heads reminds us to be cautious in movements and actions, to avoid the pain of being hurt.

"The *cross* foreshadows the labours, the persecutions and the death which threaten those who would be virtuous. We should emulate our Grand Master Jesus Christ, who willingly suffered death to bring us nearer to salvation. The *earth* buries the body; thus should the secrets of our sacred Order be buried in our hearts. It is the most important symbol of our association. The Pagans (uninitiated) spread snares for us; they are perverse enough to mistrust our associations; the very instrument of their redemption and happiness. And were they to penetrate our secret, they might force us to sustain an unequal combat.

"The *ladder* shows that virtue can be attained only step by step.

"The *bundles of sticks* denote the members, united in peace. The *ribbons* express faith: in the form of charcoal, which is black; blue is the smoke, and stands for hope; red, which is the fire, is for charity. The specimen of wood which is the badge of the Apprentices, is to be fastened to their coats at the buttonhole by a tri-coloured ribbon. Several of similar shape are stuck in the ground at regular distances, to mark the homes of Good Cousins. Its form is that of the pole of the furnace of the real charcoal-burners: the ends are cut diagonally. The Masters wear a badge of the same form in silver. The thread of that ball is the mysterious tie which unites us. The axe, the mattock and the shovel are the tools of our sacred labours."

That the Carbonari were (and may still be, for that matter) a body dedicated to revolt and to the gaining of material power may be guessed from this address to a new member. But the motives become even plainer when we see that in higher stages of initiation a different significance is given to the symbols which the member is asked to contemplate, and whose meaning he has to keep in his mind, conditioning him to aspirations whose physical achievements are explicitly and graphically given:

"The *cross* is to crucify the tyrant who persecutes us; the *crown of thorns* is to penetrate his head. The *thread* is the cord to lead him to the gallows; the *ladder* will help him to climb them; the *leaves* are nails to pierce his hands and feet. The *pickaxe* will bite into his breast and shed his impure blood. The *axe* will sever his head, just as is that of the wolf who disturbs our labours. The *salt* will preserve the head, a reminder of eternal infamy of tyrants; and the *pole* will display his head. The *furnace* will burn his body; the *shovel* will scatter his ashes to the wind; the *baracca* will prepare new tortures for the tyrant. The *fountain* will purify us from vile blood which we shall have shed. The *linen* will wipe away our stains, making us clean and pure . . ."

In spite of many Carbonari saying that there were but two degrees of initiation, it seems that there were in fact three—or there may have been more. In any case, the objective of this select band of initiates is to "find information about the signs and secret words used by men of various nations throughout the globe, towards midday and midnight." The Lodge where this ritual is carried out is made to represent a cave within a mountain. In one corner is an urn, with the inscription: "Here lies the Hero." The initiates believed that they could, by contemplation and throwing themselves into a trance, gain information about secret matters. It is here that the mystical and magical aspect of Carbonarism is briefly seen. It has been suggested that there was a whole range of higher degrees, influenced by the cult of Mithra.

Although various Carbonari secret papers claim that the Society was founded on the basis of the ancient Mysteries, including that of Mithra, there is much evidence to show that it owes at least something to the sinister and murderous associations which flourished in Italy for centuries before the Charcoal-burners were ever heard about.

It has been said by some historians that the inspiration of the Carbonari and similar societies came from pre-Christian times, for there were settled in the Alps communities which seemed to owe allegiance to Gnostic and other ideas which some profess to see reflected in Freemasonry, Templarism and the discipleship of the way of the Sufis.

Semi-political societies, purporting to avenge wrongs and to establish right in the land, have been known in south Italy since the twelfth century. The Chronicles of Monte Cassino preserve a record of a cult which was in full cry in 1186; the Avengers. These Sicilians were chiefly distinguished by their nocturnal assassinations, and their Grand Master was eventually hanged, and knowledge of the 'sect' seems to vanish at that point. Then there was the Beati Paoli, dedicated to destroying the power of arbitrary rulership. It carried on a campaign against courts, barons and prelates. Members made great use of the poisoned dagger, spread justice by burning out culprits, and thoroughly beat those who opposed them. It still existed in the eighteenth century, when the trail becomes cold, though it is said that it still functions. Its activities are still remembered locally, as those of a Robin Hood type of organization.

It was from the Beati Paoli that the Carbonari seem to have adopted their ritual cursing of defecting members. Those who incurred their wrath had their names written in a 'Black Book' and this list was read out at every Lodge meeting, to the mass imprecations of the assembled members. A trace of magical ritual survives in their habit of burning enemies in effigy, to the accompaniment of a death-curse. Although nominally Christians, the Carbonari undoubtedly had rituals which recalled other forms of religion; and they were known by the authorities as a 'sect', and did not dispute the title.

The ideas of generosity and kindness which are inculcated from the earliest moments of membership are not entirely idle ones. For it is on record that "The ferocious Lazzaroni of Naples, and the wildest brigands of the Calabrias and the Abruzzi have been known, immediately on their initiation, to perform the most striking acts of benevolence and justice". Carbonarism seems in practice to have known few social frontiers: "An assassin", says a historian, "condemned to the chain, is permitted to take his place in the Lodge of the Castle of St. Elmo, where he is confined with other galley-slaves; and the Commander of the Fort (himself a Carbonaro) has not dared to exclude him, but is obliged to sit by his side."

But if there were discreditable facts about the Carbonari, it must be admitted that their secret papers also contained 'Laws' which seemed to show that a considerable measure of personal discipline was expected from members:

"Members habitually intimate with persons degraded in the

eyes of the public, shall be suspended for a year; whoever gambles for wine, or frequents public-houses, or appears often in public drunk, shall be suspended as above. Those who abandon their families or live a dissolute life, suspended for from six months to two years."

Offenders against the honour of "females belonging to Good Cousins" were to be "given up to general execration". It is noted that, as well as ordinary relatives, "females devoted to the exclusive attachment of Good Cousins are included". It was realized that it might be the females themselves who put temptation in the way of Good Cousins, so: "Those who do not resist the criminal invitations of the wives of Good Cousins shall have their names inserted in the Black Book."

Nobody was allowed to avail himself of the weakness of degraded females; nor could a married Charcoal-burner have an 'attachment'. A special regulation (Article 74 of the Penal Statutes of the Carbonari, Section 10—*Offences Against Honour*) provided for suspension up to three years for 'seducing or carrying off female servants of Good Cousins for base purposes". Article 71, however, shows that there was some scope for the more rascally of the Good Cousins; and this was when the objects of his activities belonged to the infidels:

"Those who shall seduce the female relations of respectable Pagans shall be suspended from the Society for a period of from two to six months." At the worst, then, females of Pagans were only one-sixth as important as those appertaining to Good Cousins.

When a constitutional Government was established in Naples, the Carbonari came to the surface in such numbers that observers were astonished. "In the capital the patrols of Carbonari preserve good order, parading the streets night and day, headed by constables and agents of police, whom they have forced to become initiated, in order to become worthy of the command." Their special uniform included a death's-head badge on the cartridge-case. Since the Carbonari had their own tribunals and laws, and were forbidden to resort to courts not under Carbonari jurisdiction, we hear that "The magistrates, as well as the civil and military officers, have often been obliged to become members of the Society, in order to preserve some shadow of their authority." Something of the power of the organization recommended itself to priests as well: "The lower clergy enrolled themselves of their own free will; and seconded the views of their institution by every means in their power. The number of priests initiated, notwithstanding the severest prohibitions pronounced by the Holy See," writes a contemporary Italian author, "is a proof that the Roman hierarchy, like all other ancient institutions, is in danger from its own members."

A document on the increasing power of the Charcoal-burners drawn up by General Colletta on July 6th, 1820, says: "The number of Carbonari enrolled during the month of March in the present year amount to 642,000."

The Carbonari were revolutionaries, and in 1820 and the following year they set Naples and Piedmont ablaze. They forced King Ferdinand to take an oath to their Constitution, and to wear their tricolour of red, white and blue. But if they wanted revolution, they did not want anarchy, and this is one reason why they ruled through priests, prelates, magistrates and others who had been duly sworn in.

The revolution of the 1820s was put down through the help of the Austrians, and the Society was driven out of Italy: at least, driven very far underground. In France their exiled leaders preached liberty, equality and fraternity, and gained many converts with important results.

The Italian patriots Garibaldi, Mazzini and Cavour revived the secret society after 1830, and its members were again found to be ready for any sacrifice for republicanism and rule by the Carbonari. The effect which they had had upon the world was considerable: and it continued to be so. For fifty years they had fought in civil war; they spread to many other lands, including Germany, where they were responsible for the *Totenbund* (the Death League) which was dedicated to assassinating tyrants. They were secretly dedicated to the unification of Italy, and this they accomplished. But in the process, much blood was shed, many were the injustices traceable to them.

The Bolsheviks and their theoreticians of the Communist persuasion are traced by many as offspring of the Charcoal-burners; and if this be so, then the force of the followers of the pious hermit of Scotland is still unspent.

IO

The Garduna: Holy Warriors of Spain

WHEN Franco led his Moors into Spain to challenge the Republicans, certain units of the left-wing forces adopted as their battle-cry the slogan "Remember the Holy Madonna of Cordova!" And a secret society which may have started when the Arab general Tarik crossed into Iberia told the world that it was active again. After World War II, an important anti-Semitic German arrived in Madrid by a devious route, and sought out the house of a nobleman. He gave the password *Muerto a los marranos!*—Death to the Hogs—and it was not long before he found himself in the safety of Latin America, passed from one branch of the Garduna secret society to another. Twelve hundred years of connected history is the boast of the criminal organization which claims that it was responsible for crushing the last of Arab power in Europe, and that it was the favoured tool of the Holy Inquisition against Jews, Moslems and every kind of *marrano* heretic which infested the most Catholic land of Spain.

But it seems that the real origins of the Garduna as a unified force do not go back much further than the blood-spattered days of Ferdinand the Catholic and Isabella the Holy, who in the fifteenth century started their crusade against Moorish influence in Spain. The Moors, who civilized Spain, and the Jews, who came with them and taught in their universities, had little effective military power left by the end of the fifteenth century. Most civilians had been killed or exiled to north Africa; pockets of guerrillas remained in the mountains. Some had elected to become Christians, in order to remain in the country. They were mainly of Spanish blood and had nowhere else to go. While the Holy Inquisition had few scruples about its methods, there were still a large number of cases of Jews and Moors who professed the Catholic faith, but who were suspected of secretly practising their old religion. Some were rich, others apparently respectable members of the Church. In too many cases they could not be proceeded against openly.

This was where the Garduna came in. Dedicated to the literal destruction of every trace of non-Catholic ways, to the murder wherever possible of anyone who might harbour dangerous thoughts, the Society became the unofficial weapon of the Holy Inquisition.

In order to train its members in right-thinking, the Garduna evolved a myth. The Society, runs this pseudo-history, came into existence shortly after the first battle against the Arabs took place. The Holy Virgin of Cordova took refuge with the heroic Christians. God the Father was displeased with the Christians, and thus allowed the Moors to conquer most of the country to punish them. The only people permitted to survive were the elect, chosen to reconquer the country and wipe it clean of infidelity. In order to do this, they had to struggle for seven hundred years. It was the tears of the Cordovan Virgin which had mitigated the punishment from total destruction, and allowed that the Spanish people, if they followed the Garduna in its divine mission, should eventually prevail.

This terrible, yet in parts heartening, news was not at first revealed to the struggling patriots. Motivated entirely by pure and unselfish impulses, groups of true Spaniards took to the highlands and formed themselves into bands, unaware at the time of the details of their holy destiny.

But in the wild country of the Sierra Morena there dwelt a sanctified hermit called Apollinario, whose main activity was the worship of the Virgin. Him she chose as her messenger, to pass on the true facts of the situation. She appeared before her devotee and revealed the victory of the Moors as due to divine punishment. She was, she said, one day looking at the world and the unhappy state of the Spaniards, when she had the sudden idea to mention to Christ that the Spanish, after all, had many fine qualities. At this her Son became more cheerful, and she took the opportunity of asking Him to allow the hermit to save Spain.

He agreed. The position now was that the anchorite was to collect all patriots and lead them against the enemy in the name of the Cordovan Virgin. As their reward on this earth, the said warriors were to be entitled to all lands and other possessions of the Moors, no matter how they came into ownership of them. The wealth of the Moors was dangerous to the Spaniards; but in Spanish hands it would prove a blessing for the true religion.

The Virgin now anointed the hermit and presented him with a button, which she had herself removed from the robe of her Son. This relic had miraculous powers. Anyone wearing one like it would be saved from death, from the Moors, from heretics of all kinds.

This mandate was more than enough for the hermit, and he immediately founded the Holy Garduna, accredited to kill by the highest possible source, and directly authorized at that. This fact gave rise to the custom of religious dedication before an attack upon anyone; and the Bible was consulted for omens before taking decisions, by opening it at random and finding a meaning in the passage thus revealed.

Ferdinand and his inquisitors alike found in the Society an ally which seemed to have been created for the situation in which they found themselves. Even before Ferdinand's time, the bands had been in most active existence. They looted and burnt, combining the roasting of heretics with the burning of their houses, and also the claiming of their movable property and land. How many Garduna there were is not known, but they certainly played a large part in the crusade against the Moors, and their pious exhilaration on the field of battle has passed into legend.

When, however, the actual fighting was over, the Garduna became something of an embarrassment to the King. For one thing, they were becoming jealous of their booty and would not share it. Secondly, quite a number of genuine Christian royalists found that they were being smelt out as heretics and subjected to their tender attentions. And when the Garduna decided to descend upon a person, they completed the operation with remarkable thoroughness. Soldiers were sent out against their bands, and it seems to be at this time that the federation came about which welded the brigands into one powerful body.

Although the King was against them now, they still retained their association with the Inquisition, which tended to protect them at court. Seville became the headquarters of the movement, and the Society was given a secret constitution and shape.

There were nine degrees of membership. New Entrants were called goats (chivatos) and were little more than the servants of the fully-fledged members. From their ranks were drawn spies, scouts and porters. They were trained to imitate animal cries, which were the signals of the marauding bands. The 'covers' (coberteras) were women of uncertain morals, who had a multitude of uses. They would waylay people on the roads and engage them in conversation while the band readied itself for an attack. They wormed their way into houses on various pretexts, to spy out the land; they lured men into ambushes. For special projects which required a more refined type of character, the Garduna employed syrens (serenas) who were young women posing as ladies of breeding. These were frequently the mistresses of Garduna chiefs, and wanted for no material comfort. The bellows (fuelles) were ancient men of respectable and venerable appearance who traded in the loot, made friends with prospective victims, and negotiated with the Inquisition when the latter had special projects to be carried out.

The athletes (floreadores) were the strong-arm men, capable of every vice and villainy. They had often been convicts and bullies or galley-slaves, and they formed the backbone of the attack forces. The swordsmen (ponteadores) were more refined and could play many social parts. It was from the swordsman class that most of the chiefs (guapos) were recruited. The supreme ritualistic heads were known as Magistri, and carried out priestly and administrative functions. The commanders (capataz) were regional leaders, who carried out the orders of the chief of chiefs, the Great Brother, or Grand Master, known as the Hermano Mayor.

His word was law, and his discipline frightening.

The Garduna should not be considered as fighters alone. They had a regular tariff which included kidnapping and deportation, providing false witnesses, selling enemies as slaves, and the falsification of documents. The more refined activities were made possible through their co-operation with the priesthood. Their word was their bond where any matter of villainy was concerned. If the Garduna said that a man would be murdered at a specific place and time, he was murdered exactly as promised. Documents showed that half of any agreed fee was payable in advance, the balance on completion. Even the manner in which this money was used was controlled according to fixed rules. One-third of all money earned through 'commissions' went straight to the general funds of the Holy Garduna; a similar amount for running expenses; the remainder was shared among those who actually did the deed.

The general fund was not wasted, and the Garduna were fully aware of the needs of public relations officers and friends in high places. "That for a considerable period the affairs of the Society were in a very flourishing state is proved by the fact that they were able to keep in their pay at the court of Madrid persons holding high positions to protect and further the interests of the members. They even had their secret affiliates among judges, magistrates, governors of prisons and similar officials; whose chief duty lay in facilitating or effecting the escape of any member of the Society that might have fallen into the hands of justice."

It was not until 1822 that a really determined attempt was made to suppress the Society in the closely-knit modern form in which it now existed. When this descent upon the Garduna took place, much of abiding interest was discovered. The organization, although it was careful to have no papers dealing with its constitution and laws, was vain enough to keep a comprehensive record of its dealings. This was in the form of a book, seized in

1821 at the house of the Grand Master Francisco Cortina. And it was on the basis of this document that the Order was brought before the courts. The manuscript showed that there were branches in Toledo, Barcelona, Cordova and other cities, towns and villages. Proved from these pages was a close and intimate connection with the Inquisition until the seventeenth century. Statistically speaking this association is of interest. The Spanish authorities showed that in the 147 years of co-operation with the Holy Fathers between 1520 and 1667, almost two thousand enterprises of dubious kinds were entrusted by the Inquisition to the Garduna. The profits on this series of transactions were recorded as almost 200,000 gold francs. Detailed analyses showed that Garduna activities on behalf of the Holy Office were equally divided as follows: murder, one-third; abduction of women, one-third; robbery, perjury and the rest, one-third.

On the 25th of November in 1822, the last official Grand Master and sixteen of his chief officers were publicly hanged in the market of Seville.

As we have seen, this was by no means the end of the Holy Garduna. The South American branches were flourishing in 1846, and there are further references to them in 1949. At the present day there are said to be two branches, mutually hostile, operating in Spain. The one supports the Church and is said to be in active contact with it. The other, a left-wing organization, is reputed to have set up its own secret Church and to be dedicated to setting up a Holy Socialist State.

I I

The Cults of the Ancient Mysteries

THERE was something strange about the classical mysteries; something which attracted people to them and having attracted them made their initiates with few exceptions permanent devotees. In Egypt, Greece, India, Rome and a dozen other places and countries, sacred initiations took place in specially prepared sanctuaries. Priests of the mysteries enjoyed the profound respect of the masses: as well as that of kings and counsellors.

What were the mysteries? Until relatively recently, and relying upon comparatively scattered fragments such as Apuleius' *Golden Ass*, historians and religious writers had formed an opinion of them which has been shown to be extremely naïve. They knew that at the ceremonies symbolical teaching took place: and hence inferred that the mysteries were a relic of the times when academic knowledge was guarded by the few, and scientific truths (such as Pythagorean theorems) were given only to the elect. They knew, too, that orgiastic drumming and dancing formed a part of many rituals: and therefore told their readers that this was a degenerate form of religion, or a mere excuse for licentiousness. They found that stories of ancient gods and heroes were recited: and were sure that the mysteries constituted little more than an underground survival of prehistoric religion, magic or tribal initiation.

Times have changed. The study of 'brainwashing' and conditioning the mind within the past decade has helped to lay bare the essence of the mysteries, and has answered the riddles which surrounded them. In this process, those who had tried to keep the celebration of the mysteries alive, who had tried to revive them, have been shown up as relying upon the symbolic interpretation alone. And this revelation has been in its own way one of the most startling developments of contemporary religion. Almost anyone, for instance, can get away with telling anyone else that he was an Egyptian priest in a former incarnation: because there is so very little verifiable material available to prove the reverse. But let anyone attempt to celebrate any of the ancient mystery-cults' rituals, and unless he has a sound idea of how the human mind works, he is unlikely to escape the criticism of those physiologists who now see in the mysteries an almost open book.

Let us return to a sketch of the conventional knowledge about the mysteries. In those of Eleusis, celebrated in Greece, the candidate had to undergo fasting or abstinence from certain foods. There were processions, with sacred statues carried from Athens to Eleusis. Those who were to be initiated waited for long periods of time outside the hall in the temple where the rites were to be held. Eventually a torchbearer led them within the precincts. The ceremonies included a ritualistic meal; one or two dramas; the exhibition of sacred objects; the 'giving of the word'; an address by the hierophant; and, oddly enough, closure with the *Sanskrit* words: "Cansha om pacsha."

The elements included the clashing of cymbals, tension and a certain degree of debilitation, eating something, plus conditions which were awe-inspiring, strange. The candidate was in the hands of, and guided by, the priesthood. Other factors were: drinking a soporific draught; symbolic sentence of death; whirling around a circle.

Initiation ceremonies of secret cults of the mystery-type invariably involve tests, sometimes most severe ones. The effect of certain experiences was a carefully worked programme of mind training which is familiar in modern times as that which is employed by certain totalitarian states to 'condition' or reshape the thinking of an individual. This process produces a state in which the mind is pliant enough to have certain ideas implanted: ideas which resist a great deal of counter-influence. This was the secret of the mysteries, this and nothing else. Echoes of such training are to be seen in the rituals of certain secret societies without mystical pretensions which survive to this day: trials, terror, expectancy, drinking and the rest.

That this fact was known in the past is evidenced by the words of Aristotle, who was exiled because he was said to have revealed something about the mysteries; and he said: "Those who are being initiated do not so much learn anything, as experience certain emotions, and are thrown into a special state of mind."

What was this special state of mind? It was a plasticity, in order that the conditioning might take permanent root. The psychologist William Sargant, the greatest authority on this subject, says in his classic *Battle for the Mind*: "It seems, therefore, that there are common final paths which all individual animals (though initial temperamental responses to imposed stresses vary greatly) must finally take—if only stresses are continued long enough. This is probably the same in human beings. If so [it] may help to explain why excitatory drumming, dancing and continued bodily movement are so much used in such a number of primitive religious groups. The efforts and excitement of keeping the dance in progress for many hours on end should wear down and if need be finally subdue even the strongest and most stubborn temperament, such as might be able to survive frightening and exciting talk alone for days or weeks."

Dr. Sargant notes that Chinese experiments in mass-excitation,

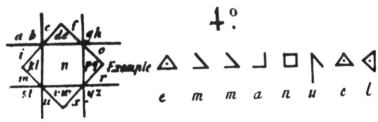

Cyphers used by secret societies.

breaking down and reconditioning are based on the same physiological principle as religious conversion and also group and individual psychotherapy treatments. These include the application of tension, fear, anxiety, conflict, to the point where the subjects are uncertain. In this state suggestibility is increased and the old pattern of behaviour is disrupted.

The fact that the devotees of the mysteries were thoroughly conditioned to them, and felt that they were important in their lives, is seen in much historical evidence. Even in the fourth century of the Christian era, the Greeks were insisting that they "would consider life unbearable if they were not allowed to celebrate those most sacred mysteries which unite the human race".

The work of those who have pointed out the function of the mysteries as mind-training and conditioning has, of course, evoked no answer from those who still think that the rituals are mere symbolic representations of knowledge or of facts. But it is interesting to note that the ecstasy which is produced by excitatory methods and is followed by manipulation of the mind is still sought by members of many secret cults who are aware of the scientific explanation. Their reaction is that the experience may well be induced by physical methods: but in spite of that "it is nothing less than actual spiritual communion with a supernatural power". This is the point at which scientists and mystics cannot agree. The mystic feels sure that he has experienced something sublime. The scientist tells him that it is an illusion. He will not believe it. The situation reminds one of the time when someone produced the soul of a departed relative to tell a spiritualist that there was no life after death. Although this is alleged to have happened in Ireland, one can visualize it taking place easily enough in the mutually heated atmosphere of scientist versus mystic anywhere.

The orgiastic side of the mysteries, too, has a place in the sphere of psychology. The catharsis (cleansing of the mind) which the secret cult of the Cathari experienced after ecstasy is paralleled by the modern therapist's procedure in bringing his patient to a state of excitement and collapse before implanting what he considers more suitable ideas in his mind.

Christianity was not behind in its use of the mystery-system for initiates. It was not until A.D. 692 that every believer was ordered to be admitted to the worship of the Christians, following the period when it was thought advisable to celebrate certain parts of worship in secret. Traces of this survive in such customs as that of the Greek Orthodox Church, where the priest celebrates divine worship behind a curtain, which is only taken away during the elevation of the Host, "since at that moment the worshippers prostrate themselves and are not supposed to see the holy sacrament".

The reason given for the secrecy of the practice of the Christian cult gives a clue in explaining that the celebrant must be prepared by expectation. St. Augustine laid down that secrecy was essential because: the mysteries of Christianity were incomprehensible to human intellect, and should not be derided by the uninitiated; secondly, because this secrecy produced greater veneration for the rites; thirdly, that the 'holy curiosity' of those to be initiated into the experience of Christianity should be increased, in order that they might attain to a perfect knowledge of the faith. St. Basil (*De Spiritu Sancto*, cap. xxvii) tells how the Fathers of the Church "were well instructed to preserve the veneration of the Mysteries in silence. For how could it be proper publicly to proclaim in writing the doctrine of those things which no unbaptized person may so much as look upon?"

The origin of mystery ceremonies does seem to be India: or, at least, the place and time when the Brahmin priesthood started its initiations. The ceremonies were based upon the Hindu myths; but the procedure followed in training the aspirant is strikingly similar in Egypt. And Egypt profoundly influenced Greece.

Prayer, fasting and study were the first requirements, when the Indian candidate prepared himself for the trials which were before him: for the actual sight of the Great Gods, and for the final 'word' (teaching) which would be implanted in his mind when it had become sufficiently prepared to receive it. If the weather was cold, he would have to sit in the snow or rain, naked. In the torrid heat, he sat in the full blaze of the sun, with four fires built around him to give additional heat. This was the first part of the undertaking; while he repeated prayers and repetitions which included the invocation for his complete conversion. This latter concentration upon the desires of the candidate is applied in more than one of the mysteries. Coupled with the 'word' which is given during the ceremonies, it means that the power of suggestion is being applied continuously, and should penetrate into the mind at every moment when it is able to receive it.

This period of dedication was succeeded by one in which he visited the underground cave of initiation. Passing through a tunnel of complete darkness, he emerged into the cavern, where three priests, dressed as gods, awaited him in resplendent and intimidating array. After being addressed and partaking in the oration of prayers, he walked rapidly around the temple several times, and was then carried through several subterranean and unlit caves. During this time there were wails and shouts from every side, while illuminated spectres and other horrors abounded. At the end of this terrible experience, the aspirant came to two doors which, when thrown open to the sound of the sacred conch trumpet, revealed a scene of brilliance and glory. This hall was full of every delight in the form of pictures, music and perfume. He walked to an altar in the room where he was again harangued: and presented with his sevenfold cord, which marked his passing through the initiation.

If we compare these proceedings with those which were said to be carried out among the Egyptians, the parallelism is startling. The candidate was taken to a well, which he had to descend until he came to a tunnel. Torch in hand, he passed through a door, which closed with a resounding noise. He was met by frightful figures, which offered him a last chance of going back. Now he passed through a fire, swam through a dangerous underground stream. As soon as he reached a door and touched a ring to open it, a blast of air blew out the lamp which gave the only available light. A machine swung him over a bottomless pit. Just as he was on the point of exhaustion, an ivory door opened, and he found himself on the threshold of the resplendent Temple of Isis. Here the priests received him into their company. After this series of tests, he had to undergo fasting and what would nowadays be called indoctrination, before he could be considered completely initiated into even the first degree. The foregoing experiences were followed by the higher degrees, those of Serapis and Osiris.

It is needless to outline the beliefs and methods used in the Chinese, Japanese, South American and other mysteries; because while the legends which are inculcated vary, the training system hardly does so at all. The real mystery of the mysteries is how and when man first discovered the use of certain procedures to condition other men: and whether the discovery was instantaneous or gradual, or simultaneous or at different times and places. But one cannot date doctrines as one can archaeological finds, by radioactive carbon.

12

False Cults and Societies

THE student of secret organizations does not go short of information about completely spurious cults, and those about whose real existence there is a reasonable doubt. It is often thought (and perhaps more often stated in the Press) that the world is riddled with sinister cults practising black magic, drug-addiction, or pure deception. It is said, of course, by those who believe that the whole basis of ritualistic organizations is delusion, that they are all false, anyway. But a number of distinctions can be made. Not all cults which are dominated by adventurers were always bogus; and some which started off in a dubious manner have achieved respectability.

We hear of this problem mostly in its Western expression: false yogis everywhere, bizarre idol worship in California, Satanism in France. But its roots go back even farther than we can trace them. Take the case of the traditional Eastern story of the Turkish Saint, which is folklore, but may be part-truth.

Centuries ago in Anatolia a sage lived with his small son in a hut beside a *ziarat*—a shrine where a holy man was buried. Over the years, the place had acquired such sanctity that pilgrims came from as far as Africa and the Indies to say a prayer and invoke the sanctity of the unknown saint. The boy, on the threshold of manhood, decided that he would travel in search of knowledge; go to seek his fortune, as the Prophet Mohammed had once said, "yea, even unto China journey—for knowledge is the most excellent of all things". His father gave him a donkey to ride upon, and the youth set off. He passed through the famed cities of Islamic learning, through Isfahan, Bokhara, Samarkand, sitting at the feet of teachers; and then turned his steps towards China. It was in Kashmir, several years later, that the donkey suddenly lay down and died. The young man was beside himself with grief. Unable to decide what to do, he buried his only friend and sat in mourning upon the mound.

Certain travellers passing by asked what ailed him. "My only friend and companion is buried here: he who never failed me, who inspired me and who was my means of progress." Deeply impressed by this, they assumed that he spoke of a spiritual teacher. They donated some money for a dome to be built over the grave of an individual who must have been of much merit if he could inspire the sorrow which they had seen. The youth— Mustafa—never looked back. More years passed, and his father found that the revenues of his own shrine were suffering through the diversion of pilgrims to this new and highly sanctified one in Kashmir. He decided to travel thence, in order to ascertain who this revered sheikh might be. As soon as Mustafa saw him, he broke down and confessed the truth. "Know, my son," said the sage, "that all is ordained in advance. It was fated that there should be a shrine here and that you should become a shrine-keeper. For let it not be concealed from you that the grave of the Unknown Sage which is my own Shrine, marks the spot where, under similar circumstances exactly, the father of that donkey of yours expired."

Apart from those who have sainthood thrust upon them in the East, there have been in the past few decades quite a number of new cults, claiming ancient origins, organized for tourists and others. Egypt is a prolific source of these bodies. Originally started by various unscrupulous individuals for the Westerners attracted to the Pyramids, the Order of Isis is a good example. Credulous believers in the fact that all wonders came from ancient Egypt joined the various (competing) branches of the 'order' in droves. It became more democratized during and just after World War II, when many young soldiers of Allied armies were enrolled, sons and daughters of Isis, inducted with the strictest secrecy. The fact that the Mysteries of Isis were traditionally only lesser ones was known to the initiators as little as to the initiated.

Libel laws prevent one from detailing some of the cults which are still running; but it may safely be generalized that some of the Yoga ones are run by adventurers. It is easier to spot a really false cult than one might think, though the knowledge of how to do so comes mostly through personal experience. The completely false cult relies upon window-dressing and impressing the individual with the atmosphere and ritual of the Order, or whatever it may be called. Few spurious cults depend upon the personality of the chief, because it is the exception when the false magus has a sufficiently impressive 'presence' to dispense with the trappings: at least in the early stages of initiation. Contrary to the sensationalist writers, secret cults and societies do not rely greatly upon drugs of addiction, perhaps because this is one direction in which the authorities are far too much in control of the situation. Hypnotism, too, is an uncertain tool, to say the least of it, as anyone with practical, applied knowledge of experimental hypnosis will testify. Cults connected with sexual perversion and other aberrations do spring up now and then, and there is always the possibility that such things may obtain in a secret organization. The fact that perverted people are fickle or feel themselves in need of a change from time to time, however, militates against the long-term use of this in a secret organization.

What, then, keeps false cults in being for any appreciable period of time? Firstly, the desire for power; secondly, the love of mystery; thirdly, a sense of being someone special; fourthly, the feeling that one is going to gain something by membership. It will be seen that the pandering to such sensations is not the province of secret cults alone. Almost every advertiser is guilty of it—though seldom to an anti-social degree.

Eliphas Lévi has given a graphic description of a cult which was false in that it was concocted by a group of politicians, but not spurious inasmuch as its leader and many followers believed in it. He calls them the "Saviours of Louis the Seventeenth". Even people who fought against them, he says, were eventually overcome by their beliefs and joined them. Certain individuals concocted a sect, and chose as its leader a certain labourer named Eugene Vintras. And he explains how they did it. It was not hard, given a rather gullible dupe, in the form of a Vintras.

The year was 1839. Vintras was sitting in his room, expecting a workman to arrive. There was a knock on the door, and there he saw an old man, dressed in rags. This apparition addressed Vintras as Pierre Michel—names which he thought nobody knew were his. The visitor complained that everyone thought him a thief, that he was weary, and so on. Vintras, touched, handed him ten sous, with a reassuring word. He left, but Vintras did not hear him go downstairs. He searched the house, but could not find him. He later found that there was a mysterious letter, with the coin which he had given to the stranger on top of it, on his table.

This letter, by its contents and 'supernatural' appearance, made Vintras (probably with some other inspiration of a similar kind) a protagonist of Louis XVII. Now Vintras appears as a sort of seer and prophet, carrying on propaganda for Louis in a field where it could do a great deal; in the twilight of supernatural belief. He had visions, all showing support for Louis; blood appeared on his body without any vestige of a wound; wine turned to blood. Even priests, who came to scoff, joined the cult in enthusiasm when they saw the miracles which they had preached about actually seemingly occur before their eyes.

Vintras was accused of being in league with the devil. Analysts certified that the blood was indeed real. But the blood appeared on consecrated hosts, and even priests could not believe—as some indeed said—that the devil had the power to cause such a change to the Body of Christ. Gozzoli, one of his former supporters, published a tract in which he made revelations of obscene rites being performed by the cult. These included black masses, ritual nudity and indiscriminate physical licence among the worshippers. By November, 1843, when Pope Gregory issued a letter condemning the cult, it had supporters everywhere. The obscenity revelations were discounted as due to jealousy or (of course) the machinations of the evil one. Vintras was not to be outdone by a mere Bishop of Rome. In his turn, he excommunicated Gregory and proclaimed himself Pope. There is no doubt that he was thoroughly persuaded that he was a messiah of some kind, and that he suffered from extraordinary hallucinations. Some of his letters survive, in which accounts of incredible experiences are preserved.

13

The High Priesthood of Thebes

A MOST detailed account of what was said to be the seven highest degrees of secret Egyptian initiation was first published in Germany in the eighteenth century. This strange and very exhaustive document combines many elements from the ancient mysteries, and may in fact be a pure concoction. On the other hand, it could be at least partly based upon some surviving esoteric practice. It seems to come from Greek sources, because many of the words used are Greek; and it may well be that we have here the modern beginnings of an attempted revival of ancient mysteries. Whatever the document may be, it is not one of those fanciful and spurious ones which used to be printed merely to attract the credulous: because it is plausible in containing the sort of material which might well have formed the content of an initiation and mind-conditioning system.

The earliest version known is in the form of an anonymous pamphlet (probably not intended for public sale) of thirty-odd pages, which was printed in 1785. It was republished in a French translation thirty years later, purporting to be the ritual of the Master degree in Freemasonry. The French editor claims that it is a composite ritual, derived from the works of some fifteen Greek and Roman writers.

This degree, we are told, was open to Egyptian kings and priests alone; and only those specially recommended by an initiate could enter it. The usual procedure was that the Pharaoh himself introduced the candidate to the priests. By them he was sent from Heliopolis to the Memphis priests; from there he went to Thebes. He was circumcised, forbidden to eat pulse or fish; and generally had to abstain from wine. He was put for several months in an underground cave, and asked to write down his reflections. When he had done this, he was led to a passage supported by the pillars of Hermes where he had to learn certain things which were inscribed thereon. As soon as he was word-perfect, the Thesmorphous (introducer) came to him with a strong whip, to keep the uninitiated at bay. He was blindfolded, and his hands bound with cords.

Now follows the procedure from the first degree of this elect body. The candidate was led to the Gate of Men, where the introducer touched the shoulder of an apprentice (Portophorus) standing there on guard. He in turn knocked on the gate, which was opened. When the aspirant entered, he was questioned on various matters by the Hierophant, after which he was led around the Birantha in an artificial storm of wind, rain, thunder and lightning. If he showed no sign of fear, Menies the Expounder explained the laws of the Crata Repoa, to which he had to agree. He was then taken in front of the Hierophant, made to kneel, and vowed fidelity with a sword-point at his throat. As witnesses he called upon the sun, moon and stars.

"His eyes were then unbandaged, and he was placed between two spare pillars, called Betilies, where lay a ladder of seven steps, behind which were eight doors of different metals of gradually increasing purity. The Hierophant then addressing those present as *Mene Musae*, or children of the Work of Celestial Investigation, exhorted them to govern their passions and fix their thoughts upon God."

The candidate was taught that the ladder symbolized the wanderings of the soul; he was told the causes of wind, thunder and lightning; and given other valuable information, such as medical lore. He was given the password of recognition of this degree, which was AMOUN, meaning secrecy. He was taught a grip, given a pyramidal cap and an apron called Xylon. Around his neck was a collar; and he wore no other clothes. His duty was to guard the Gate of Men in his turn.

The Portophorus was now able, after showing his devotion, to proceed to the Second Degree. Following a prolonged fast he was taken into a dark chamber called Endimion, the invitation grotto. He was now of the degree of Neocoris. "Handsome women brought him dainty food; they were the wives of the priests, who endeavoured to excite his love."

If he resisted these advances, he was further lectured by the Master of Ceremonies and led into an assembly, where the Stolista (water-bearer) poured water over him. Then a living serpent was thrown at him. The whole room was full of snakes, to test his courage. "He was then led to two high pillars between which stood a griffin driving a wheel before him. The pillars symbolized East and West, the griffin the sun and the wheel of four spokes the four seasons. He was taught the use of the level and instructed in geometry and architecture. He received a rod, entwined by serpents and the password HEVE (serpent), and was told the story of the fall of man. The sign consisted in crossing the arms over the chest. His duty was to wash the pillars.

When he was initiated into the Third Degree, the member was given the title of Melanophoris. He was led to an anteroom, over whose door was written 'Gate of Death'. The room was full of copies of embalmed bodies and coffins. Here too were a number of dissectors, embalmers and so on.

"In the centre stood the coffin of Osiris. The Melanophoris was asked if he had had a hand in the assassination of his master. On his denying the question, he was seized by two Tapixeites, or men who buried the dead, and led into a hall, where he found all the other Melanophores clothed in black. The King himself, who always was present on these occasions, addressed him in an apparently friendly way, begging him if he did not feel courage enough to undergo the test now to be applied to him, to accept the golden crown he was offering him."

He had already been coached to refuse the crown and tread it underfoot. At this 'insult' the King called for revenge. Raising his sacrificial axe he touched the head of the initiate. The two corpse-carriers threw him on the ground, and the embalmers wrapped him in bandages. All who were present wept. Now he was led to a gate over which was written *Sanctuary of the Spirits.*

"On its being opened, thunder and lightning struck the apparently dead man. Charon received him as a spirit into his boat and carried him to the judges of Hades. Pluto sat on his judgement seat, while Rhadamanthus and Minos as well as Aethon, Nycreus, Alaster and Orpheus stood beside him. Very severe questions were put to him as to his former life and finally he was sentenced to remain in these subterranean vaults."

The bandages were removed, and he was told never to desire blood, never to leave a corpse unburied; and to believe in the resurrection of the dead and the judgement to come. He was taught coffin-decoration and the peculiar hierogrammatical script. The sign was an embrace, to express the 'days of wrath'. He was kept in these underground chambers until thought fit to proceed to a higher degree.

These 'Days of Wrath' generally lasted for a year and a half, until the initiate was ready for promotion to the Fourth Degree: 'The Battle of the Shades'. He was handed a sword and a shield and taken through dark passages. He met "certain persons, presenting a frightful appearance, carrying torches and serpents". He was attacked, with the cry of PANIS! He defended himself bravely, but was taken prisoner, his eyes were bandaged and a cord placed around his neck. Dragging him into a hall, the spectres disappeared. He was led into the assembly of initiates, and his eyes unbandaged. Before him he saw a magnificent hall, decorated with beautiful paintings; the King and the highest dignitary—the Demiurgos—were present.

All were wearing their Alydei, an Egyptian Order composed of sapphires. Among those present were the Secretary, the Treasurer and the Master of Feats. The Orator made a speech, congratulating the new member on his fortitude. He was given a drink, called Cyce, which he drank to the dregs. This was probably the ritual drink of honey or milk, water, wine and gruel—and perhaps some hypnotic drug. He donned the boots of Anubis, took up the shield of Isis, put on the cloak and cap of

Orcus. He was handed a sword and told that he must cut off the head of the next person he met in a cave and bring it back to the King.

This cave was pointed out to him. Entering it, he saw what seemed to be a beautiful woman, but in reality was a model of one. He seized this by the hair and severed the head. This he brought back to the monarch, who praised him, telling him that he had symbolically won the head of the Gorgon, wife of Typhon, who had caused the death of Osiris. He was now permitted always to wear the dress which had been given to him, and he was entered in a book as one of the judges of the land. He was able to communicate at any time with the King, and received an allowance from the court. He was invested with an Order (that of Isis in the shape of an owl) and it was revealed to him that the secret name of the great lawgiver was JOA, which was also the password of this Degree. But the password for the meetings of the Christophori (as the Fourth Degree initiates were called) was SASYCHIS.

The Fifth Degree, that of Balahate, could not now be refused to the Christophorus. He was led to a hall to watch a play, at which he was the only onlooker. Other members of the degree went through the hall, as if looking for something. One drew his sword, and the terrible figure of Typhon appeared. He was slain. Now the new Balahate was told that Typhon represented fire, a terrible element which was at the same time indispensable. The password was CHYMIA, and the teaching was in chemistry.

In order to become an 'Astronomer at the Gate of the Gods'—the Sixth Degree—the candidate was taken to the hall of assembly, bound, and led to the Gate of Death. He was shown corpses which had been cast into water, and warned that he might be similarly treated if he broke his oath. He was given some teaching in astronomy, and taken back to the Gate of the Gods, where he looked at the pictures of the gods while their histories were explained to him. A priestly dance took place, symbolizing the course of the heavenly bodies; he saw a list of members of the Order throughout the world, and learned the password: IBIS, for watchfulness.

The last and the highest degree was that of 'Propheta', in which all secrets were laid bare. It was conferred following public processions, and when the permission of the King and all the highest members had been obtained. The members secretly left the city by night, "and retired to some houses built in a square and surrounded by pillars by the sides of which were placed alternately a shield and a coffin, whose rooms were painted with representations of human life. These houses were called maneras, for the people believed them to be visited by the *manes* of departed men. On their arrival at these houses the new member, now called prophet or Saphenath Pancah (a man who knows the secrets), was given a drink called oimellas, and told that now all trials were over. He received a cross of peculiar significance, which he was always to wear. He was clothed in a wide, white-striped dress, called etangi. The usual sign was crossing his arms in his wide sleeves. He could peruse all the sacred books written in the Ammonite language . . . his greatest privilege was having a vote in the election of a king. The password was ADON."

14

The Decided Ones of Jupiter the Thunderer

THE life of one of the most celebrated of Italian brigands runs through the story of the Lodge of Jupiter the Thunderer, which came into lusty being after 1815, when bands of outlaws were terrorizing Calabria and the Abruzzi. Ciro Annunchiarico was his name, and he had placed himself at the head of a cut-throat band, unable to live in normal society because of their crimes.

For some time the brigands were able to operate unmolested, but when the Government decided to take stern measures against them, Ciro realized that there might be scope for a general confederation of all outlaws. Ciro himself had little to lose, being under sentence "of at least perpetual imprisonment for murder". He was nobody's fool—and had no hope of being able to overcome the Royal forces; but he felt that he could muster sufficient forces to gain favourable terms when it came to the point of negotiation. His was not the most powerful gang, but Ciro had a strong personality. The Vardarelli bandits, he knew, were already so powerful that they would make the best allies; and he accordingly invited them and the chiefs of other groups to a conference, about the end of 1816 or the beginning of 1817. As a priest, he himself celebrated a Mass for the combined forces in a deserted chapel just before the deliberations commenced.

Gaetano Vardarelli, head of the other important group, felt that such an alliance might attract too much unwelcome attention from the authorities. In point of fact he was himself at that very moment in the service of King Ferdinand, for he had made his peace with him on favourable terms. At the same time, he was prepared to listen to any proposition which might give him greater profits than his current arrangements.

He awaited Ciro's suggestions. Ciro was both a desperado and a man of learning. Brought up in comfortable circumstances, he was early earmarked for the Church, came of a respectable family of farmers, and had an uncle who was known as something of a savant. The youth began his terrible career through killing a young man of the Montolesi family in a jealous rage. Whipping himself into a sense of hatred for every relation of his victim, he pursued everyone of the name of Montolesi, until only one remained alive. This worthy only escaped by shutting himself up in his house and staying there for several years. Even when Ciro was killed, he refused for some time to believe it, such was the terror which his enemy inspired in him. After four years in prison, Ciro escaped, and started his career as chief of a society of murderers. Some of his exploits cannot be recorded in a book for general circulation. His more ordinary activities were sanguinary enough. Such things as the ravaging of a woman at Martano and stealing from her 96,000 ducats were the normal routine with him. He kept in continual correspondence with a large number of brigands, and a letter to him was enough to send him off to murder almost anyone designated, providing that the price offered was sufficient. When asked by the Commission which eventually condemned him how many people he had personally killed, he said that he could not remember: but it might be sixty or seventy.

In addition to being reasonably cunning, Ciro was an expert marksman and always rode a first-class horse. Even when betrayed, he outmanœuvred ambushes by forced marches of thirty and forty miles. Such was his luck and judgement, so many were his seemingly miraculous escapes from justice, that he was considered to be a magician; and this was an impression which he sedulously fostered. Nobody dared to say anything against him, let alone curse him (in spite of the Italian penchant for such outbursts), because if they did so, "a demon would certainly inform him of it". He was also of an unusually loose moral character, and carried a "portfolio of very free French songs"—

which was with him when he was eventually arrested. Although an ordained priest, he seemed to think that he was the only genuine one, because, although he would celebrate Mass, he declared that all others were impostors. Missionaries, he stated in a published paper, were preaching untruths, and he forbade them to function in the villages of the countryside.

Ciro amused himself with whims from time to time. When he was being pursued by a General d'Octavio and a thousand men, he jumped down upon him from a garden wall, armed to the teeth. "I will spare you this time," he told the terrified commander, "but if you continue to hunt me I shall not be so indulgent." The reason why he spared the General, he told his cronies, was that it was better to be hunted by a frightened man than a new and possibly unfrightenable one who might replace him if he were murdered. He is described as being of an engaging personality, pleasant in appearance, strong, fond of women. At the time of his capture, he had mistresses in all the towns of the province through which he was restlessly ranging.

This was the adventurer who placed himself at the head of the secret society called the *Patrioti Europei*; and later another called the *Decisi*. These organizations were strengthened by the fact that they were able to corrupt minor functionaries, and also because they found enough priests to attach to all their camps and detachments, giving them a sort of implied importance or regularity. "The Archpriest Cirino Cicillo of Cacamola, Vergine of Coreligiano and Leggeri filled important situations in the sect. The signature of the last was found under the patents in quality of Captain-Reporter. The Archpriest Zurlo of Valsano celebrated Mass on Christmas Eve, armed to the teeth."

Some parts of the country were under their complete control. In other places they ranged the countryside in guerrilla fashion, dressed in fantastic costumes which served to increase their supernatural reputation. In more settled areas, hired or sworn secret assassins lurked and watched for the moment to sink their knives into the breasts of persons sentenced to death by the confederation of secret societies.

Between December 1817 and January 1818 the total number of members—all on the active list—was estimated at 20,000 men. Some lived—like the Thugs of India—seemingly respectable lives; others lived irregular and bandit-like but settled lives, forcing everyone in their home villages to sign over their property to them at the point of a poignard.

The secret society coccus was thus arranged: Lodges were known as Decisi (Decisions) of the Order of the Decided. These were the Assemblies of the Reformed European Patriots. The society was divided into Camps (of three or four hundred men) and Squadrons (of forty to sixty strong). As their numbers increased, the aim clearly became one of general revolution. Proper military formations of infantry and cavalry were organized, drilling and exercises held. Each member had a Patent, decorated with terrible symbols, and inscribed somewhat as follows:

"The Salentine Decision. Salutation. No. 5 Grand Masons. The Decision of Jupiter the Thunderer hopes to make war against the tyrants of the universe, etc. The mortal *Gaetano Caffieri* is a Brother Decided *No. 5*, belonging to the Decision of Jupiter the Thunderer, spread over the face of the earth by his decision, has had the pleasure to belong to this Salentine Republican Decision. We invite, therefore, all Philanthropic Societies to lend their strong arm to the same and to assist him in his wants, he having come to the Decision that he will obtain liberty or death. Dated this day the *29th October, 1817*. Signed: *Pietro Gargaro* (The Decided Grand Master No. 1); *Vito de Serio*, Second Decided. *Gaetano Caffieri*, Registrar of the Dead."

Part of the document is written in blood. A proper register of the dead and the manner in which they were killed, was maintained; and the names inscribed thereon, together with 'blasphemies and infernal projects'. The killings themselves, when possible, were carried out according to a special ritual:

"At the signal of the first blast of a trumpet they unsheathed their poignards; they aimed them at their victims at the second blast; at the third they gradually approached their weapons to his breast, with real enthusiasm, and plunged them into the body at the fourth signal." Four dots appear under the name of Gargaro. These indicate his power to pass sentence of death. If these stops were included thus in a letter from the Decision, it meant that the addressee was automatically sentenced to death if he did not obey the order. If there were no dots, then a milder punishment, such as laying waste his fields, would ensue.

The symbols of this society include a thunderbolt darting from a cloud and striking a crown and tiara; the fasces and the Cap of Liberty upon a death's head between two axes; a skull and cross-bones with the motto 'Sadness, Death, Terror and Mourning'. The colours are yellow, red and blue. All this may seem very melodramatic; but the fact that the Decision meant business and carried out its threats tended to outweigh such superficial criticism. Certificates cost a great deal of money, and these fees provided the society with a considerable amount of its funds.

The first really determined attack upon the secret society took place in the summer of 1817. Armed with unlimited powers and 1,200 Germans, Albanians and Swiss, completely reliable and unshakable mercenaries, General Church set off for the mountains. In many places nobody would give any information. It is reported that in five important areas only one monk out of all the population bowed to the General. In some other places, however, the inhabitants were a little more communicative when they realized that this was at last a determined effort to flush the rebels.

Ciro, surrounded by moving columns of troops, acting as 'beaters', is reported to have said, "This General is a different man from those who have been sent against me before. I have made fools of many generals—French, Italian and Neapolitan, but this one will end by making a fool of me."

He tried to flee in a ship at Brindisi, but was recognized, and resolved to stand and fight at the fortified town of St. Marzano. The town was taken after some resistance; and those who had defended it were taken into custody. Ciro's standard and other objects were captured and sent to the King; but the bandit chief escaped. He now took refuge in a fortified farmhouse, but was tracked down by Church's troops, who had been threatened with severe penalties by the General should they fail to find him. With three companions he held out for a day and a night. Tormented by thirst, he eventually surrendered.

Searched, he was found to have poison on him, and said that his companions had prevented him from taking it. He pleaded for his subordinates, saying that they had been forced to become bandits. When sentenced to death and offered the consolations of religion, the renegade priest said, "Let us leave alone this prating; we are of the same profession—don't let us laugh at one another."

As he was led to execution by Lieutenant Fonsmorte, he remarked that he would have liked to make him a Captain; and the scene is described thus: "The streets were filled with people; there were spectators even on the roofs. They all preserved a gloomy silence."

When he arrived at the place of execution, he was asked to kneel. He did so, but was told that bandits were shot in the back. As he turned, he asked a priest to stand back, in case the bullets hit him by mistake. Twenty-one musket-balls hit him, and still he did not die. "This fact is confirmed by all the officers and soldiers present at his death. 'As soon as we perceived,' said a soldier, very gravely, 'that he was enchanted, we loaded his own musket with a silver ball, and that destroyed the spell.' "

On the following day, ten of the chiefs of the Decisi were shot at the same place; none showed any repentance; and the most lurid days of the secret society were brought to a close.

15

The Order of the Peacock Angel

IT was a scene that would have delighted the heart of any Sunday newspaper reporter, and would have aroused the envy of a master stage designer. Somewhere in Putney, most respectable of London suburbs, sixty men and women were gyrating ecstatically in an underground temple before an eight-foot, glossy black statue of a peacock. As I stood in a small gallery built above the floor level, I took note of the pool of water in which the bird's feet rested; the monotonous arabesques of the wall-decoration, the criss-cross patterns of the stone floor.

Rising and falling in an incessant, all-intrusive beat, hidden drums were thudding out a tempo which made it almost impossible to keep oneself still. Each of the worshippers was robed in a white flowing garment which completely covered his ordinary clothes. On the breast of each was embroidered a peacock—some green, some black, others red.

The devotees of the Peacock Angel meet once a fortnight, carry out their complicated rituals, whirl before the effigy of their deity —and return to their respective homes. You would not be able to identify them if you met them outside; no slit-eyed oriental or turbaned sheik leads the revels. No 'obscene rites' are practised. The devil-worship attributed to the Yezidis of Kurdistan who are also peacock followers is not to be found here. Then why should an otherwise apparently sober and sometimes very ordinary man in the street become a member of a cult like this? What does he get out of it? How is he recruited?

The snake and the cock (or peacock) are symbols of power. As such they are worshipped or propitiated by the Yezidis, and have given many a headache of identification to those experts on the Gnostic mysteries who have found them engraved upon seals of uncertain origin in the Middle East. The English version of the cult was brought to Britain by a Syrian who settled in London in 1913. He converted, so runs the tradition of the Cult, five people of importance: a banker, a member of the Peerage and three ladies who were well known at that time as society hostesses. His name is known only to initiates, who introduce it in a disguised form into their conversation.

The cult grew in numbers until sixteen *halkas* (lodges) were formed, each with a minimum of seven members. Essentially the belief is that there are two powers which can be of help to people in everyday life: the powers of increase and of construction. These are known by the coded name of the peacock and the snake, because their names must not be pronounced except by the initiates. The reason for adopting these pseudonyms is that the total of the numbers in the names (worked out by numerology) is equivalent to the numbers of the names of the words 'peacock' and 'snake'.

It was this discovery, based upon the numerology of the Arab cabbala, which led to the London peacock men and women. I had let it be known that I had heard of their existence (which I had) and that I had something of interest to impart to them (which I had not) through a member who had been introduced to me, and who had mentioned the Yezidis in a general conversation on the Middle East. That he was a priest of the cult became evident when I mentioned the Sacred Number. The peacock cultist (British Branch) did not at that time know that anyone who was reasonably proficient in the *abjad* (cabbala) system of the Arabs would be able to decipher their Holy Name.

The aims of the cult are distinctly fraternal. The main objectives are the sharing of the ecstatic experience which follows the operation of the rituals, and mutual help thereafter. These ideas are by no means confined to the peacock people, for they underlie the theories and practices of quite a number of secret societies. What was interesting was to find the cult in London, to make contact, and to be able to witness the ceremonies.

Like Sufism (with which it probably has connections in the remote past), the peacock religion embraces the belief that the sharing of the rituals will make the worshippers in some way akin to one another and also conduce towards the realization of their ambitions. At a certain point in his development, the worshipper becomes 'enlightened' as to what his true vocation is—and finds the means to satisfy it. Thus the organization not only offers what might be called peace of mind in spiritual activity; it purports to bring material success in the mundane world as well.

Although they are not by any means missionaries, the cultists do try to attract members. This is in accordance with the belief that progress in the things of the world can be achieved by co-operation as well as by magic. Further, it is believed that the magical practices are more likely to succeed if there is a community within which they can be given expression. It was put to me thus: "If three members of the Cult get together and decide that they are to progress in the world, they may find that they have a 'call' to open, say, a shop. If they have the confidence that this is likely to succeed, and if they give the peacock-power the environment (the shop) in which to work—it cannot fail!"

If nothing goes on to which anyone might take exception, why is the cult so shy, why is its very existence kept secret? In the first place, much uninformed literature on the subject says that the worshippers of the peacock are devil-worshippers. The origin of their belief is the Moslem intolerance under the Turks which labelled these schismatics infidels. They are not allowed to use the name of Satan—and it is blacked out in their books. This is because they are allowed only to think of good, and must not retain the idea of evil in their minds.

Secondly, the High Priest told me, the organization is pledged to maintain secrecy because "there has been no society and no country in which ecstatics have not been subjected to persecution. We must be allowed to operate for ourselves, and with ourselves. We are not interested in casual onlookers and Press sensationalism."

The nature of the ecstatic experience which is attained by the members is of course the kernel of the whole thing. But let us start from the beginning. Members are expected to be on the watch for possible recruits. The theory is that there is, deep down inside almost everyone, a feeling that he is unfulfilled. This fulfilment is sought in the career, in promotion, in money, in marriage or hobbies. But there remain a large number of individuals who do not attain it. These are the prospective members of any cult, and especially of the peacock people.

In conversation, the member is to find out the mental attitude of the prospective recruit. What are his hopes and fears, what are his weaknesses and strengths . . . what his goal in life. Reports on these people are submitted to the High Priest. Providing that the potential member is not deeply in debt, or thought to have any unusual or perverted interests, and once he has developed an interest in fulfilling himself, he can be put on the list of candidates for missionary development.

People who already have a metaphysical commitment, or leanings towards spiritualism or organized religion in any form, are barred.

The candidate is asked whether he would like to take part in group discussions or demonstrations of contemplation and concentration, based upon an Eastern model. If he agrees, he begins to attend meetings at which he is 'developed'. This development takes the form of going through exercises which give him the power to direct his mind at will upon certain thoughts and exclude others. If he is interested in hypnotism, he may be taught this, with the reservation that the group's attitude towards hypnosis is that it is of limited value, except in the early stages of spiritual development. He brings his problems to the leader of the Circle. These difficulties are met in discussion in training how to overcome worry and confusion—again by concentration and meditation. The entire programme of mind-training is leading the candidate towards the mystical experience, although he may not yet be aware that this is so—or even that such a thing exists.

If he finds (as he generally does) that he is deriving benefit from this form of psychotherapy, he is told that he can progress further, but that in order to do so he must place himself completely in the hands of the master of the Circle—the High Priest. At this point some candidates fall out of the running, partly no doubt because quite a number of people object to being told exactly what to do. The remainder, however, carry on.

The next part of the training is to carry out specific exercises—both mental and physical—in a graduated course, until he can fill his mind with various emotions at will: joy, fear, optimism, a sensation of power. He is given words to repeat before going to sleep. Any dreams are to be carefully noted; for these are looked upon as omens, and are interpreted in accordance with fixed rules by the Master or Guide (his assistant).

There is no carefully worked-out theology in the movement. The peacock represents the power which is 'in charge' of human affairs; and anyone who wants to enter the fold must believe that there is such a power. I talked to several members who said that they had been recruited at a stage before this, however. They were curious to know how various of their friends were able to battle with life without flinching, were able to achieve what others could not, and so on. They asked: and were brought straight into the 'instructional' phase, at which there is no preaching, only practice of exercises. When the exercises seemed to work, they were told that it was through the power which was called the Peacock Angel. There are probably several hundred members throughout Britain, and I was told of three lodges in the United States. Some of the members have live peacocks, which they keep as symbols of the 'Path' upon which they have embarked.

After the ceremony just mentioned, worshippers and guests were ushered into a large, well-furnished room, where refreshments—no alcohol—were laid out on buffet tables. They had removed their outer robes, and stood revealed as ordinary men and women, much like the type whom one might meet at a better kind of cocktail party in the West One district of London. The sign of identification, I am pretty sure, is thus: the right hand is placed, with the fingers spread out (perhaps to represent the tail of the peacock) on the left breast, just above the heart. The counter-sign may have been stroking the chin with the left hand. The latter signal is one which has been in use for many centuries among mystical fraternities of the Middle East, from which the London peacock people have undoubtedly derived their rituals and probably their beliefs as well. In the Middle East, the chin is stroked with the right hand.

Out of the sixty members whom I saw at this meeting, none looked like a foreigner, none of the working class, nobody seemed on superficial inspection to be the wild-eyed crank type.

Prayers are said, in private, to a small (probably silver) image of a peacock. These, or such of them as were shown to me, did not seem to ask for much else than enlightenment, material progress and mystical experience. When it is desired to attain an objective of a more specific sort, special rituals are used, of a magical type.

I asked the High Priest about black magic and evil-wishing. "Black magic is an appeal to the power of evil. We believe that evil is not a power in its own right, but an unhealthy force which can be built up in a man's (or woman's) mind. Therefore we do not give it a place in our thoughts. To think about it would be to admit its existence and give it reality and focus. Therefore the devil does not exist for us. Those who revere evil are as bad as those who fear or hate it. We ignore it completely. The same answer gives you the explanation why we cannot indulge in evil spells and the like. They must not exist, because we do not allow evil to exist in us. Since we are aiming at removing the evil from people's minds, we cannot allow thoughts of it to enter. The thoughts which we have are all constructive."

How was the Order of the Black Peacock financed? There was certainly a good deal of evidence that money was being spent upon it. . . .

"You will see," said the priest, "one way in which money comes to the Shrine, and you can draw your own conclusions from it. But I may tell you that this organization is not run for profit. When members make money as a result of any activity for whose success they have prayed to the Peacock, they pay two and a half per cent. of that to the Shrine. This money they keep in their own possession, and they lay it out for objectives which are decided by the Council." Who were the Council? "The Council changes every year, on the occasion of our Spring Festival: the first Wednesday in April. There are two representatives for every twenty members. Elections are among all the members."

I supposed that the priests had an automatic seat on the Council.

"Not at all. In this year's Council, for instance, there is no priestly member."

Did the Order hold much property? No, it seemed, none. Who, then, financed a meeting such as this one? "In rotation of surname-initials, the members who have accumulated profits from the intervention of the Peacock in their business and professional affairs."

I had been interested for many years in ecstatic religion, and was determined, if I could, to be allowed to see the exact method by which the members worked themselves up into a frenzy, and what happened then. "It shall be as you desire," said the priest. "You are in any case invited to the Urs." This word is the standard one for the festival of a patron saint, in Arabic and Persian.

Ten days later I was picked up at Clapham Common Underground station, after a telephone message. It seemed that there was still some doubt as to whether I was working for a newspaper, or might in some way let out what little I had learned. In any case, the number-plates on the car which met me were well covered with mud, and the homely but self-possessed woman sitting in the back kept me talking all the time we were travelling to the scene of the meeting. "Do you swear on every holy book, upon your honour, upon the life and death of yourself and those dearest to you, without reservation, that you will not give others the opportunity of contacting us; that you will treat our Cult with respect; that you will help, not hinder, us and anything connected with us, while you are convinced that we are worthy of this trust and this consideration?" "I do."

In the growing dusk, the house to which we were driven

seemed an ordinary small suburban one. Inside it was neat and clean, and showed that it was a place of no great size. My friend the High Priest was there, in the front room, sitting with about ten more or less serious-faced people, some of whom I recognized from the original meeting. There were new faces, too. A tiny oil lamp burned in a niche by the door. Newcomers passed their hands over it, to purify themselves, as the Kurds do.

We were given green tea, small cakes with icing upon them. The talk was general, and seemed to be commercial rather than anything else. Any group of people, I thought—perhaps uncharitably—who met regularly and helped each other in business affairs, and who believed as firmly that there was a special supernatural blessing upon their activities, would achieve prosperity, in the long run. . . .

There were sounds of music from the next room, but much less insistent than before. One by one, the members rose and excused themselves. I sat and talked with a barrister and an accountant about my days with the dervishes in Asia and Africa, and found that they were most interested. They seemed to feel that there was a point of contact. Presently—about half an hour after we had started tea—the priest took me by the arm. "The time has come for me to go in."

A short passage led to the other reception-room of the house. As we reached the door, he removed his shoes, and I did the same. Inside, sitting on small hassocks and swaying in time to the music, were the other members of the cult. In one corner stood a smaller peacock statue, standing on a large bronze vessel of water. The water was distinctly bubbling. . . .

In one corner sat the musician, playing a guitar, from which a haunting melody seemed to creep through me. Its effect upon the rest of the congregation was even more remarkable. The hassocks were arranged in a semi-circle around the image of the bird. Some of the figures which sat upon them had their faces covered by their hands; others swayed with the eyes closed. Still others had their hands clasped around their legs. About half were women, their ages between twenty and thirty. As I watched, a man stood up, moved towards the statue, and threw a rolled-up piece of paper into the water. Nothing happened for a few minutes, as he took his place again among the worshippers, in his eyes a far-away look. Then a woman, with smiling face and hands beating out the melody on her sides, approached the silent bird and said: "Thank you, thank you!"

The same kind of action was repeated by several more worshippers. After thirty minutes I noticed that half the people had left the room.

Meanwhile, my priest had apparently fallen into a trance. He sat on the floor, his body rigid, eyes staring, unwinkingly open. Someone, about to leave the room, accidentally touched him, and became rigid in his turn, slowly sinking down upon his knees, his muscles stiffening, eyes turned towards the peacock.

Being a witness to a scene such as this is sure to have some effect upon the observer. I noted that if I looked at the statue and listened to the music, I felt wave upon wave of something sweeping over me. Whether this is suggestion or not, it was actually taking place in the only place that mattered, my mind, and the mind was influencing the body into greater and greater rigidity. I found that I could inhibit this process, by looking at something else. Finally, I decided to allow the experience to take shape. I would partake of the mystery of the power of the peacock. . . .

One did not lose consciousness, I found. The mind became more and more awake, while the body seemed to recede in some way into complete unimportance. The sensation, as it grew, was one of the most ineffable relief, of joy, or happiness, such as one had only felt before in moments of exceptional fulfilment. Time had no meaning. There was nothing in the mind, except the desire to allow this blissful state to continue; for it seemed to pour fresh strength into me.

I was able, at the same time, to take some note of what was going on around me, and also to think, if I wished, of other things. The first extraordinary development within my thinking was that, when I let myself think about a certain problem, the solution suddenly flashed into my mind. This had the same quality of certainty that exists when one dreams that one has settled one's worries. The difference this time was that the solution was in fact correct, and I was able to act upon it later.

The second phenomenon was a vast expansion of memory. Trying to recall a time about which my memory was slight, I fixed upon a moment, many years ago, when I was carrying out a study of symbols used in ancient cultures. Anyone who has had the difficulty of absorbing and correlating masses of almost meaningless designs would understand how I felt when I suddenly realized that these shapes were whirling past my mind like an unreeling film. There was all the material, available whenever I wanted to see it, stop it, reel it back. . . .

Had I been doped? I examined this thought at leisure. Yes, it was possible. I could test this by not eating or drinking anything next time, if there was to be a next time. Meanwhile, I tried to recall the symptoms of the use of various drugs—and the whole complicated data, which I had read and discussed years ago, flashed back into my amazing new mind. Yet I could not account for the symptoms: unless I was in such a state that I was in no condition to seek them in myself, physically speaking. There was no disturbance of sight; no vomiting, no sweating, no apparent difference in the heartbeat, no sensation of flying, no shortness of breath, no distortion as far as I could see in thought. . . . Was it hypnosis? It was easy enough to think that it might be, but no form of hypnotism is conclusively known without suggestion, in spite of what the sensational novelists say. It is easy to use such phrases as 'suggestibility induced by drugs', but any experimenter knows that the effects vary, and also that the phrase has less meaning than it seems to have.

If I were drugged, or hypnotized, I would be able to see by one test—could I rouse myself, then slip back into the state at will? I tried. And I could. Then there was the matter of idiosyncrasy, which the would-be dopers could not know. I was, for example, a very difficult hypnotic subject. Further, my tolerance to drugs is so low that in all cases of narcotics being administered to me, I have had a most severe hangover, and cannot be roused easily. I decided, therefore, to rouse myself, and go to the other room to see what my symptoms might be then.

I stood, shaking off the influence, whatever it was. In an instant all seemed clear again. Opening the door, I moved quietly through the passage, where a number of peacock people were sitting, talking in low tones. I sat down on a settee. Nothing seemed in any way changed. There was no explanation.

The roots of the Peacock Angel cult in the West must be sought at the Sanctuary of Sheikh Adi, north of Mosul, in Iraq. In spite of what Madame Blavatsky (who claimed to have visited them) said, the Yezidi peacock people are in fact Kurds, and their language is Kurdish. The name by which they style themselves is taken from the old Persian word 'Ized', meaning originally something which is to be worshipped; and their reputation as devil-worshippers has melted before the light of modern scholarship. The Turks, who tried to convert them to orthodox Islam, and the Western missionaries, who are somewhat baffled by their rites, are mainly responsible for the label of demonolatry, which stuck in many a popular imagination to produce a good deal of lurid fiction.

The journalistic Blavatsky is at her most imaginative in the following, which she evidently claimed to be based upon a visit to the Yezidis: "They are called and known everywhere as devil-worshippers, and most certainly it is not either through ignorance or obscuration that they have set up the worship of and a regular intercommunication with the lowest and most malicious of both elementals and elementaries. They recognize the present wickedness of the chief of the 'black powers', but, at the same time, they dread his power, and try to conciliate to themselves his favours . . . they join hands and form immense rings, with their Sheikh, or an officiating priest, in the middle, who claps his hands, and intones every verse in honour of Sheitan. Then they whirl and leap in the air. When the frenzy is at its climax, they often wound and cut themselves with their daggers . . . they coax and praise Sheitan and entreat him to manifest himself in his works by miracles. As their rites are chiefly accomplished by night, they do not fail to obtain manifestations of a varied character, the least of which are enormous globes of fire, which take the shapes of the most uncouth animals". The authoress of *Isis Unveiled* (vol. ii, p. 571), from which this extract is taken, evidently did not feel herself bound by the limitations of the human knowledge of her day.

But the Yezidis are at least partly responsible for the misunderstanding. It is only relatively recently that they have explained to all and sundry that they will not pronounce the word 'Sheitan' (Satan) because the very use of the sound, they think, is associated with the power of evil. Satan, they hold, was a fallen archangel whose period of power over mankind was limited. He is now rehabilitated, and influences the affairs of man, in both good and bad ways. The force of evil is disappearing with his guilt, but it can be contacted and delayed in this disappearance by those who think about it.

Who actually was their founder? Oddly enough, Sheikh Adi is one of the most sanctified Sufi mystics of the eleventh century. As the authoritative *Encyclopaedia of Islam* has it, it seems strange that "the Yezidis should have chosen as a national saint a Sufi Sheikh like 'Adi b. Musafir, recognized without qualification throughout the whole Mohammedan world, whose orthodoxy, as we find it in his works, could hardly have led to the foundation of a sect so heterodox and foreign to the nature of Islam as Yezidism actually is." But it is possible that the esoteric teaching which is carefully preserved by the Sufis might have been passed on in the case of followers of Adi in this form. Certain it is that some of their beliefs and practices are similar to those known to the Sufis.

The Yezidis are superficially organized in a manner similar to the Sufi dervishes, and the similarities which have been pointed out between them and the Buddhists are probably derived from Sufi origins. The laity are all termed Murids (disciples) because the entire nation is considered to be composed of would-be initiates. The clergy are called kahanas (mystical leaders) or else ruhan, which is a term signifying those who can enter a deep trance. The ordering of the various ruhans closely follows Sufism. The sheikhs are all descended from Adi, and wear white robes and black turbans. They form the highest class of ascetic. Under them come the Pirs ('ancients', or 'sages'), black-robed with white turbans; while the Fakirs, or ordinary ecstatics, form the rank and file of the mystics. They also have a sisterhood called the Faqraia, the Little Poor Ones.

No outsider is allowed to see the secret rites of the Yezidis on their own ground, but there is little doubt in the minds of those who have been partial witnesses that the rituals follow more or less closely the symbolism of Sufism. The daily ordinary ritual consists of hailing the sunrise, and then circumambulating a stone which has been placed upon the ground. This stone is inscribed with the name of Malak Taus, the Peacock Angel, and the ritual is not thought to be a form of worship. A Yezidi told a Sufi initiate whom he mistook for a co-religionist: "Let us remember the force of the good and the bad which are one; and let us now stand before it, and move around our stone." They believe in reincarnation, and that to be born again as an animal is an indication that one has lived an evil life. Those who have lived good lives are reincarnated as human beings. They receive messages from the Peacock, in a manner quite similar to spiritualistic ones, which tell them of their former lives, and explain how past experiences can help them in the current incarnation. There is a legend that large numbers of reincarnated Yezidis live in the West; but why this should be so nobody knows.

One of the more secret rituals concerns both the reaching of a satisfactory ritual and also contact with this Western group. Six dancers (Kochek) and three singers (Qawwal) assemble in an enclosed place before one of the seven important portable peacock statues. A chant is started by one of the singers, taken up by the others; it begins with the long-drawn-out repetition of the words MALIK TAUS! and continues with the rapid repetition of the four syllables. When these proceedings have been continued for about a hundred repetitions, the dancers light seventeen small oil lamps, which they place in a circle in which the worshippers assemble.

Before the rite all are in a state of ritual purity, having put on a single clean garment. Men and women do not mix in this observance.

Now the dancers begin to gyrate, moving slowly around the outside of the circle in an anti-clockwise direction. They say nothing, but their arms move and the palms of the hands are rubbed together.

As the pace quickens, the repetitions get louder. Soon the ordinary Murids begin to shake, or to appear paralysed. When the latter, they always sit facing the peacock emblem.

It is believed that during this ritual much merit is acquired, which will help towards improving the character and thus leading to a human incarnation and a westerly destination.

Fig. F

The Sufi idea of *baraka* (transmitted magical power, literally meaning a 'blessing') is also held by the Yezidis. Thus it is that a person who is thought to have such power is sought after, and asked to place his hands, in the manner of the early mesmerists, in front of the eyes of the Murid. This is described as 'drawing down the blessing'.

The focus of the religion is the former Christian monastery of Lalesh, where Sheikh Adi lived his last years surrounded by disciples and zealously performing miracles. This is the Shrine to which pilgrimages take place. This, too, is where the shiny black snake (symbolizing regeneration and reincarnation) lies, carved against the portal of the sacred precincts. The snake is blackened each morning with the soot from the olive-oil lamps which are kept perpetually burning. The symbolism of this is that "the soot is the product of the oil, which does not die, as nothing really dies; it is but changed."

The baptism which is a part of Yezidi ceremonies is not an essential feature, but is a symbolic act of dedication by the person being baptized. This is reflected in the words which are used by the officiating priest: "As in this clean water you purify yourself so shall you cast off sin, as evil has been cast off from the world, and exists not except in the minds of evil-doers: therefore, be this your resolve reaffirmed, not to think evil."

There is an institution of 'heavenly relationship', somewhat reminiscent of the system of godparents. Each devotee of the cult has a brother or a sister: an 'other brother' or 'other sister', drawn from the families of the priestly class.

Upon being initiated into the sect, the devotee is given a thick woollen cloak (such as the Sufis use) which is worn next to the skin. A holy thread, of intertwined black and red wool, is put around the neck. Like the sacred thread of the Parsis and other ancient Middle Eastern cults, this must never be removed; and it sounds like the cord that the Templars were accused of wearing when the Order was suppressed as heretic. A bright red, woven wool girdle is worn around the khirqa (cloak of the order). This initiation follows a fast of forty days, and a ritual bathing which symbolically removed all past sins from the would-be fakir.

(i) ل

(ii) ع

(iii) ٧

(iv) ٣

Fig. G

At least until recently, the peacock people of Europe had little contact with their opposite numbers in the East. The main difference seems to be that the Western branch is less interested in the reincarnation belief. Whether Sheikh Adi, when he left his mystical school to carry on in the thirteenth century, foresaw the strange developments which took place within the Order in the Levant—and the stranger ones in England and elsewhere—seems unlikely indeed.

16

The Masters of the Himalayas

THERE are people all over the world who believe that in India and Tibet there are communities of master-sages. These strange and dedicated men, shunning normal life, have discovered secret and mysterious powers which enable them to communicate telepathically, to send out what is generally called 'power', to affect the destinies of the world or of individuals. They are, of course, most sympathetically inclined towards those who believe in them and who try to make spiritual contact with them. Reincarnation is one of their tenets: and they alone hold the true secrets of life and death, of the supernatural. They are in contact with the creative and destructive power; and they therefore form the true link between the ordinary man and the immensity of all that is not man. They may even take the form of incarnate gods.

We may now visit one of their lamaseries, in that high, frozen waste of the remote Pamirs, where Russia, China and India meet; where religion and magic are the preoccupation of more people per square mile than anywhere on earth. The Pamir people are squat, Mongoloid, impassive, and their way of life has changed little since the untamed horsemen of Genghiz Khan passed this way seven centuries ago. For millennia before that they carried out their ritual practices, which much later were given that overlay of Buddhism which came to its greatest—if unorthodox—flowering in Tibet.

They are not, as we have been told, romantic, impressive, powerfully spiritual people who can at will exercise extraordinary powers which leave the mere Westerner gasping. Such things as cameras, binoculars, radio sets, far from being accepted with a superior nod of the head, excite and baffle the monks of Ta-Shi. And yet, during and after their magical rituals, they distinctly show powers which are inexplicable to the ordinary man.

They are, again, conjurers, deceiving people with tricks which involve such illusionist procedures as apparently making plants grow several feet in a few minutes. This penchant of theirs for combining religion with conjuring, their ignorance of the outside world and periods of uncanny prescience, has been responsible for producing the myths about the lamas: and the debunking. The truth is much more complex, and one searches in vain among travellers' tales and occultist literature alike for any sign that they have been studied with an open mind. But the facts have not been laid bare. The facts are that they are dedicated to achieving magical power and using it. They are also practised in deception, and use it. Both things, they think (unlike the analytical Westerner), are complementary. Why?

Rituals take two parts: those which are performed publicly, and the ones reserved for the initiates of the secret cult. On Wednesday evening, as the sun goes down over the jagged rocks dominating the valley of Ak Soka, the beating of drums announces that the rituals for making sure that the luminary rises tomorrow morning are about to take place. People of all kinds and conditions crowd into the levelled space before the gaunt monastery to watch the dance. Men and women, dressed in outlandish garb dominated by immense demonic-looking masks, jig up and down to the incessant drum beat, against a background of reed flutes and the clang of gongs.

The first part of the ritual has begun. Flaming torches illuminate the scene, carried by young would-be priests in flowing robes, their faces shaven, some of them still innocent of stubble. The atmosphere is already becoming charged with emotion, for the spirit which animates the lamas may soon manifest itself. Suddenly, under a circle of pitch-brands held high, a tiny lama steps forward. He takes from the folds of his robe a knife, then another, and a third in quick succession. These he throws at a small statue of the Buddha, which is held up by none other than the Mahatma (chief priest) himself, standing on the temple steps. His aim is excellent: each seems to hit the statue, each falls to the ground. With a shout of triumph, acolytes run forward, pick up the knives, and pass them around the crowd. It is immediately seen that the metal has been shivered as if it were glass, and little but the wooden haft is left. A shout goes up: the miracle has been performed. The conjuring trick has shown the power of the Buddha.

"The meaning of this rite," Orgun Lama said as he guided me through the rituals, "is to show that the Buddha is inviolate. He can defend himself, but does not use violence." I asked him whether the whole thing was not in fact a substitution trick. He paused for a split second. "It depends upon what you are looking for. If you see something like this and it seems to be a trick, this means that for you it is the symbolic nature of the act which matters. If, on the other hand, you believe that the miracle has actually taken place, you can proceed further in your development, on the basis of faith."

This concept of conjuring was one that I had never heard of, but it seemed to have its own logic, at least from the Lama standpoint.

The dancing became frenzied, with dancers and spectators joining in, including some of the forty-odd priests. Half a dozen of the latter, I noticed, did not move, but surveyed the scene with the wary and contented eye of the stage-manager when all is going well.

Why should it be necessary for followers of the Buddha, who believe that absorption into nothingness is the best aim in life, to ensure that the sun comes up tomorrow morning? Orgun regarded this as a rather elementary question. The activities of the believers in the doctrine of the Buddha, he said, over the past two thousand years, had caused reality to become less. Reality included things like the sun, everything which we perceive by the senses. Lamas, it was true, had attained or could attain Nirvana: the state of nothingness which is complete contentment and unity with the divine nothingness. But in so doing they were selfish if they slipped into it and left the rest of the world where it was. So they could not let this millenium (as it were) of nothingness occur until everyone was ready to be absorbed. Hence the need to keep the sun in its place.

This at least showed that Buddhists had a sense of responsibility for the community, and did not concern themselves with their spiritual welfare alone. I told him so. "That is indeed so. And this is why we keep contact with the world at large, and seek to steer it on the way which will lead all to Nirvana." It was at this point that I recognized the first of many indications that this was the source of the legend of the Himalayan masters. There are masters, he told me, throughout the world. They are in constant contact, by telepathy, of course. A part of their activities was this maintaining the *status quo* of the world.

A procession was now moving into the temple which stood at the foot of the fortress-like Lamasery, and we followed. At each step the gongs clanged and the priests intoned the mystic word of power *OOM*, which I had been told must never be pronounced, such is its physical force. Inside the temple an aisle led to the immense sitting Buddha statue, at the foot of which offerings and incense were placed. The air was heavy with a sickly odour, which seemed to interfere with the clarity of one's thinking.

When all had filed before the idol, and stood in prayer before it, the procession re-formed, and started up the long and stony climb to the monastery itself. Here, in a large but low room, sat the chief Lama, sitting with his disciples, somewhat incongruously, upon a number of gilt armchairs. Before them were low tables. A number of bowls were brought, and a mixture of flour and water was handed out, which we ate in silence from our bowls. It was yellowish, not very pleasant, and contained chopped pieces of some vegetable. The Lama spoke to me at some length. A great deal of what he said I did not understand, even through an interpreter. His mystical theories seemed to contradict one another, and when I tried to go into their ramifications, I was

met with a polite smile and an assurance that I would understand
in due course. I asked him about various people in the West about
whom I had heard as Buddhist adepts. He had never heard of
them, he said; but politely added that this might be because they
were known to him under different names. No, he could not
locate them by countries, because this was not the way in which
things were done. Yes, he was in spiritual communication with
people all over the world. No, he did not interest himself in
politics. The Dalai Lama was one of the reincarnations of the
Buddha, but reincarnation was not a real Buddhist belief, it was
a "contamination from Hinduism".

Was Buddhism as he understood it a secret cult, and was it the
same as understood in Tibet proper and by the Dalai Lama and
his followers? Yes. Why secret? Because it could not yet be
understood by the majority of people. The drums were beating
again, and I realized that something was happening within me.
There was a distortion of the things which I saw, and there
seemed to be a huge space of time between my thinking of something and my saying it. I felt distinctly annoyed by the necessity
of sitting there, and began to think that if the music was faster I
would like to dance. As if in response to the unspoken wish, the
music did get faster. Or seemed to do so. But I now found that
I could not dance if I wanted to.

An Indian had told me, when I left Kashmir: "Keep away from
those Lamas, they hypnotize you." This was the thought which
now came into my mind, but I could not hold it there. It came
and went. I looked, with tremendous effort, at my watch. An
hour had passed since I had come into the room. I looked at the
Lamas, and they seemed to be in various states of abstraction.
Only the chief man still looked at me, unwinking. There was no
sense of menace, but a definite feeling that he knew that I was
getting out of myself; that reality could not now be counted
upon. I looked at a torch, burning in a bracket across the room.
There was a distortion of its flames, and a change in their colour:
an uncanny brightness about it.

My interpreter began to talk again, and I was relieved that he did. He was telling me what the sage was saying; about life; about death; about the mission of man in the world; about the divinity of matter; about the fact that nothing really mattered at all; how a man became released through following the Middle Way.

I felt that this was right, this was true, nothing else mattered; he was right. He said that I should try to project my mind out of the body, and that in this way I would gain things which were really my need, until I came to the stage when I needed nothing. This, I thought, was real, true philosophy. I cared nothing for anything else than to sit and listen to that voice, waiting until what it said should be translated to me, waiting with confidence that this was just what I wanted to know. Then I woke up, lying on a pile of skins, in a cold and draughty cell in the monastery. My throat was dry, and I wanted water badly, but could not speak. I was still tired, but had to have some water. I went out of the cell, through innumerable corridors, found that I was below ground. Then I was out in the early morning air, gulping it, looking for the stream which I had seen near the monastery. I drank water greedily. Monks were walking here and there, none took over-much notice of me. I wandered back into the Lamasery, with no idea of where my cell had been. Deciding to go back to the central audience-hall, I was just getting to it when I saw, piled up outside, a number of the bowls from which we had eaten the previous night. Adhering to the sides of one or two of them was still some of the yellow paste. On an impulse I scraped some of it out, wrapped it in my handkerchief, and put the mess in my pocket.

I went to say goodbye to the Master, as soon as I had located the friendly Orgun, and he kindly told me that I should come back any time, as his guest; and that I would now have something to think about, and should think about it a good deal. I did. The analyst's report of the *zamba* paste showed that it contained alkaloids of scopolamine, hyoscine and atropine—all possibly derived from belladonna juice; that the chopped vegetable matter was probably mandrake, which contains scopolamine and other alkaloids which produce hallucinations. It is scopolamine which it is said makes a person malleable and open to suggestion; and both mandrake and belladonna were used in the witches' brews of long ago, when those unfortunates believed (under whose direction is still not known) that they had converse with the devil, and that they had cursing power, could fly, and the rest. Putting it charitably, there seem very good chemical reasons why the followers of this cult believe that they have the power to contact the minds of others, and even influence events at a distance. Perhaps, like the conjuring, the use of drugs is symbolic: or merely helps to open the psychic eye.

The fact that these alkaloids in the uncertain concentrations in which they occur in wild plants are highly dangerous to life indicates that if they were being administered deliberately the dosage must be extremely finely calculated. On the other hand, they might merely be a part of the local diet: though I never saw them being collected for food. Amateurs, at least, who experimented with them would probably cause death, while severe poisoning would be the least of it. Looking back, one is inclined to think that the monks used this in their food for their own purposes, because they would have had little reason to employ such drugs only upon casual travellers.

17

The Secrets of the Witches

WHEN you try to approach the question of black magic, it becomes apparent that twentieth-century man (and woman) is still very much in the psychological position of any savage in almost any jungle: he is either afraid of it, or knows nothing at all about what it might be. Prominent in his thinking is likely to be the unformed idea that it is 'evil', 'not to be meddled with', 'connected with obscene rites'. But what is it? Who are its practitioners? Does it work? Now read your newspapers. Ever since the popular Press replaced the harassing pamphlets that used to be printed and circulated at the slightest excuse, black magic exposés have been frequent. The only difficulty is—that they tell next to nothing about black magic.

Insanity, obscenity, undefined dangers are hinted at. Warnings are given, backed by the pronouncements of Churchmen, that this thing is 'dangerous'. The police are very often quoted as 'investigating' or 'interested' in what is very often called a revival of black magic which is always characterized as sweeping the country; carried out in secret: in high places; for nasty but undefined purposes.

This may all be very true and very laudable; but it is surprising that nobody seems to have approached the subject from any other point of view—particularly that of merely collecting information about the practices and the people who carry them out. Can an evil be stamped out by people who do not know what it is, who do not know upon what it is based?

Now as to definitions. Those who believe in the existence of a devil or a number of demons have asserted that the black magician is one who gains temporary power over certain fields of life through an arrangement made with one of these supernatural beings. In Western magic the price is often believed to be the surrender of the individual's soul after a fixed term of years, to prevent it being able to reach Heaven. Among peoples who do not believe that the devil has such overwhelming power as to gain possession of a human soul, his aid is sought to further the cause of evil itself: helping him, as it were, to carry on his work in this world.

There is a third group of believers in black magic. To them the art consists in cultivating what is termed by them 'destructive power' which is then projected upon the victim, probably to cause his death or other disaster. People of this persuasion may not believe in the existence of a devil, may rather feel that the power which they use is something of neutral tinge, which can be accumulated and used for good or evil purposes. They generally hold that the evil (destructive) use of this power is easier than the constructive use, because emotions of hatred are more easily aroused and projected than those of construction.

Spells and magical processes designed to curse others, when they do not involve an invocation and 'pact' with an evil spirit, come within the last category.

A considerable confusion has arisen throughout the ages by the superimposing of one set of ideas upon another, and the introduction and modification of magical beliefs, one with the other.

Thus we find, in Europe, spell-books (Grimoires) which give long and elaborate processes for conjuring and compelling demons, which undoubtedly derive from Babylonian and Jewish demonology. Christianized, some of these involve a sacrifice to, or pact made with, the spirit. Other processes clearly show that they are based upon the idea that the magician can compel the demon—an inferior being—to work for him and do his bidding, by the use of 'secret and magical words of power'. This is derived from the *hekau* (words of power) used by the priests of ancient Egypt, who believed themselves to be masters, rather than slaves, of evil spirits. Islamic demonology, which came into Europe via medieval Spain, has a similar attitude: even evil jinns (genies) were inferior creatures whom the properly trained magician could control.

If black magic is to be considered anything that is concerned with the use of supernatural force for an apparently evil purpose, then there is a third form. This includes such afflictions as the evil eye, which is involuntary. According to primitive (and modern) belief throughout the world, a person may have the evil eye and may not know it. Among the Arabs it is believed that people who are envious of others can inflict evil upon them by the mere force of that envy: by thinking about the object of dislike, powerfully enough, but not necessarily with the intention of any evil actually resulting.

Actual worship of the devil is another question. According to the records of the Inquisition and the many witch-trials of Europe, the deity of the witches was a devil—that is, a power of evil, represented by a human being who occupied a place of importance in the rituals of the cult. To anyone without especial bias in favour of preconceived theory, it seems more than likely that this was the case. Modern apologists for witchcraft may say that the witches were in fact the 'wise people' of pre-Christian times; that their horned god was a fertility figure, and so on. But they seem to have selected from among the mass of material (folklore and legal) certain aspects of a religion, and rejected the others. In order to do this plausibly, it has been necessary to claim a connected chain of tradition which they themselves alone possess. Otherwise, of course, they could be accused of 'proof by selected instances'. At the same time, they have established no proof of the truth of their fertility cult; and still less that it was not primarily an evil— or a good—one.

Writers like Montague Summers and Margaret Murray have done no service to knowledge by stretching their material almost beyond logical credence. Summers, the Catholic, felt that the devil was almost everywhere; Miss Murray, the Egyptologist, asks one to believe in divine kings and prehistoric religion as if there were sufficient evidence to establish them beyond cavil. Many of the confessions attributed to witches by their Christian persecutors may well have been obtained by force, cajolery, and prompting. But the picture that remains when the material is carefully studied seems to show that there was in fact a devil-worship cult which practised black magic, in full cry in Europe. Had the inquisitors wanted to concoct the whole story, from start to finish, they could have made a much better job of it. Further, they were well aware of the literature of black magic of the grimoire-type. Even popes were known to have practised the ritual form of magic which this kind of book contains. It would have been far more likely that, had the witch mania been deceit on the part of the Church, the latter would have modelled the confessions which they are supposed to have put into the mouths of the witches upon the form of black magic which they knew, especially from the demonology of the Old and New Testaments.

What is the form of black magic attributed to the witches? Worship and propitiation of an evil being, for one thing, represented by a human figure. Further, the carrying out of spells which differ very little, even in detail, from those which belong to the black art as practised by primitive peoples the world over. Finally, the cultivation of supernormal powers—flying, prophecy, and the like, which seem to have been induced by drugs.

It is possible to reconstruct many of the witch practices from contemporary literature.

Careful examination of the inquisition records of various countries, plus the confessions of a number of the people accused of being secret devotees of a diabolical cult or conspiracy against the Church, produces much evidence in favour of the belief that the sect was no delusion. This is not to say that it really was derived from the fertility religion, though this is what Miss Murray seems to think. Neither, by a long chalk, does it seem to accord with the theory of the Church that it was a parody of Christianity invented by the devil. There is no evidence of supernatural intervention.

Secret societies, whether political or religious, tend to remain secret; and in many cases only the piecing together of evidence can bring the story to the surface. In seeking to reconstruct the witch cult in Europe, we have to look for several things. Do the early references to the rites show, for instance, that there is a lingering of another religion below the later Christian one? Is there any evidence of absorption of another, propagandist cult from outside? Are there ceremonies of initiation, passwords, strange names, a priesthood, evidences of a purpose behind such an association? In the case of the underground organization at first dimly descried through the hysteria of witch persecutions, every one of these indications—and more—can be found. Naturally, there is no cult which can be said to be 'pure'; to contain the essential elements of its original days; and this is clearly true of what the sorcerers and witches practised. But there seems ample material to show that their movement was very much standardized, and very much in operation, until at least comparatively recent days.

The literature on witchcraft is immense, and its study is complicated by the fact that more than one school of thought has tried to produce a meaning by selecting instances and weaving therefrom a possible explanation: varying from a belief in complete invention and delusion to a theory of a meek and mild, harmless collection of gay, carefree hailers of the ancient astronomical and seasonal festivals, united in fellowship and dispensing moral and physical salves to the afflicted peasantry. Those who claim that they actively practise withcraft today form yet another class. But they can answer only for the particular rites which are their own.

Whatever one may think of the ignorance and the confusion of the medieval Church in its zeal to fight anything that challenged Christianity, it is interesting to note that among the earliest Western ecclesiastical records mentioning what later became known as witchcraft, there is more than one mention of people who worship Diana and other gods; people who think that they are carried magically from one place to another, "night-riding with Diana".

The earliest mentions of the witches' 'sabbats', which were

also known as 'synagogues', come in the eleventh century, and seem to show the assimilation of the Diana cult with another: one which involves the worship of a 'Black Man'. Then we have mention of brewing potions, rubbing on ointments, meetings and spells at cross-roads, renouncing Christianity and the use of the pierced wax image in a death-spell.

By the fifteenth century, there was a remarkable similarity between witch meetings reported or confessed to, in many countries, some without much contact with one another. Reference will be made later to the 'sabbat' rituals reported from Sweden, Spain, Scotland and France. From the seventh to the fifteenth centuries the Moors were ruling Spain and North Africa. Cultural penetration from their universities into Western Europe was enormous; while their translations of Greek and other philosophical books posed a challenge which the theologians of the West were hard put to meet.

During this very same period, a strange cult had arisen in Morocco, crossed the Straits into Andalusia, and was actively—if secretly—followed in centres of Arab civilization with cosmopolitan populations. The latter consisted of Arabized Jews, Christian scholars and wandering ascetics who travelled from one country to another in search of knowledge. The cult was called by the Arab authorities (who tried to put it down) "the double-horned", and seemed to be connected with moon-worship. It certainly was associated with magic, and its similarities to what were later reported as the witch practises are very close.

The devotees of this cult met on Thursday nights, were initiated by having a wound inflicted somewhere on the body (which left a small scar), and believed that they could raise magical power by dancing in or around a circle. Some of them claimed that they at times carried out religious services which involved the saying of the Moslem prayers backwards, and invoking *el aswad* (the Black Man) to help them. They served their priests, whom they saw only rarely, says the historian Ibn Jafar, after taking an oath of fealty of body and soul. They were drawn from all sections of the community, were of both sexes, and used ritual knives in the scarring ceremony. These knives were known as Al-dhammé or bloodletters.

Here is a typical initiation-ceremony of the Horned Ones:

"We gathered by night, where two paths met and crossed; and he who had been so instructed bore with him a cock, which was to be sacrificed as the emblem of the new day. Each carried a staff with the two horns in brass upon the head; which is symbolical of the goat which is ridden, the sign of power and irresistibility.

"This is the meeting which is called the Zabbat, the Forceful or Powerful one; and the circle of companions are the Kafan (Arabic for winding-sheet). We were thus termed, because each man wears over his naked flesh during the ritual only the white, plain sheet in which he will be buried.

"I was to be given the sanctity that night, and to join the band of the elect who would spread joy throughout the world, those of us who are companions of the Rabbana (our Lord) exemplified by the blacksmith." In Morocco to this day, blacksmiths are considered to be great sorcerers; and in the Middle East in general (as well as in the *Arabian Nights*) it is the Moor who is always a magician.

The initiate continues: "Small drums beat as we twelve came into the circle which had been drawn in the dust; two dervishes in their white kafans taught us the chant of *Iwwaiy*, which we repeated to the drums. Then, the end of the kafan over, our shoulders was put over our heads, and we whirled in dance until there was a loud shout. At this our eyes were uncovered, and we saw that the leader had appeared."

Next, the devotees were required to swear allegiance to this newcomer (Rabbana); and the cock was sacrificed with the small knife, by cutting the throat. Each initiate was nicked with the knife on the arm.

The dance started afresh, anti-clockwise, or, as witch tales have it, widdershins, ending in a form of ecstasy such as is often described following such rituals. The account mentioned is not complete by any means, for the writer, who had had a somewhat chequered career as a Jew from Basrah, a Magian and sorcerer (dhulqarneni), eventually became a Moslem, and seems quite reluctant to reveal all the mysteries of his shameful past.

From another source, however, we find that among the blue-eyed Berbers of the Moroccan Atlas mountains, a similar type of ceremony is still extant. Abdelmalik Harouni, in his *Muajizat-Ifriquia* (wonders of Africa), writing a thousand years later in Constantinople, speaks of the "Berber sect of the horned ones", who light fires and dance around them. Each member carries a staff called the goat which he throws away during the ecstasy of the ritual dance. They drink wine and are sworn to the absolute allegiance of a chief who enrols them at a ceremony in which they formally renounce not only any former religion, but their parents and relatives, and then he teaches them how to achieve a state of psychic drunkenness in which they have mystical and magical powers.

These people also believe that they have a hidden, supreme leader, called Dhulqarnen—the two-horned lord: whose name also means, by a play upon words, 'Lord of the Two Centuries'. This coincidence of meaning is considered to be deliberate, because Rabbana has a useful life of two hundred years. The first portion is until he dies. After that, for the remainder of the two centuries, he remains attached to the earth, in some sort of spirit form, able to direct the work and play of others, and attaining wisdom in this fresh dimension until he is ready to descend to the world of mankind as one of the men of perfection, in a sort of reincarnation. He chooses what form of incarnation he prefers, and retains a full and complete memory of his former life on earth.

There are a large number of correspondences between this strange cult and that attributed to the witches in the Middle Ages. It seems quite possible that medieval European witchcraft was a mixture of 'two-hornism' and various remnants of folk-belief from pre-Christian times. In 1324, the trial of Lady Kyteler in Ireland brought up the allegations that she was a witch; that she sacrificed a red cock to one 'Robin', who was called an Ethiopian; and that she carried out a ritual at a crossroads. All these factors seem curiously close to those which belonged to the Berber sect.

The use of the name 'Robin' and 'Robinet' and other variations is more than once found in European witchcraft cases. The appearance of the Black Man is not uncommon. The horns (which may account for the identification with the devil) are much in evidence. Was there a connection between the Moors and Western Europe as early as this? Most decidedly so; and much earlier, for that matter. Anglo-Saxon coins imitating Arab dinars of A.D. 774 (even to the 'There is Only Allah and Mohammed is his Messenger') were struck by King Offa. The originals were minted by the Caliph who ruled Spain.

In 1450, a tract entitled *Errores Gazariorum* gives a sketch of what were reputed to be the rites of the Sabbat of the witches in France. After being "seduced into joining" the cult, the member was made to promise that, when summoned, he would immediately leave for the meeting. He was given ointment and a staff. He (or she) is presented to the devil at the 'synagogue'—a place, rather than a building, according to the context in which this word is usually used in witch-recitals of the period. The 'devil' appears in the form of an imperfect man or animal, and not infrequently as a black cat. The initiate is asked whether he will adhere to the Society and obey it in all things. He swears this allegiance, and vows that he will obey the master; he will find as many members as possible; he will disclose no secrets unto death; will kill as many children under three years of age as he can, and bring the bodies to the synagogue; will come whenever summoned; will prevent what marriages he can by magic; will avenge all harm done to the sect and its members.

Then the newcomer must worship the 'devil' and kiss him under the tail, and promises a part of his body to him after his death. He is given a box of ointment and a staff, and instructions how to use them. A feast now takes place, in which children are cooked and eaten. The lights are put out, and all dance; after which there is indiscriminate intercourse between the members. After some time, the lights are again kindled, and further eating, this time with drinking, takes place. Sacrilegious, anti-Christian acts form the next part of the proceedings; and if anyone breaks the rules, or does anything that is not to the taste of the master, he or she is beaten.

This document is a summary of contemporary witch beliefs. Written by an inquisitor, it makes use of material obtained from many confessions. If we remove the anti-Christian part of the rite, and also discount the cannibalism, it is still possible to say that this might well be a primitive ritual celebrated by a community of ecstatics, who follow a method of producing frenzy and ultimate release: what modern psychologists call catharsis.

Now we may look at a Sabbat report which seems to be either a composite one, or to originate in Spain, for Spanish words are used in it. Satan, in the shape of a huge he-goat, sits on a throne at the place of the ritual. He has a face in front, and another on his haunches. All who are present kiss him on both faces. This Satan appoints a master of ceremonies, and with him he examines all the witches and wizards who attend, for the secret mark which identifies them as his own. Singing and dancing "in the most furious manner" follows this procedure, and then it is the turn of the new members to be initiated.

The newcomers deny their salvation, kiss the devil, spit on the Bible, and swear obedience in all things. Now the dance is re-started, while the new initiates are welcomed with the words:

"Alegremos, alegremos,
Que gente nueva tenemos!"

The meaning of which is, roughly, "We are happy to have new members!" This dance seems to continue for an hour, after which all sit down and recount their evil-doings since the last meeting. Those who have not sinned enough are beaten by the devil. There may now be a dance of toads. The devil stamps his foot and they disappear. At the banquet which comes next, disgusting things are served up and (for some reason) greedily devoured. When the cock crows, the Sabbat breaks up.

From Scotland, in the celebrated case of 'Doctor' Fian, we find a witch meeting which could well have been held by a group such as subscribed to the above activities, if such indeed existed.

Dr. Fian was a teacher, and was put on trial towards the end of 1590, accused of trying by witchcraft to do away with King James I (of England), the monarch who, not unnaturally, developed such an implacable hatred for witches and their works. Fian confessed; and although elements in the story show that some of the allegations are purely propagandist ones, there seems to be a strong association with an underground cult which believed in the use of magical power. The devil was said to want to kill King James "because he was his worst enemy on earth". Disregarding this kind of material and stripping the alleged witch meeting in a church down to its bare bones, a framework of a conspiracy-cum-cult does become visible.

Summarized, the account tells of how the witches met and performed a ritual circumambulation around a church in an anti-clockwise direction. Then the wizard blew into the lock of the door and it opened. He blew upon a candle, which lit itself. Now the 'devil' was seen to be occupying the pulpit, dressed in a black gown and hat, and was saluted with the cry "All hail, Master!"

The ritual garments and get-up of this cult functionary follow the hint in other accounts that an animal disguise was adopted. His "body was hard, like iron, his face terrible, his nose was like a beak. He had great burning eyes; the hands and legs were hairy, there were long claws on hands and feet. His voice was very gruff."

The devil called over the names of the congregation, asking whether they had been good servants, and what success had attended their magical operations against the King. He boxed the ears of a crazy old warlock who inadvertently made the automatic answer that fortunately the King was well. Now came the sermon, in which the witches were exhorted to be dutiful servants and to do all the evil they could. There was then a heated exchange between the fiend and some of his servants, because he had forgotten to bring a wax image which he had undertaken to prepare for them to curse. The ritual continued with the "eating of a corpse", then much wine which they liked, and they became "jolly". Finally the dance, with the devil leading off, which lasted until cock-crow.

The very human elements in this story—the devil's forgetfulness, his need of accumulated concentration upon the wax image, boxing the ears of the warlock, the wine and the dance—point to a ritual carried out by a local group of cultists, rather than something of transcendental meaning prompted by the theological devil of the churchmen. Again and again one is struck in such tales by the fact that, if these were (as has been alleged) entirely concocted stories by the Church, they would have been couched in the language and the spirit of traditional Christian demonology.

Even the 'widdershins' movement of the circuit of the place where the ritual was held can be better understood than by the contention that it was evil because it reversed the more 'normal' way of going around a sanctified place in a reverse direction. The most ancient ritual practices with a connected history known to us include (in the Mecca pilgrimage) counter-clockwise religious circuits, before the devotee passes between the two pillars of the Mecca running-place. Hewett, in his *Primitive Traditional History*,[1] has made a study of this matter. In ancient astronomical lore it was believed that the retrograde left-hand circuits of the Great Bear around the Pole accurately represented the circular tracks of the sun and moon through the stars. The belief in the sunwise (clockwise) motion of the sun, he says, quoting ancient practice, only began at a comparatively late period. Thus it may well be that the anti-clockwise ritual circuit is the older survival, not just an 'evil' reversal of custom.

Now to Sweden, and the Blockula Sabbats. Again we can take the bare bones of what the self-confessed witches stated they performed in the way of ritual. They went, it was stated in August, 1669, to a gravel pit near a crossroads, placed a vest over their heads and danced round and round. Then they proceeded right up to the crossroads and called three times to the 'devil': "Antecessor come and carry us to Blockula!"

[1] J. F. HEWETT: *Primitive Traditional History*, London, 1907. 2 vols.

A little old man now appears, in red and blue stockings, with very long garters. His high-crowned hat is folded around with bands of many-coloured linen. A long red beard hangs to his middle.

This apparition, who seems to be the leader of the cult, asks whether the devotees will serve him, body and soul. They agree, and make ready for the journey. In order to get there he stipulates that they have to find scrapings of altars and filings from church bells. He gives them a horn with salve in it, with which they anoint themselves. He brings beasts for them to ride upon, a saddle, hammer and nail. Now he speaks some words, and away they fly: over churches, walls, rocks. They arrive at green meadows. On Blockula mountain there is a great house, with tables to sit down at and delicate beds in which to sleep. The witches bind themselves to the service of the master, body and soul. There is a feast; the devil takes the chair, plays the harp or fiddle as they eat. Now they dance in a ring, sometimes naked, sometimes not; cursing and swearing all the time.

The flying and the ointment belong together, in this as in other tales of this kind. It has already often been pointed out that the so-called witch-ointment was one which contained such things as hyoscine, which gave the impression of flying.

This brings us to the interesting Persian sect called the *Maskhara* (Revellers), who danced madly to induce ecstasy, used henbane to produce visions, and gave the world the word 'masquerade', because they dressed in animal masks, blacked their faces and pretended to be supernatural creatures. In English and other Western languages their name is still preserved; for this face-blacking compound is known as mascara, and used by women to apply shadows to the eyes.

In A.D. 1518 Johannes de Tabia states that the *Mascarae* is a sect, and is an alternative name for witches. If the witches, the Horned Ones and the Revellers are not one and the same society, at least it may be said that all three of these cults shared certain beliefs and practices, and may be derived from a common origin. The ritual blacking of the face, the Black Man, was easily equated by the

Church with the devil. Among the Maskhara, however, the meaning of this disguise was that "death is to be followed by reawakening", and the awakening came through the ecstasy, which was produced by dancing and drugs. Wine is mentioned as used by all three sects; so is dancing and circumambulation.

There were two main objectives in the rituals of these secret

Sublimes Princes du Royal secret.

J ℈ ꓶ ⊔ ◙ ⋒ ◻ ⋂ ⊔ ∟ ⫦ ⌐ ╅ ⫞ ∻ ⋂ ⊤ ⫟ ⫝̸ ⫝̸ Ⴟ ⋇ ⫞ ∤ ⫦

a b c d e f g h i j k l m n o p q r s t u v x y z

Cyphers used by secret societies.

cults. The first was the liberation of the individual from the bonds of ordinary morality and especially of self-restraint. The second was the belief that, acting together, the congregation could achieve, by the use of their united wills, the destruction of enemies or the progress of their plans. The important place taken by the priests, or devils, and the confused nature of the reports of the drugged devotees, show that in all probability it was the master magician (or devil) who alone held the secret knowledge of how their united emotion was to be discharged as part of a magical rite. They had to obey him, and he was the person who produced the ritual ecstasy which was necessary for him to project their mutual 'psychic' power.

The actual presence of demons, and so on, has been questioned by religious commentators; and some of the most interesting indications showing that the cult was really a religious one are found in the period before it had been associated with devil-worship by the Church. Looking through these earlier records, one is struck by the fact that the writers seem to be recording remnants of a subterranean ritual. In January of 1091, Father Gualchelm of St. Albin's Church, at Angers, reports a huge collection of people, on horseback and on foot, going past him. "This," he said, "is the Harlechim, of whom I have heard, but in which I did not believe." Five hundred years later, N. Jaquier[1] reports that witnesses had actually seen assemblies of witches. The witches had agreed that they had been so observed. But there were no demons with them. "This was because demons render themselves invisible to others." It is unlikely that the cermonies of the Sabbat (Arabic Zabbat) were illusions, as Johannes Nider[2] claimed. But he did show that someone of his acquaintance could rub herself with an ointment and collapse in a coma through the effects of the drug penetrating the skin; afterwards believing that she had actually attended a Sabbat during that period. Jerome Cardan,[3] who evidently could not bring himself to believe the 'party line' that devils materialized and led people astray, records in some puzzlement that witches do identify their leaders and ritual locations so unanimously that these facts must be true.

There were probably quite large numbers of followers of the cult, in one or other of its forms. The famous poet Martin le Franc alleged in the middle of the fifteenth century that at various places as many as three to ten thousand people attended Sabbats.

Some versions of the cult may have had political ambitions. In Switzerland, the 'devil' told the seven hundred members of his cult at a meeting in 1428 that eventually they would have their own laws, and would overthrow Christianity.[4]

This strange mélange seems to be the cult of witchcraft which was most popular with the country people of medieval Europe— and a good many of their betters as well. The modern versions as practised by those who believe that they have inherited the lore of the witches, are unlikely to be strongly connected with the central theme of the real witchcraft. Of the form in which witchcraft was practised in the Middle Ages, there is little trace today. Perhaps it has died out, ritualistically speaking. There are still, however, coteries of devotees and lone practitioners who rely upon some of the legends of the witches and sorcerers. In the eighteenth century

[1] N. JAQUIER: *Flagellum Hereticorum Fascinariorum*, Frankfurt, 1581, pp. 47–9. He regards them as a sect or cult.

[2] J. NIDER: *Formicarius (Visions and Revelations)*, Helmstadt, Bk. II. 4, 1517.

[3] J. CARDAN: *De Rerum Varietate*, Basel, 1557. Chap. 80. Bk. 15.

[4] J. FRUND: *Lucerne Chronicle*, 1428.

and after, various attempts were made to revive witch practices. These can be identified quite easily as bogus because ignorance of the important Oriental elements in the cult causes errors of interpretation and ritual which point to fabrication of the materials. The Satanists of modern France are an entirely different question, forming real and bogus secret societies, based upon the Catholic concept of the devil.

18

The Cult of the Black Mother

THREE secret types of organization have given new words to the world's languages: the Assassins of Persia, the Tongs of China—and the Thugs of India. 'Thug' means, literally, one who deceives, from the Hindi verb *Thagna*; and the member of this most awful cult of the Black Goddess is one who practises a certain form of deception. He lives an open life of virtue, a secret one of destruction.

A great deal has been written from time to time about the Stranglers of India; and on analysis almost all of it is found to be derived from the eighteen-forties, when a determined attempt to put down the nation-wide cult of Stranglers had been made. Hundreds were caught, convicted of murder, sentenced—and the movement was thought to be crushed, for all time. Something which springs, however, from the very depths of the Hindu religion as it is still understood and practised, has a greater vitality than the gallant British officers who caught the Thug gangs would have thought. Thuggee is still with us, and will remain, in one form or another, as long as the goddess Kali is worshipped, and as long as the secret initiation—and training—of the Society continues.

What is Thuggee? It is a religion, a secret society, a means of enriching its members. Contrary to what has been said by some sensational writers, there has been no case of it in England; and the Thugs do not operate as hirelings, or travel great distances in search of victims who have desecrated temple idols. Originally the cult of the murderers was practised by certain tribes, who adopted the goddess of destruction as their patroness. Later, probably with the infiltration into India of members of the Assassins, it became a cult which the normally daggers-drawn Moslems and Hindus both joined. Thug villages were known; Thugs roamed in robber bands; the man next door, regardless of his apparent station in life, might be a Thug. This was common knowledge in India, before and during British rule; and very little could be done about it.

The priesthood of the Stranglers was generally drawn from Thug families, nominally of either of the two main religions, though these priests were not necessarily the leaders of the murder bands. Over the centuries, the cult grew into a full-blown religion-cum-tribe, with its own rules of behaviour, its own signs and passwords, its own argot and superstitions.

Briefly, the Thugs believed that the goddess Bhowani, also known as Kali the Black One, demanded lives as her sacrifice. In return, she gave success in this world, and a part of this success was the property of the victims and immunity from being caught.

By their own traditions the Thugs in their present form came into being at about the same time that the Mongols reduced the fortress of Alamut and drove out the nest of Assassins there. According to General Sleeman, who played a large part in the struggle against the bands, they are descended from the armies of Xerxes; but there seems little support for this theory. The bands used Persian military organization and ranks. There are resemblances between them and certain tribes native to India, which are known as criminal tribes, and it is probable that the Hindu ritualism was grafted upon the Moslem military framework.

The religion is based upon a myth, which is taught to every young Thug, and which is implicitly believed. Kali was born of Shiva, one of the three great Brahmin gods: sometimes she is also his consort: "She represents the evil spirit, delights in human blood, presides over plague and pestilence and directs the storm and hurricane and ever aims at destruction. She is represented under the most frightful effigy the Indian mind could conceive; her face is azure, streaked with yellow, her glance is ferocious;

she wears her dishevelled and bristly hair displayed like the pea-cock's tail and braided with green serpents. Round her neck she wears a collar, descending almost to her knees, composed of human skulls. Her purple lips seem streaming with blood; her tusk-like teeth descend over her lower lip; she has eight or ten arms, each holding some murderous weapon, and sometimes a human head dripping with gore. With one foot she stands on a human corpse. She has her temples, in which the people sacrifice cocks and bullocks to her; but her priests are the Thugs, the 'Sons of Death'."

While the worship of Bhowani remains a part of the Hindu religion, the possibility of human sacrifice will always remain. This is not to say that the Kali-worshippers are not divided into a number of different branches, some of them claiming that she represents certain atavistic elements of the human mind; and that her worship is necessary, to release emotions that would other-wise be spent in social violence. The fact is that the result of Kali-worship has generally proved to be an evil thing, looked at from most people's ideas of right and wrong at the time of writing.

Only one former Kali priest (not a Thug) has ever written a full account of what the training system of the Kali people is, and how her devotees actually think. This has not been published before, and here it is:

"Those of us who were born and brought up in the worship of Kali believe that the greatest expression of Deity is feminine in nature. This is the belief of many Hindus, but not all. It is the belief of those who are called Saktas; that is, worshippers of creative force, especially in the sexual sense. The male existed first, but his power is projected via an energy whose quality is feminine rather than anything else. Who is Kali? Kali is just the *form* given to Energy (force or life-spirit). She has no actual existence in any shape or form, but we worshipped her as a female because we [men] already contain the life-spirit of the masculine type. We need the feminine type until we get to the stage when we can become 'whole'; that is, until we combine the two in us, or until we gain spiritual insight into the meaning of the combination of male and female."

Kali, this former priest says, is the vulgar name for Energy in her form as Shiva's wife. Kali means Black Female; Shiva is white. Other names, all of which are used, some as passwords, by her worshippers, are Devi, Sati, Rudrani, Parvati, Chinnamastika, Kamakshi, Uma, Menakshi, Himavati, Kumari. These names, if repeated, give a special power, it is believed, to the worshipper. He can attain his aims in life if he invokes her by these names; but he must not actually shed blood in satisfying his objectives. This ruling, taken literally, may have been the origin of the use of the ceremonial noose in the bloodless killings by the Stranglers.

Kali has a constructive and a destructive side. In her name of *Bhowani*, she is destructive. She demands animal sacrifices; for as energy and force she takes life. Life cannot be taken except with her permission, whoever is taking it. As *Durga*, she is considered to be the destroyer of evil and devils. A buffalo or fruit is offered to the idol if anti-evil work is desired of her; and "she never fails to respond if the intention is pure and strong enough".

There is an attempt to harness all the human emotions into the worship of the one Kali, as one can see from the next passage in the confession of the priest: "As the Mother, Kali is called upon as *Ma*, and she is worshipped in this aspect as a giver of life. She is gentle and loving, unlike the father, who is represented by the invocant. As the wife, she is called by the name of *Parvati*, the dutiful wife and love-goddess, who can bring the love of the one desired to the worshipper. As the virgin, the emblem of purity, she is *Kumari*, and gives and sustains purity when called by this name."

The worship of the goddess may be open or secret. The 'left-hand' worshippers, who follow the destructive principle and claim that they can utilize it, worship in secret. In the higher levels of initiation, worship is changed, for both the *Tantra* (left hand) and other worshippers.

The Tantrics explain that the physical licence of the worship of Kali is needed for brutish mankind in this evil (Kaliyuga) time. This is because only a few can liberate themselves from the flesh and reach divinity direct. Kalipuja (Kali-worship) gives the brutish man and woman an outlet and an idea of how intoxicating true communion with the divine could be. For this reason, according to the priest, it is not uncommon for mass orgies to be held in the early stages of initiation of even the right-hand worshippers, so that they may get a glimpse of the physical reflection of the true ecstasy which comes with acceptance by Kali. In this latter stage, of course, there is no physical orgasm possible in the worshipper, for he or she has reached a further state, where all experience is of the mind.

This preaching gives the opportunity for a great deal of debauchery and licence, and this is one of the reasons why active Kali-worship has been looked upon askance, though tolerated, by other Hindus.

Some of the right-hand teachers reserve the ecstatic experience for a stage when the initiate can understand as well as experience it; pointing to the possibility that this experience is, in fact, a physically induced one, which has no relationship with spiritual things.

The story of the former devotee continues with the information that he was born into a high-caste Hindu family, in Calcutta—the city named after Kali. His father had him initiated at the age of six. He "progressed in the cult until, in my thirty-third year, I reached the grade of Guru (teacher), the highest degree. I had thus spent twenty-seven years in active Kali-worship. When the final secrets were told to me, I had three months to meditate upon them. My choice was either to stay with the cult to lead others and coach them to enlightenment, or to remain on as a silent Guru; one who does not tell anything: or to wander in search of knowledge."

The whole initiation-ceremonies of the cult are now exposed:

Dressed in a white loincloth, the applicant is taken to a small room, where four teachers in relays explain that Kali is the Great Mother who represents all mothers, the wife, the sister, the daughter. A man is not complete until he has experienced femininity in all aspects of relationship, in physical touch, and also within himself. The goddess must possess him. This continues for sixteen days, during which he is taught and repeats until he knows by heart the prayers to the goddess. Eventually he is to say and to believe: "I belong to Kali, and I am returning to her. If I sin, she will take me away."

Now the initiate is left to himself for some months (the period varies) and prays at sundown each day for one hour. One day during this time the four teachers come. If he has been chosen for admission, they will make the sign of prayer (palms together, hands pointing upwards) and he follows them. If not, they shake their heads and leave.

He or she is taken to an open space, which must be outside, and enters a ring of believers standing around a cross drawn on the ground. All fall on their knees, and facing inwards they pray silently for guidance:

The Guru says: "Bhowani! O Great Mother of all the World, we are your followers and slaves. Deign to accept this, your humble worshipper: give him all you can. Save him from all that may be. Prosper him in all his undertakings: for you prosper us all and you in your constructive aspect preside over every undertaking, large and small. He is ready, he is ready. If you agree, give us a sign. Give us a sign."

All now await an omen. This should be the movement of a bird or animal, or some unnatural or unusual happening. There is a long list of favourable and unfavourable omens. Cats fighting in the first watch of the night is evil; if they jump, it is worse. A hare, crossing from left to right, is evil; the other way about is good. There are quite a number of variations, because different groups of Thugs claim that they are communicated with by Bhowani in different ways, and they base their omens upon what happened immediately after a certain sign was seen.

When the omen has been seen, all cry: "We thank you, Mother, Devi, Bhowani!"

The initiate now bathes in running water, repeating to himself "Bhowani is Life; Bhowani is Death; Bhowani is All." He is taken after a further four days to a huge feast, where he is handed jasmine flowers (yellow is the Kali colour) and sprayed with rose-water. Naked girls tempt him by swaying before him, and he is given every opportunity of indulging his passions. He must not yield. Now he takes the oath by which he binds himself for ever to the service of the goddess, and he is given the white lungi (loincloth) of initiation into the lowest grade, that of *chela*, the disciple.

The manner of worship of Kali is thus:

"Anyone may worship Bhowani, but mass worship is best. Chelas worship thus, led by a Guru. At night, a statue of Bhowani or a pair of buffalo-horns to represent her, is set up. This is indoors in a house or in a specially set-aside room in a temple. A circle is drawn, with the emblem, horns or statue in the centre, and this mark [a dot within a circle] is traced in a pile of consecrated sand which stands before the emblem. The worshippers sit with their faces towards the centre. Men and women sit alternately. When women worshippers are short, temple prostitutes (divine body givers) are supplied. Only three types of women may take part: one's own wife, the wife of another, or temple prostitutes.

"Now the wine is consecrated, according to what the purpose of the rite is. The primary purpose is ecstasy, and the secondary, for which the consecration is needed, may be almost anything. For rites involving the need of money, a gold pot is used; for freedom, silver; for happiness, copper; food or works of construction, base alloy; love, crystal; stone, for power; clay for hate.

"The ritual combines, it will be seen, that of religion and magic. Kali is asked to perform a service for the worshipper, as well as being herself done honour to by those who are dedicated to her cult.

"As incense spreads its heady perfume, mounting to the ceiling of the room, the Guru fills the container with wine, and intones the mystical words: 'UM MUM KUM JUM RUM: Give power to this wine and convert it into divine nourishment.'

"The vessel of wine is placed before the chief guest, who fills small bowls from it, three of the four other *makaras* (ritual elements) are brought by the assistant priest and blessed in the same words. The five sacred elements of the power of Kali are wine, meat, fish, Indian corn and sexual intercourse. Four bowls of wine are drunk by each participant, one with each course. After this, sexual intercourse is necessary, for the fifth makara to be ratified."

This worship of Kali may take place by the uninitiated, led by the priest, and it is not unusual for it to be celebrated on Wednesday evenings (which are sacred to her); the participants behaving for all the world as if they were carrying out a ceremony of the greatest gravity.

Chelas often are invited to these ceremonies, in order that they may become accustomed to the atmosphere. To continue with the training of the disciple, however, we find that he is not promoted to the second degree—called 'bliss'—until his master is satisfied that he is pliable enough to assimilate further conditioning. Those who have reached this stage are told to fast for four days, drinking only milk. Four more days are spent now in contemplating destruction in as many forms as the chela can conceive. Now the youth is taken and given coconut juice to drink, standing before the idol; meditating how evil he is and how evil he might be able to be. He takes a new oath of secrecy and hatred of all but his fellow-believers; then another vow, by which he binds himself (if necessary) to hatred of all but his teachers. A temple woman, at a signal from the priest, steps from behind the Kali statue, and hands him a small effigy of the goddess. This he places to his private parts, then kisses it. He is now given a flower with five petals, symbolizing the five makaras. That evening, during the worship of the idol, he is gashed in his right arm, from which he drinks some of the blood, and rubs it with consecrated raw sugar: the sacred *Gur* of the Thugs.

Special ceremonies are now open to the initiate, who attends dancing sessions at which men sit and watch naked women dancing until they themselves pass into an ecstatic frenzy. In these rites, the Guru takes no active part. His function is to chant hymns of praise (some made up on the spot) and concentrate upon invoking the energy-principle. The effect of these proceedings is greatly increased by the flickering of numerous temple lamps, the heady incense and the repeated assurance by the priests that Kali is actually present, looking through the bloodshot eyes of her awful statue.

The third stage comes when the Guru sees that the initiate is ready for anything. He watches him for signs of frenzy; seeing just how quickly the ecstasy develops on successive evenings. He is taught the use of more magical words and phrases. He is also allowed to use some of the temple funds, if he wants to build up a small business. At the same time he is subjected to tests to shake his faith. He is branded with eleven marks in front of the idol, on the right or left arm, according to which path he has taken. The rituals include making him scream repeatedly, until he falls in what is described as a fit.

The words used for this strange procedure are: BHOWANI, MA, MU, UM, KLING!

He is asked at this juncture whether he is prepared to kill anyone—even his own child—for the sake of the goddess of destruction.

The fourth stage in the training comes only when the worshipper is able to throw himself into a trance on a word (such as A–KA–SHAA); and when he can, he no longer needs the idol or the rituals: he is part of Kali. This is not to say that he does not do homage to the symbols of the cult; but he does not rely upon them. They are explained as part of the training system.

Those who have reached this advanced stage believe that they have great magical power; they are told the final secrets by their Guru. "There is no such thing as Kali, no power but energy, no right and wrong; nothing but you and those like you. You are of the nature of a god. You have been led to this stage by the only avenues possible for a man of your type, as you were: through the path of the physical senses, because they have to be killed. Now you have lost the power to employ your senses, the sexual urge, the need for wine, for corn, for meat and other things.

"Three months are given to you to meditate upon this, without any idol or ritual to guide you. You have to choose to stay here as a Guru and train others; to become a wanderer or a silent holy man; or carry on the search."

These Gurus, it will be seen, while they may be training others to become anti-social through the implications of the worship of destruction, did not themselves take any part in socially evil actions. It is the less advanced, those who followed the literal path of destruction, who became Thugs, and formed the major part of the recruits for the murdering bands which roamed India. Ordinary Kali-worshippers, it is true, may easily develop homicidal tendencies, carried away by the fact that Kali must have a sacrifice; and cases are not unknown of people killing their own children because they felt that Kali demanded this offering.

In the case of the priest whose confessions we are following, however, "I chose the last alternative, because I realized that there was more to be known. My teacher said 'You have chosen well; I always knew that you would discover truth'. I wandered away, and met many men with whom I discussed things of occult and magical importance."

After three years of wandering through India, living on the charity of the peasants, he came to the sanctuary of a mystic belonging to a very different cult: that of the dervishes

"I came then to the Circle (halka) of Janbaz (he who has thrown away his life) and asked if I could take part in his rites. He allowed me to stay in his compound, and for over two years I talked with him in his majlis (assembly) but still was not admitted to the rites. But I knew that I was on the brink of something, because I felt it. He was modest and did not try to impose ideas upon me. To my great joy one day he gave me an exercise to perform. I carried it out faithfully, though he did not refer to it again."

This is a typical method of some of the Sufi dervish teachers. The object of giving some small repetition-formula or Yoga-like exercise to the postulant is to see whether he will carry it out faithfully and report any effect that it has upon him. If he does so, it shows that he really is anxious to develop the powers and experiences which the dervish purports to be able to produce. If not, he will wander away, or lose interest. Hence, probably, the two years' wait. Janbaz was an anchorite with more disciples than he needed, and could afford to treat them with a certain amount of disinterest, thus selecting only the keenest ones.

"As soon as I felt a tingling at the base of the spine, running up, I realized that it was having some effect. He gave me another, and seemed pleased. I asked if I could take the oath (of allegiance) but he told me to ask one of his companions. I asked Aslam Abasi, and he took me to Janbaz as my sponsor, and I was accepted. After being a *salik* (disciple) I never thought about Bhowani again, as I realized many, many years had been wasted until I got to this path."

The Thugs, while completely wedded to their Kali rituals, spent far less time in their devotions.

They had to study, after acceptance, the signs and signals of the sect, the various omens which told them what Kali was thinking, and the method of strang-

(i) (vi) (ii) (vii) (iii) (viii) (iv) (ix) (v) (x)

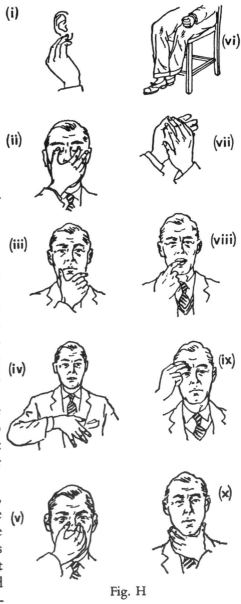

Fig. H

ling with a rupee tied in a knot within the folds of a large kerchief. Thug gangs carried no killing knives, but the priests bore the sacred pickaxes, of which many wonderful stories are told. When, for instance, a gang camped for the night, captured Thugs averred, the pickaxes—of silver—would be thrown into a well or some other inaccessible place, for safe-keeping. In the morning the axebearer had only to call the axe and it would fly through the air into his hand.

Certain people were tabooed as Thug victims: wandering holy men, women (because Kali was a female) and certain classes of merchants. The Thugs believed implicitly that if they sinned against Kali by breaking any such taboos, they might be caught. And this, strange though it may seem, was the cause of the exposure of Thuggee and the suppression of a large number of gangs by the British. A Thug labouring under a burden of sin against the goddess was caught. Believing that his capture was ordained by Kali because of his unfaithfulness to her, he confessed all to the almost incredulous British officers, implicating numerous confederates. And this brought on a chain-reaction: the others in their turn reasoned that they had been betrayed because it was their fate to come to such an end. The organization's weakness was just this fatalism.

A revival of Thuggee in a more efficient form was rumoured following the partition of India and Pakistan in 1947. A number of students, relatively well educated, dispossessed of their property and hopes by the upheaval which scarred the whole of the sub-continent, banded themselves together and swore that they would oppose both India and Pakistan, their hand would be against every man, except the worshippers of the Mother Goddess. The movement started in Bengal, which has always been a home of the Kali cultists. It was given additional strength because that province, which has a sense of national unity, was divided between the two new powers. Bengalis of both the Hindu and Moslem religions are closer in their ways of thinking than members of the rival religions elsewhere. This time, it seems, Kali-worship is to some extent political; though while the strong ritualistic element remains, it will be a difficult thing to suppress.

19

The Rosicrucians

NO authentic document has ever been seen by an impartial observer to show that the Rosicrucian Order is of the antiquity which is usually claimed for it. Its very elusiveness is, however, part of its charm: because, it seems, people want to believe and have since its existence was announced always wanted to believe that there is such a thing.

The work of the student is not helped by the fact that there have been several organizations which claimed to be the true Rosicrucians: to hold the only secrets which are worth having, to preserve certain ancient wisdom which will in some magical way give the aspirant what he needs. The approach is, in any case, psychologically sound. There are few people who feel completely fulfilled. Of the rest, at least some of them at any given time want a short-cut to what they think they need.

In 1597 we find the first traces of the Rose Cross Brotherhood. During that year a certain alchemist is said to have travelled through certain parts of Europe, seeking to found a society which should carry out alchemical researches. Little is known about his success, but eight years later was published a book which gives a Rosicrucian constitution. It was, however, in 1614 at Cassel that the *General Reformation of the World* appeared. This work included a tract called the *Fama Fraternitatis*, which purported to give the history of the founding of the Order.

According to this work, Christian Rosenkreuz was a German nobleman who founded the Order in the fourteenth century. He had been sent to a monastery in 1378, to learn Greek and Latin. One of the monks took him to Cyprus on the way to the Holy

Land, and died. Christian, now alone, and sixteen years of age, journeyed to a place called "Damcar" (which is supposed to be in Arabia, though there is no record of any such place) to visit certain holy men. He travelled in Arabia (which would have been very unlikely for a Christian at that time) and studied at Fez and in Egypt.

He brought his knowledge back to Europe. In Spain (which is the only place in the West where his alleged Arab learning of the time would have been readily acceptable) he says they would not listen to him; although only the most northern part was under non-Moorish rule. Perhaps, as one writer has observed, Rosenkreuz was too mystically minded a person to notice this.

He retired to Germany, where he made many disciples, having formulated the great wisdom which he had received into a system which was to save mankind. He died at the age of one hundred and fifty years: not because he had to, it is noted, but because he wanted to—which seems a good enough reason. The organization was secret; the work which the disciples did was to heal the sick. In the year 1604 one of his followers caused his tomb to be opened, and found strange inscriptions and a manuscript in golden letters.

The Rosicrucians claimed that they felt no hunger, nor did they ever suffer from thirst. They could command spirits and make themselves invisible. They attracted to their persons precious stones and jewels. The objective of the organization was to restore the supposed lost secret of science, particularly medicine. In addition, they were dedicated to providing the world's rulers with treasures so that they could look after their subjects better. Small wonder that people wanted to believe in the existence of such a fraternity. The selfish and unselfish alike clamoured to join.

The requirements of members were not difficult of granting. They were to cure the sick without fee; wear the clothes of the land in which they lived; attend one meeting of the Order each year; choose a successor when on their death-bed. Finally, the members had to keep the secrets of the Order for a hundred years.

Since the appearance of the *Fama*, the excitement about the

Rosicrucians has continued, if not unabated, until the present day. No sooner had the first edition of the *Fama* been issued than it was sold out. People claimed that they were members, illuminati of the Order, and many of them lacked no disciples. Others wrote pamphlets stating that the whole thing was a fraud. Some of the defenders of the Order who burst into print are almost pathetic in their entreaties to be admitted to the fraternity. There is no doubt that much of the literature which sprang up as a result of the publicity is bogus. Rosicrucian literature, especially among the Germans of the eighteenth century, indicates a strong preoccupation with alchemy. But this is an alchemy of the soul, not actual transmutation of metals. It is the transforming of the ordinary man into something more sublime. The possible actual transmutation of metals is denounced by the *Fama*.

The episode of Johan Valentine Andrea is an interesting one in the Rosicrucian story. This writer was a Lutheran, and it seems certain that he used the Order for the dissemination of Protestantism. The organization was eventually penetrated by Catholics, who turned its bias towards support for Holy Mother Church. Andrea now denounced the Order, and founded another, called the Fraternitas Christi. Then another Order—the "Blue Cross"—sprang up. But later, with the inspiration of Andrea, Rosicrucianism spread far and wide. Before 1785, when the Order was suppressed by the Austrian Emperor (who spared the Freemasons alone in his drive against secret societies) the society had a well-established method of initiation.

The room of initiation was carpeted in green, and on it were a number of objects. A globe of glass, stood on a pedestal with seven steps, was divided into two parts, symbolizing light and darkness. Three candelabra were placed to form a triangle, and nine glasses indicated the 'male and female properties', the quintessence, and other things. A brazier, a circle and a napkin completed the ritualistic items.

The initiate was brought by a sponsor, who first took him into a room where these objects were laid on a table: a candle, bare sword, pen, ink and paper, sealing wax and two red cords. Now the candidate was asked whether he was still strongly of a mind to become a student of true wisdom. If he answered that he was, he surrendered his hat and sword, and paid his fee of three gold pieces. Now his hands were bound, a red cord placed about his neck, and he was taken to the door of the lodge. His sponsor knocked three times, and the doorkeeper opened it.

The following secret dialogue ensued:

Doorkeeper: "Who is there?"

Sponsor: "An earthly body, hiding, imprisoned in ignorance, the spiritual man."

Doorkeeper: "What is to be done with him?"

Sponsor: "Kill the body, purify the spirit."

Doorkeeper: "Then bring him to the place of justice."

The party enter, and stand in front of the circle, making the candidate kneel. The master stands on his right side, with a white wand, and the sponsor on his left, sword in hand. Both wear aprons. The next part of the initiation takes place:

Master: "Child of man, I conjure you through all degrees of profane Freemasonry, and by the endless circle which embraces all creatures and contains the highest wisdom: tell me why have you come here."

Candidate: "To acquire wisdom, art and virtue."

Master: "Then live! But your spirit must again rule your body. You have found grace. Arise and be free."

The initiate is unbound, and enters the circle. The master and the sponsor hold their instruments crosswise, and the candidate lays three of his fingers upon them. There is a pause, until the master says the words: "Then listen". This is the signal that the oath is to be repeated. This takes the form of an affirmation that the brother will have no secrets from other members and that he will live a chaste life. He is ceremonially handed the regalia: the seal, password and sign, the hat and sword. Certain mysteries are explained to him.

These are the mysteries: there is a mystical table, divided into nine vertical and thirteen horizontal sections. The first column of nine give the numbers, the second the names, of the various degrees of initiation. The lowest rank is that of juniors, who have been told almost nothing; the highest are the Magi, who know all, their jewel is an equilateral triangle.

What was the meaning of the rose and cross device? It is more than possible that there was no such man as Christian Rosenkreuz (Rose Cross); but it is a singular coincidence that Andrea was a fervent Lutheran—and Martin Luther's coat of arms bore a rose and cross. Other guesses have also been hazarded to account for this symbolism. The cross, according to the alchemists, stands for Light: so the meaning may be 'Light of the Rose'. If this is so, there is a curious parallelism with the Arabic school of illuminati who followed Abdelkadir Gilani. His device is a rose, and he is known as the Light of the Rose. The path of practical mysticism which this Sufi established in the twelfth century at Baghdad was (and is still, for the Kadiri Order is an important one) called *Sebil-el-Ward* (The Path of the Rose). Still stranger, in some Eastern countries, the word *Sebil* (Path) is sometimes mispronounced colloquially as *Selib* (Cross). But the initiation and other ceremonies and tenets of the Rosicrucians do not seem to accord in any one particular (save that of spiritual alchemy) with those of the followers of the Path of the Rose. It is just possible that the Baghdad Order did influence Western mysticism, if only because practically the totality of the alchemy of the Middle Ages was passed to Europe by the Arabs. Among another secret mystical cult of Syria, the word *Wird* (which means secret conjurations, repetitions of words of power, devotional exercises, and is a technical term of Islamic mysticism) is represented by a symbol (the rose) which is *Ward*, as a mnemonic. The *Path of the Wird*, if this were taken as a direct translation, would be immediately understood by any member of an Arab, Persian or Pakistani mystical order to this day.

The only trace in Western literature which might connect Rosicrucianism with Sufism, however, apart from the strange coincidence of names, is the mention of the practices of the Spanish Illuminati. They are mentioned at times as being connected with the Rosicrucians. There are grounds for believing that they had associations with a Moslem mystical Order; but it is their method of carrying out their spiritual concentration which links them strongly to the Sufi mystics. As with the Sufis, the Illuminati (Alumbrados) of Spain, before they were suppressed as heretics by the Church, practised concentration upon the will of their master or teacher in a supernatural or 'illuminated' union of minds. The Alumbrados were put down in 1623, by an edict of the Grand Inquisition.

If Rosicrucianism was in fact an adaptation of sublime Eastern thought or not, it soon deteriorated from its marvellous claims— at least in the person of those who professed or supported its doctrines.

In England the mystic, Robert Fludd, became its staunch protagonist in 1616. The true Rosicrucians, he said (although he was plainly not one of them), were continually travelling through the world, unknown by the vulgar mass. They were sublime personages: the sons of God were not known to the world; because they did not want to be known. Heydon, who was born in 1629, was another of their followers and defenders. This lawyer wrote that they were the real guardians of the sublime secrets, that they were of the nature of Moses, Elias and others and they were seraphically illuminated. Heydon felt that it was a criminal thing to eat; for there was nutriment in the air for those who knew about it. Those who wanted to satisfy their appetites could inhale the aroma of a plate of cooked meat—placed on the stomach.

A Rosicrucian Society was formed in London by a number of savants whose names are still well known. Among them were Elias Ashmole, William Lilly, Dr. Thomas Warton, Dr. Hewett and Dr. Pearson. They were less secret in their ways than most hidden cults, for only the recognition signals were reserved for the initiated. The rituals which they practised (and probably concocted for themselves) were a mixture of Masonic ones and the symbolism of the alchemists. The objective was to refine mankind by spiritual means. The carpet in their Lodge was representative of the pillar of Hermes, who knew all sciences. There were seven steps, standing for the four elements and salt, sulphur and mercury (the main ingredients used by the alchemists) which led to a stage upon which were displayed symbols of the creation, which took place in six days.

A Rosicrucian who recorded some of his dreamings (or a part of his beliefs, according to your prejudice) was Joseph Francis Borri, a Milanese who fell foul of the Inquisition because he attacked Papal abuses. He was condemned to perpetual imprisonment, but left behind the fascinating *Key of the Cabinet of Signor Borri*, which is a romance in which many Rosicrucian notions are to be found. This is also known as the story of *The Count of Gabalis*, published in 1670 by the Abbé de Villars. It is made clear in the pages of this work that Rosicrucians do not believe in witchcraft, sorcery or incubi and succubi. The whole of mankind is surrounded by elemental spirits which can do him service. These could be brought to his will by the Rosicrucian by imprisoning them in a ring, a mirror or a stone, and compelling them to appear when desired. Here is a distinct parallel with Arabian cabbalistical literature, some of which, folklorized, is in the *Arabian Nights*.

These jinns were not subject to such limitations as those of space and time, but were limited by not being immortal. They could win eternal life, however, by gaining the love of a human being. The description of these spirits almost seems to echo the sort of thing which modern man is told about radioactive substances. They were made of pure elements from the matter which they inhabited. And, like radioactive isotopes, they lived for a restricted period of time: a thousand years.

At least some branches of the Rosicrucians seem to have practised or attempted the chemical transmutation of base metals into gold; and there may have been a good deal of magical experimentation as well. The celebrated Paracelsus, alchemist, philosopher and magician, is named as the *Monarcha* of an alchemical Order in a book published in 1607. The Society was formed by a Count Bernard in Germany, after being initiated into a circle of fifteen in Italy, which claimed to have been founded in 1410. This society is said to have been merged with the Rosicrucians in 1607, and a further document, which was discovered in the eighteen-seventies, gives further information as to their signs and activities.

Dr. von Harless, in *Jacob Bohme and the Alchemists*, tracks the Order down in Germany in the year 1641. He quoted a document of 1765 which contains the statutes of the Order of the Rosicrucians, and is named the Testament. Directions are given for alchemical operations, and warnings to avoid Roman Catholics, as enemies of Protestants.

The chief of the Order was called the Imperator, and all members were to change their places of residence every ten years. Their very existence was to be kept a secret. Apprenticeship lasted for no less than seven years. Recognition signs are also given; the salutation being *Ave, Frater*, and the answer: *Roseae et aureae*. Now the first continued: *Crucia*, upon which both chorused: *Benedictus Deus qui dedit nobis signum*. Each now produced his copy of the Seal, which they were to carry.

The various splinters from the Rosicrucians themselves formed Orders and cults, which cropped up almost everywhere that credulous or gullible people could be found. Some of them became quite powerful, others centred around a leader or Magus, who merely made money out of admission fees. The Asiatic Brethren is an offshoot of Rosicrucianism.

Collecting within its fold people of all creeds (including "Jews, Turks, Persians and Armenians") the Order of the Brotherhood of Asia was founded about 1780. The teachings concerned such matters as how to tame spirits and employ them through the seven Arabian seals, how to make gold, and how to prepare miraculous medicaments. The Order was not officially termed Rosicrucian, but purported to contain all the elements of the earlier Order. Initiation was in five degrees, two of them probationary and three Chief Degrees. For fourteen months the members of the first degree (the 'Seekers'), who were limited to ten, waited for promotion. Each fortnight they attended lectures, and they wore a distinctive costume. Seekers, to be properly dressed, had to wear round black hats with black feathers, a black cloak, a black sash with three rose buttons, white gloves, a sword with a black tassel, and a black ribbon supporting a double triangle. The triangle symbol was also embroidered upon the left side of the cloak.

The Seeker became a 'Sufferer' when his period of probation was over, and he was now expected to carry out practical researches during the seven months in which he remained a member of this degree. There were ten members, dressed in black hats with black and white feathers, black cloaks with white linings and collars, upon which the double-triangle symbol was embroidered in gold. Their black sashes and white edging and three rosettes and their swords had black and white tassels.

The 'Knights and Brother-Initiates from Asia in Europe' wore white, black, yellow and red; red crosses and green roses, and so on.

The initiation into the degree of Sufferer was thus:

The candidate was led into a room hung with black, and the floor and furniture covered in black cloth. The room was lit by a central candlestick in the shape of a human figure, with a white robe and girdle of gold. There were also six other five-branched golden candlesticks. The seat of the Master stood on a dais below which were three steps, under a square canopy of black, and "the back wall was partly open, but held back with seven tassels, and behind it was the Holiest of Holies, consisting of a Balustrade of ten columns, on the basement of which was a picture of the sun in a triangle, surrounded by the divine fire. Under the centre candlestick was the carpet of the three Masonic degrees, surrounded by nine lights, a tenth light standing a little farther off at the foot of the throne. There stood, on the right, a small table, on which were placed a flaming sword, with the number 56 engraved thereon, and a green rod, with two red ends; to the left lay the Book of the Law."

It was not until the higher degrees that the revelation of secrets began. Whether there ever were any such secrets is open to the most serious doubt, partly because what are generally referred to as 'secrets' in mystical orders are connected with ecstatic experience. The training for the receiving of this experience does not seem to have been given in any form by the Rosicrucians. There was a great deal of symbolism, but nothing is said (even by apostates from the Order) about mystical experience. If this is not true of all Rosicrucianism, it certainly was of the Asiatic Knights, which were rightly called "a fee trap of no mean order"—like the spurious Masonic degrees.

In 1781 a man called Fraxinus was Provincial Grand Master of the four United Masonic Lodges in Hamburg. Unknown to the Masons, he was running a Rosicrucian Order from whose members he obtained a good deal of money. He was eventually cornered by one Cedrinus, who felt that he had been overcharged at 150 dollars for various initiations. Cedrinus published an attack upon these activities, but was expelled as being 'corrupted'. This is a mere sample of numerous spurious and other initiations whose candidates were kept on tenterhooks, expecting that one day, when they attained a high enough degree, all would be made manifest to them. It seems that it never was.

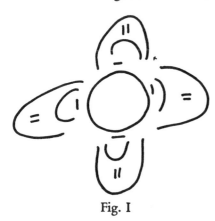

Fig. I

But Rosicrucianism was able to survive the most adverse publicity, and the association of the worst scoundrels with its tenets. It spread from one country to another; lodges were set up here and there. The only country where it had but limited success was France. In 1623 there had been a determined publicity drive. Notices appeared posted up in the streets of Paris, informing the populace that Rosicrucians dwelt and walked invisibly in the city. But perhaps due to the power of Catholicism, the movement seems to have made little progress here.

The movement still thrives. Lavishly produced and privately published books continue to appear, purporting to contain the truths of Rosicrucianism. They are, of course, unintelligible to the general public. It is not until he joins and reaches the requisite degree of initiation (and has shown his patience) that the candidate can partake of these delightful mysteries.

The position today is so confused that it is more than possible that some of the various societies known as being of the Rose Cross are teaching doctrines which differ widely from those which have become known as Rosicrucian ones. A recent writer goes so far as to suggest in this connection that teaching and knowledge changes with the age in which it is given out. Hence, for all that anyone knows, new truths and real knowledge may be available from such sources. The English Rosicrucian Society told its members in 1871 that it was purely interested in antiquarianism and literature, and not in the supposed secrets of the original Order.

20

The Holy Vehm

WESTPHALIA during the Middle Ages was subject to very little law and order. But in the middle of the thirteenth century a mysterious and powerful society, eventually to have at least a hundred thousand initiates, rose and claimed revenge in the name of society for wrong-doing of almost every kind. The secret courts of the Holy Vehm are surrounded by an extraordinary degree of mystery. Nobody knows what 'Vehm' is derived from, or when it was first used. Some say that it is from the Latin *fama*, fame or repute; others that it is a corrupted form of the German *fahne*, a flag, standard. The men who had been through the rites of initiation called themselves *The Wise*—and hence some have seen in the word (pronounced *Fehm* in German) the Arabic *Fehm*, wisdom, imported during the Crusades by the Germans who went to fight in the Holy Land. Certain it is that the methods of trial and execution were as summary as anything that might have obtained under the special and lawless conditions of the Crusades, when no mean proportion of the participants were dissolute adventurers at best, at worst, criminals.

In spite of the paucity of documents about the Vehm, there is sufficient information available to show that justice was in its early days generally adequately dispensed; although the cruelty with which it was applied is alien to our present-day thinking.

Popular novelists (such as Sir Walter Scott) are said to be mainly responsible for the general impression that the tribunals were held in dark and subterranean places; that the whole proceedings were shrouded in great mystery and danger, that the populace was terrorized by the sinister figures behind the movement. But it should not be forgotten that there are folk-legends still surviving which accuse the Vehm of strange barbarities, just as much as there are those which paint the Vehmists with the rosy colours of chivalrous knights.

It seems very possible that both types of story are in part true. There is a tradition that some tribunals put their victims to death in a singularly unpleasant manner:

"The victim was told to go and kiss the statue of the Virgin which stood in a subterranean vault. The statue was of bronze and of gigantic size. On approaching it so as to touch it, its front opened with folding doors and displayed its interior set full with sharp and long spikes and pointed blades. The doors were similarly armed and on each, at about the height of a man's head, was a spike longer than the rest: the two spikes being intended when the doors were shut to enter the eyes and destroy them. The doors having thus opened, the victim by a secret mechanism was drawn or pushed into the dreadful statue and the doors closed upon him. There he was cut and hacked by the knives and spikes. In about half a minute the floor on which he stood—which was in reality a trapdoor—opened and allowed him to fall through. But more horrible tortures awaited him; for underneath the trapdoor were six large wooden cylinders in . . . three pairs. The cylinders were furnished all round with sharp blades; the distance between the uppermost pair of parallel cylinders was such that a human body could just lie between them; the middle pair was closer together, and the lowest very close. Beneath this horrible apparatus was an opening in which could be heard the rushing of water. The mechanism that opened the doors of the statue also set in motion the cylinders, which turned towards the inside. Hence when the victim, already fearfully mangled and blinded, fell through the trapdoor, he fell between the upper pair of cylinders. In this mutilated condition, the quivering mass fell between the second and more closely approaching pair of cylinders, and was now actually hacked through and through on the lowest and closest pair, where it was reduced to small pieces which fell into the brook below, and were carried away, thus leaving no trace of the awful deed that had been accomplished."

The Holy Vehm was holy because its first interests was

Seal of the Holy Vehm.

in the upholding of the Ten Commandments and other aspects of the Christian faith. Before long, it seems, the tribunals discovered that almost anything could be construed as affecting the welfare of Christianity, and their scope became wider and wider. As an example of what the members of the society thought about their powers, we have a document recording their decision at Arnesburg in 1490 as to their main scope; they were determined to proceed against:

1. Those who revealed the secrets of Carolus Magnus.
2. Those who practised or introduced heresy.
3. Those who fell from the faith and became heathens.
4. Those who committed perjury.
5. Those who practised witchcraft or magic or entered into any treaty with the Evil One.
6. Those who revealed the secrets of the Society of the Holy Vehm.

These were the subject of the deliberations of the Secret Tribunal of the Vehm. The Public Tribunal of the same body was concerned with:

1. Wilful injuries to churches and churchyards.
2. Theft.
3. Rape.
4. Robbery of women in childbirth.
5. Public treason.

6. Highway robbery.
7. Arbitrary persons.
8. Secret and open manslaughter and murder.
9. Wandering vagabonds.
10. Those who committed sacrilege.

Other lists have also been discovered containing such items as a determination to proceed against "those who act against honour and justice and are therefore not to be answered in honour". By these provisions, almost the whole populace of the immense area of medieval Westphalia was virtually in the hands of the Vehm.

There were odd exceptions. Because of sex and age, women and children did not come within their competence. Jews, heathens "and the like" could not be tried, because they were beyond the pale of such an important and sanctified body. Nobles were exempted, because they had to be tried (by the universal custom of the Middle Ages) by their peers, and it was not practicable to find enough people of the same quality to try them. The Vehm considered itself incompetent to try members of the clergy. Expediency is said to have been the reason for this provision.

It was probably as obvious to the Westphalians as it is to the reader that membership of the Vehm could be a highly desirable thing. It conferrred a status such as few other attainments could in those very unsettled and terrifying days. The main body of the Society were the *Schoppen*, who were recruited after being nominated by a Lord of the Tribunal and undergoing initiation ceremonies. Until such time as he was properly admitted, the Schoppen was known as Ignorant, when enrolled, as Wise or Knowing (*Wissende*).

In his initiation, the candidate had to appear bareheaded before the assembled tribunal and answer questions as to his qualifications. Then, kneeling with his thumb and forefinger on a naked sword and a halter, he swore his Great Oath before the Count of the Society:

"I swear on the holy marriage that I will from henceforth aid, keep and conceal the Holy Vehms from wife and from child, from father and from mother, from sister and from brother, from fire and wind and from all that the sun shines upon and the rain covers, from all that is between sky and land; especially from the man who knows the law; and will bring before this free tribunal under which I sit all that belongs to the secret jurisdiction of the Emperor: whether I know it to be true myself or have heard it from trustworthy people, whatever requires correction or punishment, whatever is Fehmfree, that it may be judged or with the consent of the accuser put off in grace; and will not cease to do so, for love or for fear, for gold or for silver or for precious stones. And I will strengthen this tribunal and jurisdiction with all my five senses and power; and that I do not take on me this office for any other cause than for the sake of right and justice. Moreover that I will ever further and honour this free tribunal more than any other free tribunals; and that what I thus promise I will steadfastly and firmly keep, so help me God and His Holy Gospel."

The allusion to the Emperor was made because the Vehm considered itself directly under the monarch—whether he liked it or not. It is not to be supposed that he always did like it. In 1470 the Vehm summoned the Emperor Frederick himself to appear before their courts ("under penalty of being held to be a disobedient Emperor"); and although he did not do so, he swallowed the insult.

Vehm tribunals had a habit of spreading from one district to another: but it can be said to their credit that they did not always do so without warning. In the year 1608, says a manuscript life of Duke Julius of Celle, "when the Fehm-Law was to be put into operation, all the inhabitants of the district who were above twelve years of age were obliged to appear without fail on a heath or some large open place and sit down on the ground. Some tables were then set in the middle of the assembly at which the prince, his councillors and bailiffs took their seats. The Secret Judges then reported the delinquents and the offences; and they went round with a white wand and smote the offenders on the legs. Whoever then had a bad conscience and knew himself to be guilty of a capital offence was permitted to stand up and to quit the country within a day and a night. But if he was struck the third time, the executioner was at hand, a pastor gave him the sacrament, and away with him to the nearest tree."

The general procedure of these bizarre courts, once they had been established in the land, was fierce and without any waste of time. The first thing that happened was that the accusation had to be made by a member—a *Freischoppe*; upon which an order for the appearance of the defendant was issued. If he did not present himself, he was hounded. If, during the period of his absence the accuser could produce seven witnesses to the fact that the accuser was a person whose word could be believed, the case was considered proved. The charge was not gone into. The Imperial Ban was pronounced by this terrible Court: sentences were always the same.

"The sentence was one of outlawry, degradation and death. The neck of the convict was condemned to the halter, and his body to the birds and the wild beasts. His goods and estates were declared forfeit, his wife a widow and his children orphans. He was declared *Fehmbar*—punishable by the Vehm—and any three initiated that met with him were at liberty, nay, enjoined, to hang him on the nearest tree."

If the defendant had the courage to appear before the Court, he found himself before a Court whose table held a naked sword and a halter of osier. He could bring thirty friends as witnesses and could be represented by their attorneys. He also had the right of appeal to the General Chapter of the Secret Closed Tribunal of the Imperial Chamber, held at Dortmund. As soon as final death was pronounced, however, he was immediately hanged. An accused person who did not appear before the Tribunal, himself being a member of the organization, was sentenced to death immediately and hanged where found.

Although the Ban was made in the name of the Emperor, and appeals could be made to him, the ruler was not allowed to be present at the Dortmund sessions unless himself initiated. Anyone who found his way accidentally to a meeting of the Secret

Tribunals was immediately seized and hanged. Anyone who warned a person that he was under sentence was similarly treated. Each Emperor at his coronation at Aix-la-Chapelle was formally initiated by the hereditary Count of Dortmund. The Archbishop of Cologne, who had certain Vehm rights, must also have been initiated, or he would not have been allowed to have exercised them.

The secret Vehm judges, who dwelt among the general populace, were in some places reputed to be quite human. Although not allowed to warn anyone verbally or in writing that he might be subject to proceedings of the Society, they might make some sort of sign that they were watching him. This sometimes took the form of a mark on his door, or "passing a can near him at a drinking-party". One old law book gives the Brunswick procedures of the Vehm court. The *Fehmenotes* were selected secret informants who watched the citizens and passed information about suspect persons to the councils of the Vehm. If conditions were said to be bad in any particular place, a day was appointed for holding a Vehm court there. Members of the Council from various parts of the town or other area would meet at midnight and arrange for every entrance to be blocked. At daybreak the citizens were informed that the Court was to sit, and all had to repair to a designated spot at a certain time.

"When the bell had tolled three times, all who had assembled accompanied the Council through the gate of St. Peter, out of the town (of Brunswick) to what was called the Fehm-ditch. Here they separated: the Council took their stations on the space between the ditch and the town gate, the citizens on the other side of the ditch. The Fehmenotes now mingled themselves among the townsmen, enquiring after such offences as had not come to their notice and communicated whatever information they obtained and also their former discoveries (if they had not had time to do so in the night) to the clerk, to be put by him into proper form and laid before the Council."

Now the alleged offences were examined. Those which were under the value of four shillings were excluded from the deliberations. Those who had had goods stolen from them were first examined, and asked whether they knew the thief. If they did not, they had to swear by the saints that they spoke the truth. If they named anyone, and it was the first charge against him, he could clear himself by an oath. If, however, it was the second charge, he had to bring six others to swear along with him. Now he had to wash his hands in water, and undergo the trial of the hot iron. A piece of metal, heated to glowing red, was picked up by the accused, who had to carry it for nine paces without his flesh being burned, to establish innocence.

Another Vehm court, described by one writer, has been said to have existed only in the imagination. Under the castle of Baden are labyrinthine vaults, formerly (we are told) consecrated to secret Vehm rituals and trials.

"Those who were brought before this awful tribunal were not conducted into the castle vaults in the usual way; they were lowered into the gloomy abyss by a cord in a basket and restored to the light, if so fortunate as to be acquitted, in the same manner; so that they never could, however inclined, discover where they had been. The ordinary entrance led through a long dark passage which was closed by a door of a single stone as large as a tomb-stone. This door revolved on invisible hinges, and fitted so exactly that when it was shut the person who was inside could not distinguish it from the adjoining stones or tell where it was that he had entered. It could only be opened on the outside by a secret spring. Proceeding along this passage you reached the room, where you saw hooks in the wall, thumbscrews and every species of instruments of torture. A door on the left opened into a recess, the place of the *Maiden's Kiss.* . . . Proceeding on farther, after passing through several doors, you came to the vault of the Tribunal. This was a long spacious quadrangle hung round with black. At the upper end there was a niche in which were an altar and crucifix. In this place the chief judge sat; his assessors had their seats on wooden benches along the walls."

Another writer says that this description is fanciful; not because any of the details of the place are challenged, but because there is no document extant which states that such courts were held in this place or under these conditions. For these reasons some say that the place described might in fact be a relic of the Inquisition. Whether absence of documents can be considered a proof for or against anything is an interesting point.

Although the Courts were greatly respected, and probably because they administered the sort of rough justice which was required in those days, it was not long before the Holy Vehm became a word of such terror that people crossed themselves whenever they passed any place associated with its sittings. People of the most dissolute character were admitted in the end to its membership, and one writer of the time, with considerable daring, states that "those who had authority to hang men were hardly deserving to keep pigs, that they were themselves worthy of the gallows if one but cast a glance over their lives." Several notorious cases which are recorded show just how far things had gone. Duke Ulrich of Württemberg was unhappily married. A powerful young nobleman named Hans Hutten at his court was friendly with the Duchess Sabina, and was incautious enough to show off a ring which she had given him. Enraged at his lady's unconcealed liking for the youth, the Duke at a hunting party in the forest ran Hutten through and hanged the body with his belt. When the murder was discovered he stated that he had been told to commit it as a sentence of the Holy Vehm. Eventually the truth came out, but the case ended with the Duke and the Hutten family coming to 'an accommodation'.

The foregoing case, it is said, showed at the time that the tribunals would have allowed the Duke to get away with the murder had the Emperor not intervened. A worse case was the one of Kerstian Kerkerink. The Vehm tribunal of Munster had been told that he was an adulterer. Instead of trying him, or sending him any sort of warning, they sent men to get him out of bed in the middle of the night. Their representatives lured him out on some pretext, took him to a lonely place and informed the Council, which assembled at daybreak.

When they appeared, he begged for a lawyer. This being refused, he was sentenced to death without further ado. The condemned man asked for a stay of execution of one day, to settle his affairs and make his peace with God. This request was summarily rejected; and he was told that he might now make a confession, and that a priest was in attendance to receive it. He made one more appeal for mercy. As a concession, his judges said that they would have him beheaded and not hanged. A monk was called over to hear his confession. As soon as it was over the executioner (who had been sworn never to reveal anything that he had seen) was sent forward to strike off his head. Meanwhile word had somehow spread in the town, and the people poured out to watch the last act of the tragedy. Guards carefully posted prevented them from seeing anything, and all that they found when the tribunal withdrew was the body in a coffin.

These terrible courts were never formally abolished. They were reformed by various monarchs, but even in the nineteenth century it was said that they still existed, though very much underground. The Nazi 'werewolves' and resistance organizations fighting the Communist occupation of East Germany claimed that they were carrying on the tradition of the 'Chivalrous and Holy Vehm'. Perhaps they still are.

21

Devotees of the Guardian Angel

ABRAMELIN the Mage is the supposed author of a book which is to be found in an eighteenth-century hand, in the Bibliothèque de l'Arsenal in Paris. This 'Book of Sacred Magic' was first translated into English in 1898, and since that date it has formed a part of the occult training of a good many would-be magicians. From the magical point of view, it may well be called a cult on its own: for it is a complete magical training system, which requires preparation and dedication, and which promises, through concentration and the use of certain figures, magical power derived from the aid of supernatural beings.

Eliphas Lévi and Aleister Crowley (the Great Beast) are only two of the famous names which are associated with this manuscript; but the present writer has come across quite a number of practitioners of the magic art of whom the book is the be-all and end-all of ritual magic. There have been several small cults whose members have based their supernatural hopes entirely upon this document; in spite of the fact that, even though it may be partly based upon more honest originals, many indications in the text show that its antiquity is not as great as it claims. It was translated into French from Hebrew, it claims, in the year 1458. It is supposed to be the work of a Jew, ("the sacred magic which God gave to Moses, Aaron, David, Solomon, and to other Holy Patriarchs and Prophets . . .") and this Abraham leaves it to his son Lamech, with many a warning that it is to be used in accordance with the precepts contained therein.

But if the book contains inconsistencies, it also is the origin of a mystery, because actual practitioners of the magic art claim that processes extracted from it do in fact work miraculous results: even when research has shown that certain spells have been mistitled or transposed. How does a magician come to believe that he has done a 'work of destruction' when he has been using a spell erroneously included under 'works of construction'? Can a magician get results through using magical processes which are wrongly understood by him? This is a problem for the psychologist, but it does provide some interest for the student of secret cults. It may show, for instance, that a basic element underlying all these strange groups is belief in the truth and reality of what they are dedicated to. It is a case of faith—faith in anything at all—being expected to move mountains, in the literal sense.

How is the Cult of Abramelin carried out? If you are a prince or a king, dismiss any thought from your mind that you can become one of its devotees: this is the first taboo. Another important one is that children and animals are to be guarded from contact with the mystical diagrams with which the book abounds; because they can be unwittingly affected thereby. But it is not necessary to be a Jew to carry out the Sacred Magic; for Abramelin tells us that anyone can attain to power through these pages, providing that he does not change the faith in which he was reared.

Before he can call the spirits which will give him his every wish, the magician must have a properly prepared place. The book gives the choice of two possibilities: urban and rural surroundings. If he is in the country, he should find a small wooded place, and in the middle erect an altar. This is covered by a shield of small branches, to protect it from the rain. Seven paces from the altar a ring of flowers and shrubs is planted. If the ceremonies of the angelic cult are to be performed in a town, the would-be magician should have a room with a window which gives on to an open balcony and a small hut or lodge. This latter must have windows, so that the invocant can see in all directions from it. The evil spirits, we are informed, cannot enter the hut, but will be able to manifest themselves on the balcony, and can be negotiated with from a place of safety.

Detailed directions continue, to the effect that the oratory should have a floor of white pine, the balcony has to be covered with a couple of inches or more of fine sand. There are to be such objects as a bronze censer, an olive-oil lamp, two robes, a crown, wand, oils, girdle and incense. One robe is a large white linen tunic, with sleeves; the other red and gold, reaching to the knees. The magician is implored to have these vestments brilliant and clean. The girdle is silk, and white. The crown is made of silk and gold.

The holy anointing oil, which is an indispensable part of the requirements, is detailed in a careful recipe:

Liquid myrrh, one part; fine cinnamon, two parts; galangal, half a part; and half of the whole weight of these in the finest olive oil.

This resembles the traditional recipe for Holy Anointing Oil of the Jewish dispensation:

Pure myrrh, 500 shekels; sweet cinnamon, 250 shekels; sweet calamus, 250 shekels; cassia, 500 shekels; olive oil, one hin.

A perfume of incense, aloes and storax is also needed, and an almond-wood wand.

The magical ceremony, during the first two moons leading up to the appearance of the spirits which are to aid the magician, is carried out with fervour and dedication. Every morning of these first two months, the whole body is washed and clean clothes donned. Fifteen minutes before sunrise the magician enters his oratory, and kneels before the altar. He invokes God, thanking Him for all that has been done for him, confessing his sins, asking for pardon. Now he asks for an angel to guide him. The prayers take no special form; for in this cult Abramelin says that the prayer will develop as the time goes by.

The window, which was open, is now closed; and the oratory is not to be used by anyone else. The magician lives in a room which is near his oratory. He must observe certain conditions: the place, including the bed, must be clean; he must avoid his wife during her courses; change the bed-linen every sabbath eve. The eve of the sabbath is Friday for Jews, Saturday for Christians. The room is to be perfumed each Saturday; no dog, cat or other animal may enter it. In the four months (moons) after the first two all sexual intercourse must be avoided.

These are the main taboos. The practitioner should live a quiet and—if possible—a solitary life. If he is not his own master, the magician may not be able to observe these restrictions, notes Abramelin; but in any case he must be patient in what he does.

Two hours every day are devoted to reading holy books. He should not eat, drink or sleep overmuch, and especially flee drunkenness. He should have two outfits, so that he can change on the eve of every sabbath; wearing his dress only for a week at a time. He must be generous to the poor. If he becomes ill, he may continue the prayers in his bed.

During the second two moons the same prayers are said. Before going into his oratory, the devotee washes his hands and face with fresh water; he calls for the aid of angels and guidance. The prayers are lengthened. During the first four moons, the prayers and perfumes are made twice daily. The third and last two moons require the prayers and perfumes to be given three times a day.

During the third period of two moons, the prayers and perfuming take place morning, noon and night. The same confessions, prayers and supplications for the aid of angels are carried out. People of independent means should avoid all business and everyone except wife and servants.

The third period of two months is started thus: shoes are removed before the invocant enters the oratory. He opens the windows, puts charcoal in his censer, lights the lamp. From the cupboard which he has made within the altar he takes his vestments (the crown, girdle and wand) and these he puts upon the altar. He takes the holy oil in his left hand, throws some of the perfume upon the fire, goes down on his knees, and prays:

"O merciful God; O most patient, kindly and generous; thou who givest thy blessings in a thousand ways to a thousand generations; thou who forgivest the evil-doing, the sins and the harm done by mankind. . . ."

The devotee of the cult of Abramelin speaks of his unworthiness, asks for pity, purification, understanding and sanctification. He asks for power of control over spirits. The words, according to the Master, may be varied.

Now the cultist rises, touches the middle of his forehead with a spot of anointing oil, and smears a little of it on the four top corners of the altar. The oil is also applied in a similar way to the ritual garb, including the crown, girdle and wand. The final use of the oil is to trace with it upon the sides of the altar the legend:

"In such place as remembrance of my name is made, there I will come to you, and I will bless you."

The consecration is at an end. The ritual vestments are replaced in the altar-cupboard. The invocant kneels again and repeats his ordinary prayer. Nothing which has thus been consecrated is to be removed from the oratory.

The follower of the secret cult must now introduce an assistant: a small child of about six years of age, and not more than eight. He must be dressed in white clothes and be completely clean. On his forehead is put a thin white veil, which covers the eyes. This is the medium who will be able, we are assured, to make contact with the Guardian Angel who is to watch over the magician and his works. The operator wears a veil of black silk. The two enter the oratory; the child puts the fire and perfume in the censer and kneels in front of the altar. The magician prostrates himself upon the ground, asking that the Angel appear to the child, and that, if necessary, he will become visible to the master as well. He must not look at the altar.

A silver plate has been placed upon the altar, and the child is instructed to wait for the appearance to him of the angel, and to wait for the Angel to write upon the plate. As soon as the Angel has inscribed his message upon the plate, the child brings it to the master, and they leave the oratory. Nobody must re-enter the place during the first day; and the child may be sent away. The window is left open, and the lamp still burning.

The whole room, it seems, will be filled with a divine effulgence; light of unparalleled brilliance; and a delightful odour. Both participants feel that they are in the Angel's presence. The dedicated one must speak to nobody during this day, except the child. In the evening a small meal is eaten, and the magician goes to bed alone. These observances are carried out for seven consecutive days: the Day of Consecration, the Three Days of Convocation of the Good Spirits, and the Three Days of Convocation of Evil Spirits.

On the second morning, the procedure is very much the same as on the first: the robes of mourning, the lighted censer and lamp, and so on. This time, however, the prayer asks for a vision of the spirits—the Holy Angels. The devotee has to increase the fervour of his emotion; must try to summon up the spirit, for three hours.

It is on the third day of this part of the proceedings that the magician will know whether his rituals have succeeded or not, says Abramelin. If all has gone well, the Guardian Angel will actually manifest himself in a form of great beauty. He will speak, and what he says will bring joy. He will counsel good living and repentance. Finally, he will teach the True Magic; telling how to overcome the Evil Spirits, and will promise to stay with the devotee throughout his life, and never to abandon him. Since this is a day of such moment, its observances should be noted with care. On the evening before the magician washes himself all over. He enters the oratory the following morning in his normal garb, but with bare feet. The glowing charcoal and perfumes are placed in the censer, the lamp lighted and the white robe assumed. Throwing himself upon his knees, the devotee now renders thanks to God and to the Guardian Angels. It is at this point that the marvellous is to be expected.

No time is lost during this third day to take advantage of the instructions of the Angel. The magician leaves his oratory only for one hour in the afternoon. For the rest of the day he takes copious notes of the directions of the Angel regarding the Evil Spirits and how they may be commanded.

When the sun sets, the evening prayer is said, thanks given as the perfumes are burnt, thanks also being given to the Angel for manifesting himself.

Although Abramelin's manuscript is composed of no less than three 'books', totalling four hundred and thirteen written pages, the substance of the process for producing contact with the Angel occupies only a part of it. The rest is partly autobiographical material by Abraham the Jew to his son, and much is occupied with various diagrams (word-squares of a cabbalistical nature) which purport to be those which can be used in commanding spirits. It is not necessary to detail them here, as they do not form a part of the requirements of the ritual as detailed above. Further, of course, the Guardian Angel in his explicit instructions should be able to convey all this arcane knowledge to the devotee without the need of a book, even by Abramelin. The magician, as has been told us, is allowed to take notes; and the British translator of the manuscript mentions that some of this material is out of place in the copy from which he worked. Careful magicians would therefore probably prefer to verify the processes from the Angel's own mouth.

How many people follow the cult of Abramelin? There is no way of telling; but references to it are not rare in literature, and the processes form a part of the repertoire of a large number of the practising magicians of our time—in the West, at any rate. If we widen the scope to include Oriental countries, we find that ceremonies of a very similar type occur among the Arabs, Persians and Indians; probably all derived from the magical schools of the Middle Ages. The work of El-Buni, the Moorish sorcerer (which is the source-book for several well-known grimoires in use in the Moslem East), contains ceremonies for conjuring jinns which are very close indeed to Abramelin. Jewish magic was one of the studies which the Arabs cultivated in such institutions as the occult university of Salamanca in Spain; and there are said to be a number of manuscripts by "Ibrahim the Jew" in the ancient library of Fez, to which many Moorish scholars repaired after their expulsion by Ferdinand and Isabella.

The type of magical ceremony represented by the Book of

Sacred Magic is undoubtedly a cult in most senses of the word. Its one unusual aspect is that the seeker is self-initiated and acknowledges no spiritual mentor during his period of preparation for the final experience. In respect to devotion, vestments, ritual, secrecy and other characteristics of a cult, however, they are all to be found in Abramelin.

22

The Illuminated Ones

THE sixteenth century saw the rise of a powerful society based upon a secret cult, in the mountains of Afghanistan —the Roshaniya, illuminated ones. References to the existence of this mystical fraternity exist from the time of the House of Wisdom at Cairo, several hundred years before. It seems likely that small branches were founded in various parts of the Near and Middle East; which would account for the special usage of the names of the eight degrees of initiation among them.

The earliest figure named in the history of the cult is one Bayezid Ansari, of Afghanistan, whose family claimed descent from the Ansar—the 'Helpers', who assisted Mohammed after his flight from Mecca nearly fourteen hundred years ago. As a reward for this service, he stated, his ancestors had been granted initiation into the mysteries of the Ishmaelite religion: the secret, inner training which dated from Abraham's rebuilding of the Temple at Mecca, the mystical Haram.

Bayezid's own father, however, was known to be as narrowly conventional as anyone in the country, and one account of the rapid rise of the sect has it that Bayezid, after a period of preparation for the normal priesthood, was converted to his strange doctrine by a missionary from the Ismailis, the sectarians holding a secret doctrine supposedly handed down in the family of the Prophet, who maintained hidden lodges throughout the world of Islam and also claimed (after the Crusades) to have penetrated with their ideas even Spain, Germany and parts of Britain.

However this may be, the Illuminated Ones soon became more than a headache for the governors of Afghanistan, the Mogul rulers of India, and their Persian neighbours. Not far from Peshawar, which is now in the north-west of Pakistan, Bayezid set up a small school, where he carefully coached those who had been initiated by him in the knowledge of the supernatural that he claimed. A period of probation was expected from each candidate, during which he would go into periods of concealment or meditation, known as *khilwat*—silence. During this time he was to receive the illumination which was emanated from the supreme being, who desired a class of perfect men—and women —to carry out the organization and direction of the world.

Bayezid collected in this way, over a period of three years, about fifty staunch disciples, whom he had trained in obedience and to whom—so we are told—he had shown a way whereby they could liberate their 'inner powers'. This meant that they were ready to follow his further instructions. These orders, according to what his opponents say, were that the whole sect would now become bandits, to prey upon the rest of the world. Little information is available from the other side, but three letters said to have been written from one branch to another contain in outline a plan to reshape the social system of the world: first taking control of individual countries, one by one.

But something does survive of the degrees of initiation. The first was *Salik* (seeker); followed by *Murid* (disciple); *Fakir* (humble devotee); *Arif* (enlightened one); *Khwaja* (master); *Emir* (commander); *Imam* (priest) and *Malik* (chief or king). This succession does not follow the usual pattern of promotion in the Moslem mystical secret societies, the tarikas; and seems to have been specially devised for this one. In the first three degrees, the candidate perfected himself by repetitions of certain phrases which were believed to carry power. Examples are these: *rabba; aferinaa; hayya; hafida; quwwaya.*

Of these words (all Arabic or Persian) the first stands for the concept of lordship, the second for creation, the third for life, the fourth for protection, and the last for absolute power. If they were repeated, with deep meditation upon various forms of their manifestations in human life, it was believed, the appropriate

power would come into the devotee. No special deity was worshipped; but it was believed that there was a supreme overall
power, which was known by the sum of its individual powers
(lordship, protection, and so on); and that when one had medi-
tated upon them all, and they had become the 'property' of the
invocant, he would thenceforward be a man of complete power.
This kind of idea underlies a good deal of religious and magical
thinking, in many faiths; though it is seldom put in as concise a
manner. The Enlightened One of the fourth degree was he who
could attain, during the rituals, complete identification with this
overall power, and was guided by it in all that he did. This
meant that, apart from the guidance of the chief, he was free
to suit his own pleasure in life. No theological or social bonds
limited him.

It is at this stage, said the Illuminated, that the *Arif* could perform acts of wonder and magic; influence the physical world,
and know the secrets of others. He attained this degree through
the acceptance of him by the master, to whom he had confided
his dreams and mystical ecstasies. The master alone really knew
whether these were true or false experiences, and promoted him
accordingly. Some people proceeded to the higher degrees
without going through all the lower ones; because they were
helped by the spirits of former Illuminates who had died.

The Master, Emir, Imam and Malik degrees were reserved for
the very highest men and women initiates. After the fifth degree
the segregation of the sexes in rituals was no longer practised.
Anyone of the degree of Imam and higher could start his own
lodge and make disciples.

Bayezid decided to move his headquarters into the most
inaccessible mountains of Afghanistan, where he set up a large
and luxurious castle; and from which he directed his military and
bandit operations, designed to overcome the rest of the East. His
missionaries were sent far and wide, but received little official
support. The cult did, however, spread among merchants and
soldiers who thought that this gateway to mystical experiences
was something to enter. They contributed lavishly to the chief's

upkeep and his most expensive military, political and espionage system.

The heady wine of this success seems to have affected the prudence of the head illuminate more strongly than it should; for his claims became more and more extreme and public. There was, he now preached, no after-life of the kind currently believed in: no reward or punishment, only a spirit state which was completely different from earthly life. The spirits, if they belonged to the Order, could continue to enjoy themselves and be earthly powers, acting through living members. But that was all. The preaching of this spiritual vampirism seemed to delight his followers as much as it infuriated his enemies, because Bayezid now gave out more and more of the new doctrine based upon his no-after-life creed. Eat, drink and be merry. Gain power, look after yourself. You have no allegiance except to the Order, he told them: and all humanity which cannot identify itself by our secret sign is our lawful prey. The secret signal was to pass a hand over the forehead, palm inwards; the countersign, to hold the ear with the fingers and support the elbow in the cupped other hand.

Bayezid took to himself the style of *Pir-i-Roshan* (Sage of Illumination), and founded a city at Hashtnagar, which was to be the centre from which Illuminism was to spread all over the world.

Each member of his following was given a new name upon entry; and this name depended upon the guild to which he in theory belonged. According to Bayezid, all humanity was divided into professions; his were lamp-makers. Some members were the makers, others sold lamps. Some were known as this kind of lamp, some another. 'Lamp of the Darkness' was a typical example. Among the other guilds noted are those of the Builders (probably no connection with the much later Moslem Brotherhood, also organized as builders); soldiers, merchants of various kinds and scribes.

Writing in the nineteenth century, an Afghan scholar who was by no means fond of the society of the Roshaniya, claimed that they were in fact an organization devoted to fighting against the tyranny of the Moguls, and that the banditry and strange doctrines attributed to them were untrue allegations by interested parties. He bases this upon two manuscript copies of the objectives of the Order, which seem to have stated that it was dedicated to influencing people of importance throughout the East and West towards greater justice and self-training into the immense capacities of the human mind, whereby wonders can be caused, and through which the harmony of the world will be established. "These ideas are taken from those enshrined in our ancient literature and practices, as well as those of the Persians, many of whom followed the True Illuminated Path before the New Message [probably Islam] was revealed."

In the end, the Imperial Mogul decided that something must be done about the widespread power of the militant mystics of the Hindu Kush mountains. The Governor of Kabul arrested Bayezid, clapped him in irons, and paraded him through the streets, to show that here was no supernatural being. To give further point to the proceedings, his hair and beard were half-shaved. But this Governor, Mohsin Khan, was under the ascendancy of his religious guide, one Sheikh Attari—who may even have been a secret adherent of the Illuminated One, for the cult was spreading with rapidity. In any case, he told the Governor that Bayezid was undoubtedly a man of great and holy attainments, and that considerable suffering would inevitably attend anyone who treated him harshly. Bayezid was allowed to esape.

The indignities to which he had been subjected kindled his Illuminism still higher. Calling his numerous companions, he retired to tribal Tirah, where he set up a military and court atmosphere which is still remembered for its glamour, fervour and mystery.

India and Persia were to be overcome by force of arms, he announced. To that end, many more were to be enrolled into the ranks of the Illuminated. Enthusiastic scenes throughout Afghanistan resulted from the proclamation, which was carried far and wide, to the accompaniment of kettle-drums and wild sword-dances. When he was ready Bayezid, attended by his *halka* (circle) of dervishes, led the campaign into the lush land of India. Intercepted by the Mohsin Khan whom he had earlier escaped, he was wounded, put to flight, and eventually died as a result of the encounter.

His son, Omar Ansari, proclaimed himself leader, and immediately ordered an attack upon the Pathan tribe of the Yusufzai who had allied themselves with the Mogul. He was killed by the hillmen, and his own son, 'The Servant of the One', took over the leadership. By the middle of the seventeenth century this youth had been killed defending his castle against a Mogul expeditionary force. His infant son escaped with some of his followers, into Afghanistan proper, where the cult was restarted. The descendants of this Abdul-Qadir (Servant of the Powerful) continued to rule the fanatics, and to send their teachers far and wide. The creed split into two divisions: the military and the religious, and nowadays it is only the followers of the latter Way who survive, still a secret cult, which might, given the right conditions, have touched off a movement as important as that of the Assassins.

Forty years after the last religio-military leader of the Afghan Illuminated Ones died, a society of the same name (the Illuminati) came into being in Germany, formed, it is said, by Adam Weishaupt, the young professor of Canon Law at Ingolstadt University. Coincidences of date and beliefs connect these Bavarian Illuminati with the Afghan ones, and also with the other cults which called themselves 'Illuminated'. The beginning of the seventeenth century saw the foundation of the Illuminated Ones of Spain—the Alumbrados, condemned in an edict of the Grand Inqusition in 1623. In 1654 the 'Illuminated' Guerinets came into public notice in France.

Documents still extant show several points of resemblance between the German and Central Asian Illuminists: points which are hard to account for on the grounds of pure coincidence, and yet which still might, one supposes, be nothing more than that. The Prophet Mohammed, for example, is claimed as an initiate by the Western Illuminati. Their calendar is the very same which survived in current usage in the former Iranian territories among the Afghans of the time. New Year's Day with them was the same day as the Persian (and Afghan) Nev Roz festival. Further the degrees of initiation, although seemingly artificial ones coupled with some of the degrees of Freemasonry, were also eight, and there are parallels in the naming of the individual degrees. Like the Roshaniya, the Illuminati stated that they had the objective of gaining important converts for the purpose of improving the state of the world. A comparison of the degrees shows the similarity:

Roshaniya:	Illuminati:
Seeker	Apprentice
Disciple	Fellow-craft
Devotee	Master
Enlightened One	Illuminatus major
Master	Illuminatus dirigens
Commander (emir)	Prince
Priest	Priest
King, Chief	King

The early stages of initiation were designed to admit people into the brotherhood, to test them for reliability, and possibly to train them for responsible tasks connected with the greater diffusion of knowledge. Even in higher degrees it seems that tests are also applied. Those who were to become priests, for example, were taken to a secret place, where a throne stood, with before it the choice of priestly or royal regalia. The aspirant had to make his choice. Those who opted for the symbols of worldly power were dismissed; but candidates taking up the sacred vestments were saluted with the phrase: "Hail, O Holy One!" The members of this degree were considered teachers, in whose hands was the training of disciples.

Priests identified themselves with a secret sign: both hands, crossed, were placed flat upon the head. In shaking hands, the priest extended his palm, with the thumb held vertically upwards. The countersign was a fist, with the thumb enclosed within it.

Princes were those who could influence events at a very high level, either in academic or political affairs. The room in which the initiation to this high and secret degree was celebrated was hung with red; the garments which the prince was to wear were red and white. These are, of course, the colours of the Ismailis as well. In the ritual the candidate is presented as a slave, and states that he wants to liberate society from tyranny. The sign of the degree was the extending of both arms. As the countersign, before taking the hand of another, the prince gripped both his elbows.

In 1786 a raid upon the house of an influential lawyer, Zwack, revealed secret papers connected with the Order, and it is through these that many of the inner workings of the organization became known. Men were to be influenced through their women folk, and a large-scale plan for initiating women members was at an advanced stage of development. The following cipher was used by members in the lower degrees:

A	B	C	D	E	F	G	H	I	J	K	L	M
12	11	10	9	8	7	6	5	4		3	2	1

N	O	P	Q	R	S	T	U	V	W	X	Y	Z
13	14	15	16	17	18	19	20		21	22	23	24

The secret writing of the highest degrees of the Order was quite different:

It has been widely claimed that many of the charges which were made against the German Illuminati were false; and that the possession of instructions, for instance, on forging seals was due to the fact that the lawyer Zwack had a collection devoted to that subject, as a matter of legal interest to him. It is also said that the project of enrolling women and young girls had in actual fact been taken from the aims of a very different society, the Mopses. While this matter still remains open, however, one may as well examine some of the documents which are stated to have belonged to the Society.

Zwack had written, in his own hand, a document describing the manufacture of a strong-box which would blow up if it were tampered with. He also had a collection of impressions of the seals of several hundred important persons; and the already mentioned data on how to forge or substitute them. These, he stated in a letter of protest, were a part of the exhibits in his criminological collection.

The famous memorandum detailing the plan to win over women to the cause comes from papers seized at the home of Baron Bassus, one of the members. The document states that women are the best means of influencing men. They should be enrolled, and into their minds put a hope that they might themselves in time be released from the "tyranny of public opinion". Another letter asks how young women can be influenced, since their mothers would not consent to their being placed under the Illuminati for instruction. Five women were suggested by one member, as a start. They were four step-daughters of one of the Illuminati, who were to be placed in the care of the wife of yet another Illuminated One. They, in their turn, would enlarge the society through their friends. It was further mentioned that women are not considered to be really suitable for such an undertaking, because they are "fickle and impatient". But the Order was most sorely hit by the fact that something quite discreditable to the character of the founder was discovered; and it was thought that he might be trying to use the organization for personal reasons.

Weishaupt, upon the suppression of the Order, refused a pension which he was offered after he had been dismissed from his professorial chair. He attributed his downfall to the machinations of the Jesuits, whom he hated and who had opposed him as he was not of their number, whereas they considered the university post which he held to be a long-standing prerogative of their own.

He and Zwack were both banished, and little is heard of them thereafter, although there are rumours that they carried on the Society respectively in Saxe-Coburg and the Netherlands.

Illuminism had spread to France, however, some years before its suppression in Germany. Influential personages were members, many drawn from the ranks of the important Masons of Paris. As in the case of the German branch, it was soon alleged that they pursued terrible aims and practised frightful orgies. An extract from a French book (almost certainly grossly exaggerated) of the seventeen-nineties—*La Secte des Illuminés*—will give a fair idea of this:

"The huge château of Ermenonville near Paris was one of the chief lodges of the Illuminated. It belonged to the Marquis of Gerardin, who protected Rousseau and later gave him a tomb on his estate. St. Germain, the notable impostor, presided over it. He claimed to be a thousand years old, and to be able to make gold. He was said to be immortal, but died in 1784. On the day of his initiation, the candidate was conducted through a long, dark passage into an immense hall draped with black. He was able to see, by the faint light of sepulchral lamps, corpses in their shrouds. The altar, built of human skeletons, stood in the centre. Ghostly forms moved through the hall, leaving behind them a foul odour. At length two men, dressed as spectres, appeared and tied a pink band or ribbon smeared with blood around his forehead. Upon this was an image of the Lady of Loretto. A crucifix was placed in his hand, and an amulet hung around his neck. His clothes were removed and laid upon a funeral pyre, while upon his body crosses were smeared in blood. Then his pudenda were tied with string.

"Now five horrid and frightening figures, bloodstained and mumbling, approached him and threw themselves down in prayer. After an hour, sounds of weeping were heard, the funeral pyre started to burn, and his clothes were consumed. From the flames of this fire a huge and almost transparent form arose, while the five prostrate figures went into terrible convulsions. Now came the voice of an invisible hierophant, booming from somewhere below. The words were those of these oaths, which the candidate had to repeat:

" 'In the name of the crucified one, I swear to sever all bonds which unite me with mother, brothers, sisters, wife, relatives, friends, mistress, kings, superiors, benefactors or any other man to whom I have promised faith, service or obedience;

" 'I name the place in which I was born. Henceforth I live in another dimension, which I will not reach until I have renounced the evil globe which has been cursed by Heaven;

" 'From now onwards I shall reveal to my new chief all that I have heard or found out; and I shall also seek out and observe things which might otherwise have escaped me;

" 'I honour the *aqua toffana*; it is a quick and essential medium of removing from the earth, through death or robbing them of their wits, of those who oppose truth, and those who try to take it from our hands;

" 'I shall avoid Spain, Naples, and all other accursed lands, and I shall avoid the temptation to betray what I have now heard;

" 'Lightning will not strike as rapidly as the dagger, which will reach me, wherever I may be, should I betray my initiation.'

"Now a candelabrum, bearing seven black candles, is placed before the candidate, and also a bowl containing human blood. He washes himself in the blood, and drinks a quantity of it. The string around his pudenda is removed, he is placed in a bath to undergo complete ablution. After this, he eats a meal composed of root vegetables."

While it is possible that such ceremonies as this have actually taken place, it will be recalled that such items as 'human blood' are generally not of the genuine variety in any society other than those reputed to be dedicated to criminal or perverted ends. But, as with the initiations of other societies, there is no doubt that the candidate may have been made to believe that he was actually going through an initiation which involved horrible things of this nature. Initiation into the ancient mysteries was often accompanied by the exposure of the candidate to fear and other emotions, in order to make him receptive to the oath or message which was to be made manifest.

It has been said that the European version of the Order of the Illuminati contributed in no small measure to the development of revolutionary doctrines which eventually culminated in the Russian and other Communist machines. There is little doubt that the Order was dedicated to the overcoming of princely power as it was then known, and to the diffusion of anti-religious ideas. This can best be seen by examining the development

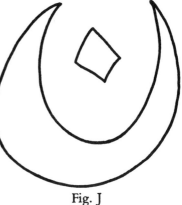

Fig. J

of the teaching of the member, as he progressed from one degree of initiation to the next.

Many young enthusiasts with a taste for mystery and a desire to fight oppression in any form were drawn, through a deliberate plan, from the ranks of the Freemasons. After an oath of obedience and silence had been extracted from the candidate, he was handed over to a Director, to be taught that the Order was one of discipline and effort, and that the final objectives were to do good through leaving aside all preconceived notions and upon the basis of free thought to lead mankind to salvation.

Those who managed to show that they were likely to accept the next stage in teaching, were advanced to the rank in which he was made to swear that he would work under the orders of his masters without doubt or question. He would not use his critical faculties in any way in any matter connected with such instructions.

In the lower ranks—the 'nursery'—the member was very much in the dark as to the way in which the Order was run, and how it should accomplish its design of freeing the world. As he progressed, however, he found that a part of his service to the Society was to gain financial and social power, and to place them at the disposal of the group. He was expected to be a diligent Mason, and to try to gain control over Masonic funds. It was not until the tenth rite of promotion had been completed that the member was given—with the grade of Priest—certain definite knowledge. This included the fact that the Illuminati were proposing to destroy princes and prelates throughout the world, and were to remove for ever the feeling of local nationality from the minds of men. The ways in which this was to be done involved infiltrating high positions in education, administration and the Press.

The very highest degrees showed that the rationalism and materialism of the thinkers who developed it were determined to stamp out belief in religion. God and any faith in a deity, the initiate was told, were human inventions, and had no real meaning. Subsequently this was developed further, and the member who arrived at the highest position (that of Rex, King) learned that he was now equal to a king, and that all men were capable of equal advancement: hence the need for kings over ordinary mortals was an illusion.

23

Tongs of Terror

"A PERSON who has committeed a murder shall conceal himself, cut off some of his hair and tie the same round his right arm. And when he goes to seek refuge among his brothers he shall wipe his left eye: and the brotherhood shall provide him with expenses and means of escape." This is one of the Rules of the *Toh Peh Kong* Secret Society among the Chinese; who, of all peoples, have developed clandestine associations to the ultimate pitch of efficiency.

The origins of Chinese secret societies are almost all legendary, some are most poetical, most are patriotic, many are criminal in the usual sense of the word. Inside China itself, they have functioned as resistance movements against the Manchus, as welfare organizations, as espionage networks. The 'Boxer' Rebellion of 1900 was started and maintained by a secret society. The republican leader Dr. Sun Yat-sen worked largely by means of one such association, which eventually became the Kuomintang, the Nationalist Party of China. When the Republican Government fled to Formosa, the Kuomintang remained, and still is, the major political party of the Free Chinese. The Communists, led by Mao Tse-tung, were early organized as a secret society. Between the years 1950 and 1960, both of these opposing elements sought to gain control of the tens of millions of Overseas Chinese who lived in Malaya, the Philippines, and elsewhere throughout South-East Asia.

At the same time, Communist and Free Chinese secret society influence sought to penetrate the communities of Chinese in America, Europe and Africa. The Formosa Government maintained contact with their supporters on the Communist mainland through these societies, which the Peiping Government still seeks to crush, and which it vilifies frequently in the official Press.

The Chinese take their secret societies seriously, and there are few of them who are not members, affiliates or entitled by hereditary right to membership. The time cannot yet be foreseen when this kind of activity will cease to play a large part in Chinese thought and life. The half-crazed, slit-eyed assassin of fiction, the opium-den of the tong, the kidnapping, gambling-dens and the horrid rituals of initiation, are still with us, and they will remain so for a very long time to come.

Chinese records of nearly two thousand years ago tell of the Carnation-painted Eyebrows Society, with painted faces, whose leader nearly became ruler of the country through banditry. They were defeated when the loyal troops painted their faces in the same bizarre pattern and attacked them. The Carnation-Eyebrows were confused and routed. This was a time of general anarchy, and among the secret societies which ranged the country in armed bands were such picturesquely named bodies as the Copper Horses and the Iron Shins.

Chinese secret society seal combines names of planets. The centre rectangle contains the name of the chief at the time: Yun Ching (Triad Society).

In the second century of the Christian era, a Taoist magician called Chang Kioh declared himself to be a god and gathered around himself a numerous following in the north-east of China. Within a few years there were so many members of the cult that they had to be split up under thirty-six generals. In a month these Yellow Turban Rebels had subdued the whole of the north of China, helped by their secret associates among the apparently law-abiding populace.

But one secret society's activities could give birth to another. It was in the struggle against the Yellow Turbans that Kwan Yu took an oath with two other warriors to liberate the country from them. His activities caused him to become deified as the God of War, and the patron of yet other secret societies, among them the Triad Cult.

It is not until a period when the Crusades were raging in the Near East that we have a record of the actual oaths taken by secret society members, upon which many of the present-day oath-taking ceremonies are modelled. In 1102, one hundred and eight men took this vow:

"We, one hundred and eight persons assembled in this hall, regard the stars as our brothers and Heaven and Earth as our father and mother ... every heart is spotless. We bind ourselves to share each other's happiness and sorrow. May anyone who is unkind or double-dealing be attacked by devils. . . . May knives and swords cut our bodies and thunderbolts destroy every trace of us; may we everlastingly sink into hell and not be reborn as human beings; may Heaven and all the gods look down upon us as we swear." The members swore to meet in every single incarnation. Then they drank each other's blood mixed with wine.

It was two hundred years later that the notorious White Lotus Society was formed. The Mongols had beaten down Chinese resistance, and the fearsome Kublai Khan was in full control. A rumour started that a certain omen would herald the liberation of the country: "When stirs the one-eyed man of stone, this dynasty will be overthrown." Shortly after this slogan became current in the mouth of every urchin, a stone image of a one-eyed man was found on the banks of the Yellow River. The White Lotus Society, which had been founded some years earlier (and which perhaps started the 'one-eyed man' rumour), now proclaimed itself destined to liberate the land. The Buddhist Messiah was at hand, said its leaders, and tens of thousands joined them, including three powerful bandit chiefs.

One of these latter claimed royal descent, dressed his followers in red turbans, and tried to seize the throne. The White Lotus remained active, though not completely successful, for centuries after this. Numerous rebellions and other unsavoury undertakings are ascribed to this group. By 1761 the Emperor Keinlung had to issue an edict against the Lotus and the Illustrious Worthies and White Cloud societies, which were patriotic (anti-Manchu) and also semi-criminal organizations. The society worked under the pretence of being a religious sect, purporting to cure diseases through incantations.

Pretenders, supposedly descended from the rightful heirs of the usurped Ming Dynasty, rose from time to time and were supported by the Lotus organization. This development is important, because the Lotus and its descendants—especially the powerful Triad Society, which still exists—are founded upon a royalist and patriotic myth. The eventual object of the Society, so runs the teaching, is to restore the Mings; a resolve which appealed to a great number of the people who felt themselves to be oppressed. But in the higher degrees of initiation the secret was revealed to initiates that the word 'Ming' stood for 'Light' (this is its literal meaning in Chinese) and the objective of the Triad and others was to obtain power over all China for the Society, which considered itself as the Light. This is why today, with very little likelihood of an Imperial Ming restoration, the Triad and other groups can remain in operation and retain their immense power.

Startling evidence of the power of the secret societies and their real objective as political and financial power came with the victory of Dr. Sun Yat-sen. In January, 1912, Sun was installed as President of the Chinese Republic. As his first official act the republican president went to the tombs of the Ming Dynasty and in a public ceremony informed the spirits of the Imperial Mings that the Manchus had been driven from the country. Dr. Sun was, of course, a Christian; but this action, as a member of the Triad Society, was one of Chinese religious and secret society import. And, of course, he did not restore the Mings to the throne. But his Kuomintang Party, descended from the Triad secret society, remained the official power in the land.

It has been said that the Triad Society was not derived from that of the White Lotus, but merely used its rituals and some of its history; but there are grounds for supposing that they are in reality one and the same body. The fact that the Lotus men helped to place the first Ming on the throne in the fourteenth century was somewhat marred by their intervention against the Mings in the seventeenth. This resulted in the triumph of the Manchus: and this could be the reason why Triad men are not always anxious to be identified with the Lotus.

Towards the end of the eighteenth century, a White Lotus chief—Liu Chi hieh—produced an 'authentic' descendant of the Mings as the candidate for the imperial throne. Lotus rebellion was in full flower, and the story circulated was that the pretender (Wang Fasheng) was a genuine, royal Ming, whom Liu had reared secretly outside China for the great day. Over a hundred thousand Lotus men were in arms, fighting for six years until Liu was captured. Then for a further four years the civil war raged, costing the Society and the throne millions in money and lives. When the revolt was put down, the young pretender disappeared.

In 1814, the Imperial Palace was attacked by what has been described as a coalition of several secret societies: the White Lotus, the White Feather, the Three Incense Sticks, the Eight Diagrams and the Rationalists. It is probable that at least some of these names were merely alternatives used by the Triad, because this society uses as symbols some of the objects mentioned above.

The rebellion was well organized, and came as a complete surprise to the authorities. It was planned by secret society leaders who claimed occult powers and who had bribed palace officials with immense sums of money. This rising failed only due to a mistake in the dates upon which it should have taken place, and was put down. The second son of the Emperor, it is recorded, realizing that this was an occultist activity when he could not kill a rebel with his ordinary musket-balls, tore off one of his silver buttons and fired it at the man, who now toppled to the ground. Magic and the reputed ability to see the future has always played a large part in Chinese secret society activities. In the 1814 rising the loyalist elements invoked the thunder gods; whereupon, we are told, "a large number of the rebels were killed by lightning in a terrible thunderstorm which broke out".

The inner workings of the minds of these cultists is interesting to note: whenever opportunity arises. Although their seers were generally supposed to know the future (and hence could be expected to know whether a revolt would succeed or not) they ultimately maintained that the future was only partly pre-destined. The revolution would succeed, they said, providing that the emotional pitch and dedication of the members was sufficiently great. To this end rituals and initiations were devised and rigidly practised. This note runs through the frenzied dedication of all the secret societies of this nature.

The 'Boxers' (actually members of the Fist for Protection Society) who attacked the legations in Peiping in 1900, were trained to a pitch of zeal and fanaticism which has seldom been equalled. They had been initiated in darkness alternated with light, in the depths of temples to the accompaniment of fasting and invocations. They had to recite meaningless phrases taken from Taoist magic, and undergo complicated gymnastics. They swallowed a variety of drugs and potions, as well as mystical diagrams written on red paper. The result was to condition their minds to ideas of success, supernatural aid, invulnerability, insensibility to pain, enthusiasm and blind obedience.

The 'Boxers'—also, and more literally correctly, often called the 'Fists for Righteous Harmony'—were a mystical organization derived from the Big Sword Society. And the Big Swords is one of the names used by the Triad Society, which lurks behind so many of the activities of Chinese secret associations. Their training is supposedly based upon that of the Fighting Monks of Shao Lin Monastery, who preserved certain secrets of meditation which made them invulnerable and endowed with various supernatural powers.

It is these very militant monks who are the supposed originators of the desperate Triad Society. Every member must try to emulate the virtues of these monks; and all revere the tale of their doings. Members are put through a form of training which is supposed to be the same as that which the militant anchorites devised; thus making them superior to all other men. It is fitting here to study the myth of the mysterious monks.

In A.D. 1674, the initiate is told, there lived a community of monks in Fukien Province. They had been there at least a thousand years, and had perfected certain arts which raised them to a position of superior men. In addition to having supernatural powers through their Buddhist meditations, they were masters in the arts of war.

The brothers initiated and taught those who came to seek knowledge, and their institution became a famous place of religio-military importance. A foreign prince had invaded China and inflicted numerous defeats upon the national forces. The Emperor had been compelled to call upon the entire nation to help to defend the realm. An honoured graduate of the monks' military academy heard the proclamation and hurried to consult the Order. The one hundred and twenty-eight sages who dwelt there immediately formed themselves into a chivalrous band and hurried to the court. There the Emperor received them and accepted their services, raised each one to the rank of general and offered whatever men or money they might need. They asked only for food and horses, and—tarrying only to choose a fortunate day—set out to give battle.

Bamboo summons to Tong member, calling him to a meeting.

In under three months, and without casualties on their own side, the warrior monks completely subdued the enemy, even cutting their way into his country and forcing him to pay tribute.

The Emperor was delighted with the victory, and again offered the monks anything that they desired. But they did not want worldly goods. The warlord disciple, however, who had first thought of bringing the sages into the fight, was showered with presents and given a high military office.

Thus far, the myth prepares the mind of the member by glorifying fighting and self-sacrifice; ascribing a high antiquity and religious sanctions to the movement; linking it with imperial commands; and showing the power of dedication and discipline. The actual mystery of how the monks obtained their supernatural powers is reserved for the leaders of the Order.

To continue the history: the monks were rewarded with a tablet and scrolls written by the Emperor himself. They were personally escorted to the gate by his sublime majesty on their departure. They received a tremendous welcome from the country people of their region, to whom they showed the Imperial commendations. These items are important, in that they contain slogans which the Triad member must memorize and keep before him. On the tablet was inscribed: "Imperial Favour, Kindness and Honour". The scrolls stated: "First in Bravery, Matchless Heroes"; and "It was not by learning that they got to court, through warlike skill they saw the Emperor." These messages convey to the initiate that he need not spend half of his life in study before he can distinguish himself.

Now the legend takes an interesting turn. There were two traitors at the Imperial court. They desired to overcome the Emperor, but realized that while the terrible monks of Fukien still had their power, there was no chance of their success. They therefore hit upon the design of telling the monarch that the monks were a danger to the Throne, because none could stand against them, and they were known to be training young men in the military art and their secret powers.

The Emperor was alarmed, and asked them what he should do, which was just what they wanted. They sought, and obtained from him, forces of the Imperial Guard, with whom they proceeded to Fukien, armed with large supplies of gunpowder, to destroy the monastery.

The traitors fell in with a monk who had been expelled from the devout community for irregular conduct, enlisted him as an officer, and with his help found their way to the monastery, surrounded it with inflammable materials and set it ablaze. Now the founder of the Order, who had become an immortal, saw the flames as they ascended to heaven, and summoned two other immortals to help the community.

By pushing back one of the walls, the immortals enabled eighteen monks, one of whom carried the Emperor's triangular Seal (which he had bestowed upon them in token of their absolute authority), to escape. They were severely burned, and thirteen of them died. In memory of this treacherous occasion, all members curse their opponents and vow to destroy them for they are considered to be "like the traitors, just as the present members are like the monks".

The Five Patriarchs, who escaped, were helped by certain boatmen, to whom they taught certain secret signals in token of their gratitude. They continued on in persecution for some time, saved again and again by the hovering immortals ("just as our members are saved by the Society when in trouble"). Finally, just as they were ambushed at their devotions by a party of soldiers, a miraculous peach-wood sword appeared. When this was shaken at the enemy, heads fell off like peach-blossom before the wind. On this weapon was inscribed "Subvert the Tsing and Restore the Ming". With the sword the monks performed many miracles. They recruited five further stalwart warriors as henchmen, known as the Five Tiger Generals.

The monks were still being actively persecuted on the instigation of the traitors: they had no food, homes or possessions. They desired life in order to get revenge; at the same time they wanted death to relieve them of their troubles. Now in their wanderings they met Chen Chin-nan, the person reputed to be the actual founder of the Triad Society. He had been driven from the court for honourably objecting to the proposed attack upon the monks in the first place. He took the wanderers in and looked after them. He gave them a spacious building—his beautiful Red Flower Pavilion—in which to carry out their rites and practise warfare.

One day the monks were strolling near this delightful retreat when they saw, floating in the Kungwei River, a large stone tripod incense burner with two ears. Shouting "How wonderful!" they examined it, and found inscribed on the bottom *Fan Tsing, Fuh Ming*: Subvert Tsing, Restore Ming. This they carried to their altar, where twigs which they placed in it miraculously ignited themselves. They prayed for guidance, and were told that they must obey the inscription on the stone.

The monks consulted Chen, who issued a call to arms. One hundred and eight warriors responded; and also a comely lad called Liu who mysteriously appeared. He revealed to the patriots that he was a legitimate Ming descendant, and was un-animously chosen as the new ruler by the small force. The army was organized as a secret society with Chen as Grand Master (*Hsiang-chu*) and the Red Flower Pavilion as the lodge. Various astronomical miracles accompanied this happy event. The name of the organization was *Hung*, which signifies both 'Flood' and 'Red'; the former because they were to overwhelm China like a flood; the latter because the sky was a glowing red at the time. They called themselves also the Brotherhood of Heaven and Earth; and the name Triad is derived from these three elements: brothers, heaven, earth.

The revolt did not succeed. One of the greatest heroes of the Hung was killed, and the army became discouraged. They post-humously raised him to the rank of duke, wrapped the ashes of his body in red silk, and buried him in a lucky place with a trian-gular 'ten thousand ages' monument, talismanically decorated with sixteen characters all based upon the sign for water. This done, the congregation sought the young would-be emperor. He had disappeared and was never seen again.

It was now evident that for some reason the precise time for the destruction of the dynasty had not yet arrived. Chen addressed the band; and after describing how the involuntary bending of his fingers had revealed to him supernaturally that there would be a further period of waiting continued:

"Gentlemen, I now advise you to disperse. Some of you are to take to the fields, others to the rivers. All must conceal themselves, conserve their strength and practise virtue. Transmit from mouth to ear the secret aims of our Society, so that in future we may be successful. Gentlemen, I now bid you farewell!"

Before splitting up, secret signs were arranged, and a special verse of recognition composed:

"At parting five a verse composed;
Which heroes carry undisclosed.
But when their brothers this do see
They know the sign of unity."

Five provincial Grand Lodges were also established, one under each of the monkish patriarchs. The rituals of admission to the Triad Society are largely based upon these supposed happenings. These proceedings are exceedingly complicated and even tedious. The effect of the whole is to direct the mind of the member, so that his every thought is concentrated upon the Society and its rules, which are inculcated at almost every stage of the symbolic proceedings.

Many of the principles are praiseworthy ones, but the result of the entire teaching is to make the organization a 'state within a state' and the only organization to which the member owes any real loyalty. He must obey his chief implicitly, and is not allowed to act against a fellow-member. Law cases must be brought before the Society, not the ordinary courts. He must always protect a fellow-member against the Government of wherever he happens to be. He must be loyal and must fight when asked. The Twenty-One Rules or Laws of the Society forbid: adultery with a woman connected with a member; committing a crime and imputing it to another member; obtaining money for the arrest of a member; falsely claiming a superior rank in the Society; informing anyone about the existence of the Society; parting with his book of ceremonies or certificate of membership; insulting or oppressing the weak; stealing from another member; failing to respond to a call or order; malconverting the Society's funds; non-payment of dues.

There are numerous signs of recognition, many poems which only the initiated know, and methods of identification based upon the way in which one drinks cups of tea.

Abundant proof of the fact that the Triad is not really

concerned with the Manchus and the Mings at all, but is a society dedicated to the acquisition of money and power, has been noted in the activities of the organization abroad. Several well-documented studies have been made, for instance, of the organization and depredations of the Triad in Malaya, where at times a large majority of all Chinese residents in Singapore and elsewhere were members. The gambling industry, opium trade, prostitution and other activities of the society, as well as the struggle against the British authorities and the Christian missionaries, had little to do with the fight for the imperial throne. There is little evidence that the Triad abroad ever bothered about who was ruling China proper.

On the other hand, there is a mass of material to show that the Triad and other secret societies worked ceaselessly for their own good and for the welfare of their leaders. There is also no doubt that the individual member received many benefits: but they were often the dubious ones of influence used to subvert the course of justice.

The British in Malaya, especially in the nineteenth century, had an extraordinary and ever-shifting policy towards the societies. Some officials thought that they were not dangerous; others that they did not exist. When disturbances arose through fearful tong-fights, it was often said that these were not due to the secret societies at all. British traders stated that as the societies only persecuted each other, they should be allowed to carry on freely in their own way. For decades the authorities were handicapped by having nobody who spoke Chinese to deal with the organizations, and relied from time to time upon the 'co-operation' of chiefs of the tongs themselves. Malays, Indians and others were enrolled, and some Malays started their own societies, two of which were Islamic. The aims and objects were getting farther and farther from the restoration of the Mings as each day passed.

In 1869, a law came into being in Malaya, providing for the registration of 'Dangerous Societies'; and all associations except mercantile companies and European Freemasons had to register and furnish information about their places of meeting, members, signs and rituals. Many did so, but provided bogus details which were accepted as genuine. This ordinance had, of course, no effect. The Governor is on record as believing that it had worked well; although the only effect had been to register the societies incorrectly, and they were increasing in numbers and influence.

By the end of the nineteenth century, the societies were better organized than ever before, in spite of policies of registration, suppression, partial suppression, and so on.

After the middle of the twentieth century, the terrible tongs of China were operating, apparently without restraint, throughout South-East Asia, and wherever Chinese people were to be found. Extortion, racketeering and murder were rife. Not even a theory as to how they might be approached, controlled or suppressed had been produced. In the nineteen-sixties, after probably more than two thousand years of connected villainy, there was no indication that the question would ever be settled.

24

Primitive Initiation Societies

ALL secret societies require an identity of desire: the Society must be working for something, and that objective should be known to the members. The custom of having degrees of initiation has in many cases been taken advantage of to inculcate different views of the world—or of the object of the Society—into the minds of the initiates as they proceed from one stage to another. This process is one of the marks of the less primitive, more sophisticated society which practises initiation, preparation and secrecy.

The tribal initiations of Africa, Amerindia or Polynesia are training systems, designed to initiate the men (and often the women, separately) into the cult in which the community believes. At the same time, the 'conditioning' technique is employed to make the new member submissive to certain rules, and to certain elders or chiefs. The objective of these societies is generally consistent: the protection of the community in the material and spiritual sense, and the maintenance of the privilege of those who are too physically weak to assert it otherwise.

Frazer, in his *Golden Bough*, and elsewhere, has stressed the magical and ritual aspect of these initiations at the expense of the purely expedient character, to which he paid little attention. Since his time, of course, many writers have pointed out the various weaknesses of his work. Professor Hutton Webster (*Primitive Secret Societies*, New York, 1908, pp. 46, 47f.) was one who showed with remarkable clarity that the supernatural beliefs of the initiators were far less important than the fact that they were working effectively upon the minds of the initiated, and not necessarily for altruistic motives:

"The long fasts, the deprivation of sleep," he says, "the constant excitement of the new and unexpected, the nervous reaction under long continued torments, result in a condition of extreme sensitiveness—*hyperaesthesia*—which is certainly favourable to the reception of impressions that will be indelible. The lessons learned in such a tribal school as the puberty institution constitutes, abide through life."

This is not the time or the place to emphasize this point unduly; because it does not take into consideration the fact that the initiate believes that his experiences are connected with the supernatural. It is the argument used nowadays by all materialists against all believers in religion: that the physiological mechanism, and nothing else, is responsible for training and conversion. It is unlikely that a time will ever come when this view is accepted by all, even if only because so many people want to believe in the supernatural in one form or another. A follower of the contemporary British witch cult recently said, in words very similar to those which would be used by a devout member of any religion: "You have not experienced this feeling of initiation, this contact with the divine. How can you judge it?"

Suffice it to say that the most primitive secret societies known to man carry out ceremonies, rituals and processes which are not to be distinguished from those employed by modern brainwashers. If these activities have a divine basis, or liberate in the mind something more than the physiologist or even psychologist would expect is not the point.

The mechanisms which are used can be summarized as:

1. The desire to participate in the ritual, and expectancy of something happening.

2. Isolation, vigils, hunger or abstinence, causing debilitation and time for reflection.

3. Noise.

4. Real or symbolic potions (sometimes narcotic and hypnotic).

5. Threats or frightening happenings, generally staged and not genuine perils.

6. Symbolic death and resurrection, with probably a renaming ceremony.

7. The use of special signs and signals and 'key phrases' which will help to awaken the conditioning (training) for special or general purposes at different times.

More than just a trace of these practices is to be found in the ceremonies of most of the world's great religions, even in the public devotions of the practioners. In the case of mystical and other dedicated orders, training systems and rituals in far greater detail are found, generally bearing out the above thesis.

The effects of conditioning and group-feeling can be felt without an appeal to supernaturalism. The sentiments experienced by patriots upon hearing key words which are associated with their country or monarch; the reactions to advertising slogans; the habits automatically performed at certain times by everyone, are the results of training which has been deliberately or unconsciously passed on from one generation to another. Secret societies use this training to take advantage of the human propensity for obedience to repeated or inculcated stimuli.

A shared experience, undergoing something which produces emotion under unusual circumstances, going through a ritual which has been expected and which exhausts the body and overwhelms the mind: these are the elements of the secret society training early discovered by primitive man and still applied by those who seek to train others.

A remarkable correspondence between tribal initiation among the North American Indians and that of a Bulgarian student body should prove the point. There is little likelihood that the Indians of North Carolina had much cultural contact with the Bulgars of the nineteenth century—or even earlier. It is more likely that by trial and error certain procedures, applied in a certain order, were found to have a conditioning effect.

Lawson, in his *History of Carolina*, speaks of the *Huskenaw* ceremony, which is designed to make the Indian braves at puberty "obedient and respectful to their superiors; and as they say it is the same to them as it is to us to send our children to school to be taught good breeding and letters."

Once a year, the young men who have not undergone the ceremony before are herded into a large cabin. They are kept in the dark and half starved. This continues for three weeks, during which they are lectured on their rights and responsibilities. When they are brought out, they are kept under guard, having been administered "intoxicating plants". They "either really are, or pretend to be, dumb, and do not speak for several days; I think twenty or thirty". They look "ghastly and changed". Now they are fully fledged members of the secret society of the tribe.

Although this writer does not specify the "intoxicating plants" given to the initiates, this custom is common to many other Indian nations. In the case of the Walapai of Arizona, the leaves, roots and flowers of *Datura stramonium* are steeped in water and administered. The Powhattan Indians of Virginia used Wysoccan —a decoction of the leaves and twigs of *cassina* or *ilex*. The Diegueños of Southern California made their brew for subduing the lads from roots of *Datura metaloides*.

The initiates of these societies within the tribe are dedicated to such things as obedience to the elders, the maintenance of certain principles of conduct, and the welfare of the tribe.

The Bulgarian initiation is preserved in an account by the Turkish author Jawad Bey. At certain Bulgarian seminaries which he visited in the early days of the nineteenth century, he says, he saw the ceremonies of admission of the students. These were young boys, scarcely old enough to bear arms. They were taken by the priests and told that they were about to undergo the test which would determine whether they were fit persons to serve the Lord Jesus Christ. A large wooden house which was used for no other purpose was used, and sometimes the place was quite full. There were no lights in the hut, and only hard planks to sleep upon. Their food was of the most meagre gruel, while for drink they were given a thirst-producing drink which contained henbane. For forty days they continued thus, "ceaselessly exhorted by the priests to repent, to determine to reform, to resolve to become loyal, submissive and dedicated men."

When brought out from the hut, they were made to run several times through files of priests who beat drums and shouted "Dumb, dumb!" at them. When spoken to they did not reply, but made signs only. In a month, all had "recovered their power of speech, but were solemn, fearful and alternately happy, completely submissive to the priests, and I believe much changed for the good; although their faces were not pleasant to look upon."

Jawad Bey notes that he had seen some of these peasant lads before they were taken to the hut, as they lounged about this monastery, and found them "uncouth, disrespectful and as they said only entering the seminary because they would starve outside." He contrasts this with the change in their appearance and behaviour afterwards, and mentions that divinity students to whom he had lectured in Constantinople "were many more months before the sense of vocation captured them than these Bulgars, tamed like animals, which they are."

The remarkable thing about these two accounts is that they agree in almost every particular. The hut is there is both cases, the segregation, darkness, potion containing alkaloids, periods of time (42 and 40 days; then 20 or 30 days and one month), dumbness, change in appearance. The motives for the training, of course, are almost the same.

Rituals and practices of the people, civilized and aborigine, of India, Australia, Africa, Siberia, show similar characteristics. Secret society and secret initiation rites seem to be practised most widely among primitive people at puberty, perhaps because that is the period when the youth is most in need of training and discipline. It is, of course, very possible that the priesthood in many cases themselves believe that these and other rituals have a magical sanction. The fact that they are able to influence initiates to such an extent may be taken as meaning that a supernatural power is at work. There is evidence of this in the training of medicine-men and witch-doctors. In such ceremonies it is not usual for the trainee to be conditioned to blind obedience of any individual.

His loyalty is transferred to a totem, god or spirit, and this is said to be the source of the magical power which he will exercise. In the secret initiations belonging to primitive and highly developed religions alike, the initiate may believe that he has experienced contact with a divine power which may henceforth guide his steps.

Index